CERAMICS

A Potter's Handbook

HOLT, RINEHART and WINSTON
New York · Chicago · San Francisco · Toronto · London

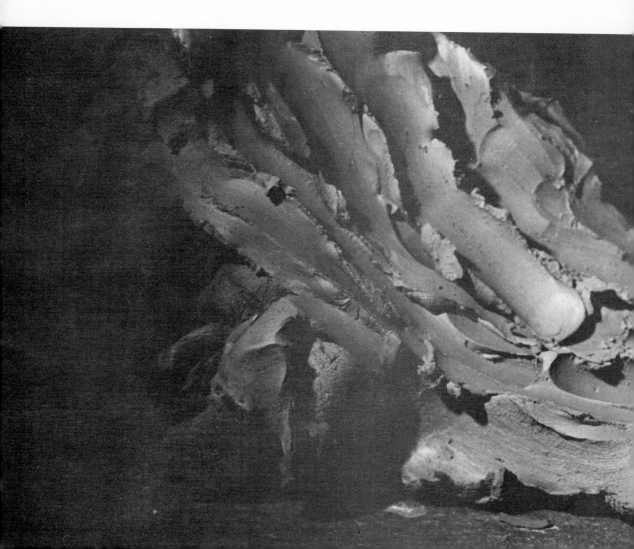

CERAMICS

A Potter's Handbook ● SECOND EDITION

GLENN C. NELSON

University of Minnesota, Duluth

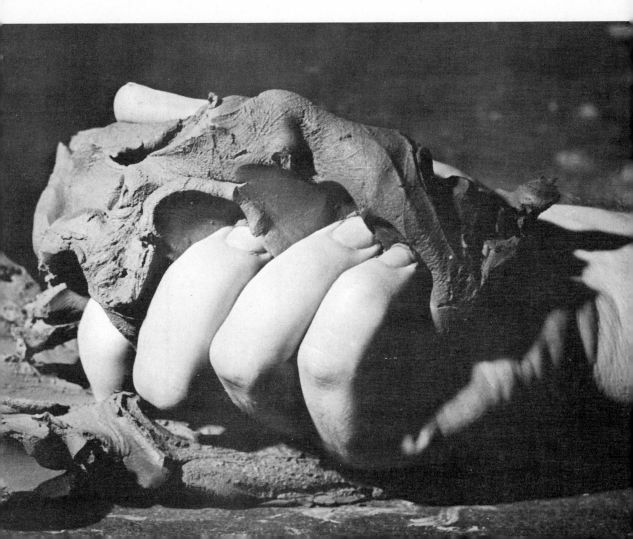

PREFACE *to the Second Edition*

In preparing a new edition of *Ceramics: A Potter's Handbook*, I have considerably reorganized and expanded the material. My purpose has been to produce a book more distinctly responsive to the needs and interests of my own students and those of numerous other teachers who have used the first edition over a period of years. To suggest somewhat more completely the rich tradition out of which modern ceramics has emerged, I have rewritten and enlarged the historical chapter and placed it at the beginning of the text. Following it, in what I hope to be a more logical sequence, is the chapter on contemporary ceramics. To the revised material here I have included additional information on the ceramics of other cultures and a wholly new section on the stimulating ceramics of Japan. A third chapter has been introduced in this edition, and its purpose is to comment on the elements and principles of ceramic design. In style, however, this material is different from the other, more explicit parts of the book; I have attempted to treat design in a broad manner and as a general concept. Design is so distinctly related to evolving ideas in the studio, is so organic to the relationship of the plastic clay shape, the student, and the teacher-potter, that I have thought it better to leave a more direct discussion to classroom instruction. For the later, technical section of the book I have prepared two chapters of material that are new to this edition: One on kilns, their operation and construction; and a second on mass-production methods.

In all, the book is substantially reorganized and enlarged in the revision. Its principal focus, however, remains on the sequence of operations from the raw, wet clay to the fired piece. The illustrated sections on techniques are retained as are the sections dealing with the characteristics of glaze chemicals; kilns; production methods; equipment; supplies; the glossary of ceramic terms; and the appendix with reference tables, glaze recipes, and clay bodies.

Because the book is intended to serve as an introduction to the world of ceramics, I have always considered the illustrations to be as substantive as the text. In this edition, the number of illustrations has been significantly increased in nearly all the chapters, and there is among them, I believe, a more accurate representation of the range and diversity in the style and form ceramic art has taken through the ages. Many excellent photographs of handsome, original pieces are now available; it has been exciting to select among them for the illustrations to accompany textual discussion. In assembling them, I have wanted the illustrations to play an expressive role in demonstrating the modern approach to ceramics, from the functional tea pot to the "one-of-a-kind" museum piece. The presence of four-color reproductions, new to this edition, makes possible a fresh dimension in the discussion of glazes and decoration. There is variety too in these illustrations, representing, for instance, an ancient Peruvian sculpture pot as well as a section from a modern ceramic mural.

I should like to acknowledge here several individuals and organizations who have aided me greatly in this revision. I am most grateful to my many potter friends who have contributed valuable ideas and criticisms to this new edition of *Ceramics*. The numerous illustrations of contemporary ceramics may be its most valuable feature. The kindness of these potters in supplying these excellent illustrations is most appreciated.

I am equally pleased for this opportunity to show the work of many foreign potters, too few of whom are known in America. Individual potters were most cooperative as well as were their national organizations. In this regard, I am indebted to the Craft Centre of Great Britain and to Murray Fieldhouse, English author, potter, and former editor of the late *Pottery Quarterly;* to Mr. J. W. N. Van Achterbergh of the Dutch Ceramic Society; to the Italian magazine *La Ceramica* and to Director G. Liverani of the International Ceramic Museum of Faenza; to Director Mia Seeger of The Council for Industrial Design in Germany; to Mr. Anders Møen of *Den Permanente* in Copenhagen; to Mr. Stig Lindberg of the Gustavsberg Studios and Carl-Harry Stålhane of the Rörstrand Studios in Sweden; to Director O. H. Gummerus of the Finnish Society for Crafts and Design; to the Norwegian Society of Arts and Crafts and Industrial Design; and to the Japanese Embassy, Dr. Hugo Munsterberg, and Mr. Allen Landgren for the Japanese illustrations.

Many art museums have also been most helpful in supplying illustrations from their collection to complement the historical survey of ceramics. To my numerous requests for information and reproductions, the manufacturers of ceramic equipment have been equally cooperative.

Mr. Jules R. Gulden, of Syracuse China, was most kind to furnish photographs and considerable information on commercial production. I am similarly indebted to Pete Slusarski for his contributions on product design.

The process photographs, which will interest many students, were taken by Ken Moran; for his friendly patience and professional skills, I am indebted.

Duluth, Minnesota   **G. C. N.**
April 1966

PREFACE *to the First Edition*

I suspect that most of us still recall with pleasure childhood experiences after a summer rain—wading through pools of rain water and feeling the pliant clay squeeze between our toes. For girls, perhaps making mud pies was more the order of the day.

The great interest of recent years in ceramics stems in part, I believe, from such memories, mostly forgotten but subconsciously retained. Certainly the plasticity of clay has made it one of the more exciting mediums with which to work. In its fired state it is one of the most ageless materials. Its three-dimensional qualities plus the effects of glaze, color, and texture make ceramics potentially the richest of all art forms.

Unfortunately ceramics is a rather fickle mistress. While in essence clay is the most elemental of materials, there are many "dos" and "don'ts" involved in working with it. Novice potters have many difficulties with the idiosyncrasies of clay. This book is an effort to develop a reliable guide for the amateur as well as a reference work for the more advanced potter. Ceramics is the most technical of all art forms if the ceramist hopes to achieve a complete understanding of the medium. Unfortunately unless the potter has a good background in ceramics, his potential results are bound to be limited.

Students and other learners will find the illustrations of step-by-step forming methods very useful guides. However, I do not believe that ceramics can be taught solely from the printed page. For this reason the critical aspect of ceramics—design—is left entirely to the studio presentation where it must be resolved in a mutual interaction between the student, the material, and the teacher.

Both the novice potter and the new teacher have equipment problems. Chapter 12 is devoted to this area and the Appendix lists, by geographic area and type of supply, major supply dealers.

The emphasis upon both contemporary and historical ceramics is unusual in a book of this nature; yet it may well be its most important feature.

After all, the final potted form is my paramount concern. All technique is subservient to it. Many cultures have produced lasting works of art with a minimum of facilities.

The enthusiasm of the novice potter is, as it is for all human endeavors, the most important ingredient for learning the art of ceramics. I hope that in providing information on techniques and equipment and by illustrating forming methods, I have helped to eliminate some of the initial frustrations of clay-working. The ironic feature of ceramics is that in spite of all this discussion about technique, opening a kiln is much like coming downstairs on Christmas Day—one never knows quite what to expect. For the practicing potter firing may well be one of the more intriguing aspects of ceramics. It gives credence to the old story that the ancient Chinese habitually formed a figurine to be placed on the kiln door to ward off evil spirits. Evil spirits or no, it is my hope that this volume will be of assistance to the pottery student as well as an aid to the many potters who, like myself, are involved with the teaching of ceramics.

Duluth, Minnesota
February 26, 1960

G. C. N.

CONTENTS

ILLUSTRATIONS

Contemporary Ceramics

Historical Ceramics

Kilns and Studio Equipment

COLOR PLATES

CERAMICS
A Potter's Handbook

CHAPTER 1

CERAMICS OF THE PAST

THE PREHISTORIC WORLD

Due to the imperishable nature of the fired clay, ceramic artifacts left by early man provide the most continuous record available of his gradual change from the nomadic hunter and cave dweller to the urban artisan of ancient cities. This development was not one of steady advance but reflects the wanderings of barbarian tribes over the earth's surface in search of food and a kindly climate, a progress frequently retarded by the disasters of nature and war.

The mysteries of life and death have been with man since the beginning of time. Fairly elaborate burial rites were a feature even of the paleolithic era. Even before man made the important discovery that a seed planted in the ground would reproduce itself, he had some awareness of the mysterious forces of birth and life. Feeling a need to propitiate these forces, he would usually carry a magic amulet and often placed one with the dead. It is largely from uncovered burial sites that we have gleaned most of our knowledge of prehistoric man. The fortunate discovery of the fabulous Magdalenian cave paintings in Altamira, Spain and Dordogne, France (circa 25,000 to 15,000 B.C.) reveal a skill so advanced that one can wonder whether man has really changed so much in the ensuing millenniums. Perhaps the oldest known of all human artifacts, dating even before the

An Aztec-Toltec ceremonial doll with the forceful vitality of the cultures we condescendingly choose to call Primitive. Teotihaucan, Mexico, ca. 600. Height 11 in. Permanent collection of International Business Machine Corporation.

cave paintings, is the famous small limestone carving, the Venus of Willendorf. Somewhat misnamed, it is basically a fertility fetish; its crude bulbous forms are typical of the earliest clay figurines found at other sites scattered throughout the world.

Due to the plastic quality of clay, it is likely that early man modeled objects from clay and sun dried them long before he discovered how hard and permanent clay became when baked by fire. It is assumed that pottery making developed when man first built a more or less permanent home, leaving the nomadic life of the hunter and seed gatherer to plant crops and tend herds. Initially, all pottery was made by the woman as a part of her household duties, for the man still spent most of his time at hunting and fishing. At this point in the dawn of history, the ice ages had long been forgotten. Paleolithic man no longer hunted the hairy mastodon and the elk. Instead he sought a milder climate and concentrated his settlements along the great river valleys of China, India, and the Middle East.

NEOLITHIC AND BRONZE AGE CERAMICS

It has been conjectured that clay may have been used as a lining material for woven baskets to enable them to hold fine seeds and that the burning of a discarded basket and the resulting fired clay form led to pottery making. The earliest pottery fragments whether from Asia, Europe, or the Americas have an over-all pressed cord decoration or banded incisions giving the effect of a basket weave. Considering the tenacity of customs, this theory may possibly be true. There is little doubt that pottery making developed independently in various areas of the world.

Early ceramic pieces exhibit a rounded or pointed bottom since tables were not in use, and a gourd may have been the original model. The oldest settlements along the Nile and Euphrates rivers are estimated to be about eight thousand years old. In each are found pottery fragments of a blackish color indicating the use of a primitive kiln, perhaps little more than a bonfire. Glazed tiles with a green copper colorant found in Egypt and dating from 5500 B.C. are our first examples of ceramic glazes. Many years pass, however, before glazes are used on pottery. Perhaps as early as 5000 B.C., the first pottery with colored slip decorations appeared in Harappa sites in India. This would indicate the development of a kiln with a chamber and a

Save for their elaborate headdress, these crude but expressive figurines are typical of all fertility symbols. Central Mexico, ca. 200 B.C.–300 A.D. Height 3 in. Permanent collection of the International Business Machine Corporation.

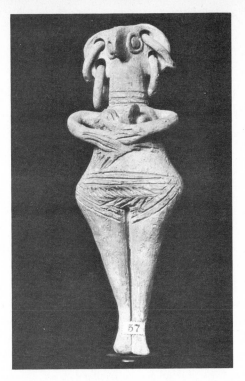

The unusual headdress would indicate a ritual background for this statuette. Cyprus, ca. 1500–1200 B.C. Courtesy of the Metropolitan Museum of Art, Cesnola Collection; purchased by subscription, 1874–1876.

The mother goddess concept evolves from the fertility fetish and also expresses fruitfullness and abundance. Susa, Iran, third century B.C. Terra cotta, height 7 in. Courtesy of the Metropolitan Museum of Art, Rogers Fund, 1951.

A coiled Predynasty pottery jar with slip decorations depicting the journey of the soul. Egypt, ca. 4000–3400 B.C. In the Brooklyn Museum Collection.

Predynastic pottery jar with spiral decoration in thin slip. Egypt, before 3400 B.C. Courtesy of the Chicago Natural History Museum.

controlled oxidization fire. Slip-decorated ware was made in Egypt by 4300 B.C. and at a similar period in Mesopotamia. Similar ware was also common in China about 3000 B.C. but not until 500 A.D. in the Americas. The rounded base continued in the slip-decorated pottery as in the earlier black corded ware. The basic forms were a wide-mouthed jar and the tall vase shape called a beaker. Combed decorations consisting of series of incised lines represent a transition design of greater freedom than the early corded technique. Inspired by the shape of the pot, many slip designs are spiral or circular in nature. An unusual phenomenon is the common occurrence of the double spiral motif in such distant sites as Northern China, Southwest Russia, and later in North America. The pointed, hollow, three-legged cooking pot is another example of similar but independent developments in both the Americas and China.

The construction of more efficient kilns is doubtless related to the smelting and casting of metals as they have a roughly similar time sequence. Even at this early date, the history of borrowing form and decoration from other media was common. The earliest pots resemble the gourds and baskets that were the older containers. The early bronzes were rare and of much greater value than a clay piece and therefore influenced the design of ceramic pieces. This practice generally worked to the detriment of the copy since the character of the material so determines possibilities of form and shape that such transfers are seldom functional. For example, the thin flared lip or foot so traditional in the metal form is not practical in the more fragile ceramic piece.

CERAMICS OF THE PAST

The slips first used were ordinary clays that due to impurities fired either white, buff, or brick red in color. After decanting to remove coarser particles, the liquid slip coating was applied to obtain a smoother surface on the pottery form. By burnishing the leather-hard slip with bone tools, a semiglossy coating not unlike a mat glaze was developed. The body of these pottery pieces were not waterproof. In time mineral additions, largely impure metallic oxides, were added to give a variety of colors.

MEDITERRANEAN CERAMICS

There is little doubt that the Fertile Crescent of the Nile and the Tigres-Euphrates river basins contain some of the oldest continuous settlements of man, and that ceramics evolved here at a very early age. Pottery with a turned foot, indicating the use of a potter's wheel, has been found at a site in Northern Iran dating from about 4000 B.C. The use of the potter's wheel spread slowly, partly because of the additional skill required. The large storage jars were still more easily made by a thick coil or partial mold. The potter's wheel seems related to the size and prosperity of settlement. Only the larger community could afford the services of a potter, a smith, a brewer, or a baker. At this period, pot making ceased to be part of the household duties of the woman and became a shared task or one wholly performed by the man. This situation has varied through the ages, but it is largely dependent upon economic factors.

Pottery jar with double spiral design in slip. Kansu, China, 3000–2000 B.C. Courtesy of the Chicago Natural History Museum.

Unglazed pottery jar with a thin slip decoration. Kansu, China, ca. 2000 B.C. Courtesy of the Metropolitan Museum of Art.

Glazed tiles from the predynastic period (before 3200 B.C.) have been found in several Egyptian sites. These glazes had an alkaline flux and were quite low-fired. A chance bonfire in a desert area containing soda compounds and sand very likely led to the first glaze. In spite of this early discovery, glazed pottery was not widely made in Egypt. The common people used unglazed earthenware. The Egyptians were stone carvers without equal, and the vases made elsewhere of glazed pottery were carved here of alabaster and marble. As the rich farming lands of the Nile delta were exploited, the Pharaoh, the priesthood, and wealthy land owners used vessels of silver and gold. Although Egyptian pottery and glazes appeared very early, they never achieved the skill of their contemporaries in Crete or of the later Persians.

The Egyptians did, however, use the alkaline glaze extensively as a decorative material. Tiles, numerous jewelry items, furniture inlays, and small statuettes were frequently made of faience. The term, faience, when applied to Egyptian ware is misleading. Faience originally referred to a pottery made in France during the sixteenth to eighteenth centuries that was covered with lead-tin glaze. The term was derived from Faenza, which was the most important pottery center in Italy during the Renaissance.

Early French archeologists made the mistake of assuming that the French lead-tin–glazed ware was similar to Egyptian alkaline glaze and the term has continued. The multitude of gods and the strong influences of religion and ceremony resulted in a tremendous demand for small cult statues. The Egyptian faience body was high in silica and borax type fluxes. As little clay was used, press molds were common and desirable for shaping the non-plastic faience. When the body dried, the soluble fluxes were drawn to the surface. In many cases, no further glaze was needed. Brush decoration was commonly employed on the faience pieces. Copper greens and turquoise were used at a very early period, and by 2000 B.C. a cobalt blue and manganese black were being used. By 1500 B.C., a great variety of additional colors were available such as the manganese purples, chrome yellows and orange, iron reds and opaque whites from tin oxide.

Turquoise hippopotamus. Egypt, Twelfth Dynasty, 2000–1780 B.C. Faience. In the Brooklyn Museum Collection.

Coinciding with the Egyptian civilization were settlements in Mesopotamia and the Aegean Islands. Lacking an oppressive priesthood, protected by the sea from easy attack, and engaging in open trade, the small island of Crete was able to develop an amazingly rich culture. The legendary King Minos was one of the later Kings of Crete. The Cretan period of 3000 to 1500 B.C. compares chronologically with the great period of Egyptian history. While Cretan sculpture and architecture did not compare with the Egyptian, their ceramics were far more varied and interesting. As a trading nation, Crete was stimulated by contacts throughout the Mediterranean. Cretan ware was certainly more advanced than that of other Aegean Islands. The snake goddess shown is a delightfully fresh piece, almost contemporary in feeling. It is a far cry from the fertility fetishes seen early in the chapter. The Cretan ware displays a variety of form in tall stemmed wine cups, handled vases, pitchers, and large storage jars. After 2000 B.C., the wheel was commonly used although large jars may still have been made by the thick coil and paddle method. Early ware was unglazed and slip decorated with geometric and later curvilinear designs. Banded decorations

Polychromed Snake Goddess. Crete, ca. 1575 B.C. Height 12 in. Courtesy of the Metropolitan Museum of Art.

became popular with the introduction of the wheel. Both alkaline and lead glazes were used. The finest period is usually regarded as that featuring the floral and sea motifs of a flowing design matching the form of the pottery (circa 1600 to 1500 B.C.). (See illustrated bottle.) As the island prospered, gold and silver objects were also made; and we find pottery with embossed figures in imitation of the metal forms.

During the closing years of the Minoan period, a series of barbarian invasions into Crete were launched from the north of Greece. These people were the Achaeans mentioned in Homer, and they gradually overran the

Copy of the famous octopus bottle. Crete, ca. 1600–1500 B.C. Courtesy of the Metropolitan Museum of Art, Dodge Fund, 1914.

CERAMICS OF THE PAST

mainland of Greece and finally the Aegean Islands. Remains of the Great Palace at Knossos in Crete indicates a partial destruction at about 1400 B.C. and severe fire and complete abandonment in 1200 B.C. The island never regained its position as a trading center, and the quality of the pottery rapidly declined.

Mycenae, in Southern Greece near present day Corinth, became the new center of power and wealth. The barbarian culture was dominated by the concept of warfare with the warrior chief as the ideal figure. Trade continued with Egypt and the Middle East but at a reduced pace. The evolving Greek pottery forms were influenced by the earlier Minoan ware. Banded geometric decoration was the early favorite with occasional battle scenes of warriors and horses. The *geometric* style lasted roughly from 1000 to 700 B.C. The subject matter—warriors, offerings to the gods, funerary rites, and battle scenes—crystalized and continued through Roman art. In many ways the geometric ware, with their conventionalized stick figures forming a sort of textural pattern over the surface of the piece, are more effective than the later and more technically advanced decoration. The slips used were usually white or a brownish black on a red earthenware body.

Terra cotta of a warrior on a horse, spirited but primitive compared to the previous Minoan culture. Cyprus, ca. 1000–600 B.C. Courtesy of the Metropolitan Museum of Art, Cesnola Collection; purchased by subscription, 1874–1876.

Mycenaean terra cotta bull with slip decoration. Late Helladic Period, ca. 1400–1100 B.C. Height 3½ in. Courtesy of the Metropolitan Museum of Art, Fletcher Fund, 1936.

An ingenious wine bottle derived from a horse and chariot which pivots on the front wheels to pour. Cyprus, ca. 1200–1000 B.C. Courtesy of the Metropolitan Museum of Art; the Cesnola Collection; purchased by subscription, 1874–1876.

During the seventh century B.C., the *oriental style* became popular. While the pottery form and banded decoration continued, the motifs were the curving forms of winged animals, birds, and flowers as in Assyrian and Egyptian ware. As conflicts occurred between the various Greek city-states and the growing Persian empire, this style became unpopular. Through the centuries, the Greek pottery forms evolved into a number of standardized vase and bottle shapes. They have graceful if somewhat hard and unclay-like outlines. The warring Greeks had a primary interest in weapons and the art of the smith was in high regard. The pottery took on a metallic quality derived from the weapons and the costly silver and gold vessels. The handles were often fragile and the flaring footrims were most impractical in clay. Everyday ware of coarse, undecorated pottery was less elaborate in design. The pieces shown here were all found in burial sites and are ceremonial and decorative in nature.

By the sixth century B.C., the prevailing style was the *black figure* ware. Banded decoration was still employed as in the geometric ware, but only a single band of figures was used. The so-called black varnish of the Greeks is an incorrect name given by archeologists to the black sliplike glaze, since it is neither a varnish, nor even a true glaze or a simple slip. This glaze appears identical to the terra sigillata of the Romans. It is prepared by making a thin slip of a high iron content clay. By successively stirring and pouring off the top layer, after allowing the heavy particles to settle, a fine slip of a glazelike quality is formed. Further gloss is developed by burnishing. Depending upon the clay used, the colors may be white, cream,

CERAMICS OF THE PAST

right Proto-Corinthian oinochoë in the late geometric
style with a handle more
proper to a metal form. Unglazed with slip decoration.
Greece, thirteenth–seventh
centuries B.C. Courtesy of
the Metropolitan Museum of
Art. left *Woman working
wool*, Athenian lekythos in
the black-figured style,
Greece, ca. 560 B.C. Courtesy of the Metropolitan Museum of Art, Fletcher Fund,
1931.

light red, brown, or black. The black is the result of a reduction during part
of the firing cycle. This was not, of course, a true glaze and it is not completely waterproof. The desire of the Greeks to tell a story seems to have
prevented them from ever using a true glaze although they were familiar
with the glazed pottery of Crete and Egypt. The black-figured ware con-

Storage jar in the famous
diphlon style. Geometric
period, Greece, eighth century B.C. Courtesy of the
Metropolitan Museum of Art,
Rogers Fund, 1914.

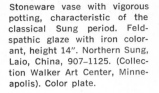

Stoneware vase with vigorous potting, characteristic of the classical Sung period. Feldspathic glaze with iron colorant, height 14". Northern Sung, Laio, China, 907–1125. (Collection Walker Art Center, Minneapolis). Color plate.

above *A Victorious Charioteer and Nike,* column Krater in the red-figured style in which decoration becomes more detailed. Greece, ca. 460–450 B.C. Courtesy of the Metropolitan Museum of Art.

right Two views of a graceful but somewhat fragile red-figured Kylix. Terra cotta. Attica, Greece, ca. 490–480 B.C. Courtesy of the Metropolitan Museum of Art, Joseph Pulitzer Bequest, 1953.

left Tanagra figurine characteristic of the trivial and sentimental nature of later Greek sculpture. Fourth century B.C. Terra cotta. Courtesy of the Metropolitan Museum of Art, Rogers Fund, 1906. **right** Tanagra figurine reflecting increased interest in movement and detail. Tarentum, Greece, third century B.C. Terra cotta. Courtesy of the Metropolitan Museum of Art, Rogers Fund, 1913.

tinued to emphasize the warrior and the battle scene along with the mythological gods. The draftsmanship improved greatly over the years although the profile view was still predominant.

By the fifth century B.C., a new technique of *red-figured ware*, which allowed for greater detail, superseded the black-figured ware. The decorative designs of the top and bottom panels were eliminated and the figure dominated the pottery. Reflecting the advances in sculpture and mural painting, the figures were now more fluid in movement and often were shown in a three-quarter view. The effect was that of a painting rather than of a pottery decoration. In fact, for the first time the piece was signed, usually only by the vase painter but occasionally also by the potter. This does not occur again until Renaissance times. There is no doubt that the painted figures and the pottery form do not belong together. During the fourth century B.C., the decoration and the form are even less related as the *florid* style develops with its crowded composition and the introduction of mountains, clouds, and atmospheric effects. This corresponds with a similar decadence in sculpture, which reflects the cultural breakdown that followed the futile wars among the Greek city-states and their colonies.

CHINESE CERAMICS

China has had a long and a relatively unbroken tradition of high achievements in ceramics. Pottery seems to have developed at a slightly later date than in the Nile–Euphrates regions, but this is uncertain since fewer archeological excavations have been made and information is meager. Neolithic ware from northwest China, circa 3000 to 2000 B.C., was pictured early in the chapter. Typical of hand-built ware, it is round bottomed, unglazed, and decorated at first with corded textures and later with clay slips. By the Shang period, 1766 to 1122 B.C., the potter's wheel had come into common use. A hard white body was used as well as the older and more common red earthenware. No glazes were available, although the burnished slip often gave this appearance.

The Shang period was notable for its great advances in metallurgy. Decorative bronzes of a variety of shapes and with intricate low reliefs became an important part of religious ceremonies. At first the early bronzes copied the older pottery forms. Finally the potter, influenced by the more highly

Wheel-thrown earthenware vase, with a banded and incised surface suggestive of a metal form, unglazed. Kansu, China, Shang Dynasty, 1766–1122 B.C. Courtesy of the Metropolitan Museum of Art.

regarded bronzes, made virtual replicas in clay. Over-decorated and with thin, breakable handles, this ware represented a regression from the simple, yet powerful, fluid ware of the neolithic era. The force of tradition has always been a great factor in the stability of Chinese culture, enabling them to eventually absorb with little change the numerous conquering Tartar and Mongol tribes from the north. The reverence for the ancient bronzes, however, has been disadvantageous to the Chinese potter. We are able to see down through the centuries his unfortunate attempts to merge metal and clay concepts.

Pottery lampadere candlestick, showing interest in bird and animal forms typical of the Han Dynasty. China, 206 B.C.–200 A.D. Courtesy of the Metropolitan Museum of Art.

Stylized horse's head, fragment of a tomb sculpture. China, Han Dynasty, 206 B.C.–220 A.D. Height 9 in. Courtesy of the Metropolitan Museum of Art.

We have little pottery from the Chou period (1122 to 249 B.C.) as it was an unstable period when China was plagued by numerous invasions by nomadic tribes of the north and west. It was the custom of these nomadic horsemen to bury their chief in a large tomb with his wives, attendants, soldiers, and even his favorite horse. As conditions stabilized, there was a long period of peace and prosperity. The great Chinese philosophers Confucius and Lao Tzŭ (circa 500 B.C.) were writing and attracting followers. In such a cultural period, the primitive burial rites were bound to change; we owe much of our knowledge of the Han Dynasty (206 B.C. to 220 A.D.) and the following dynasties to the custom of substituting clay objects for the live burial of people and animals.

A great age of ceramic sculpture occurs during the Three Kingdoms (Wei) and Six Dynasties period, 220 to 589 A.D. and the T'ang Dynasty, 618 to 907 A.D. Particularly significant are the many studies of horses that had never been modeled with such vitality before, or since. Numerous guardian and warrior figures were common as well as the mythological beasts intended to ward off evil spirits. The personages about the court, ladies, dancers, and traveling merchants were depicted with great skill. They are charming and at times amusing without being overly ornate or sentimental. The traveling merchants are of interest as they indicate that trade routes across southern Siberia to the Middle East existed at that time. None of the sculpture shown, except for the roof finial, is glazed. The clay is an earthenware of a buff or red color; it is decorated with slips or a chalky paint, much of which has flaked off from the effects of burial.

Glazes are thought to have been introduced into China from the Middle East during the late Chou or early Han Dynasty, somewhere between 300 and 250 B.C. Hellenistic and Near Eastern sculptural forms as well as their ceramic influences are also evident. At first alkaline and later lead fluxes were used. The initial glaze colorants were primarily iron and copper compounds that gave a variety of yellow-tan, brown, and green hues. The clays used were more of a stoneware type and were fired higher than in the Middle East. By late Han times, about 250 A.D., a grey stoneware was made using a feldspathic glaze possibly fluxed with wood ashes. The term kaolin is of Chinese origin and together with *petuntse*, a material similar to feldspar, it formed the basis of their porcelain body. White slips of a porcelain character were used on stoneware bodies as early as 250 A.D. A mixture of 3 parts of this porcelain slip and 1 of calcium will produce a high-fired glaze. Undoubtedly, porcelain and high-fired glazes originated in China.

Essentially there is no difference between a high-fired stone body and a porcelain body save for the presence of iron and other impurities that give the stoneware its characteristic grey color. But, it will be many centuries before the Chinese either find large pure stoneware clay deposits or refine them sufficiently to produce their famous translucent porcelain wares. Porcelain fragments from China with a hard even glaze have been found at Samarra, Persia at a site definitely dated between 834 and 883 A.D.

Terra cotta horse with the animation typical of the Wei Dynasty. China, ca. 250. Length 20 in. Courtesy of the Museum of Far Eastern Antiquities, Stockholm.

T'ang mortuary horse, slightly less detailed than the Wei piece shown. Seldom has sculpture been more dynamic. China, T'ang Dynasty, 618–906. Height 16½ in. Courtesy of the Royal Ontario Museum, Toronto.

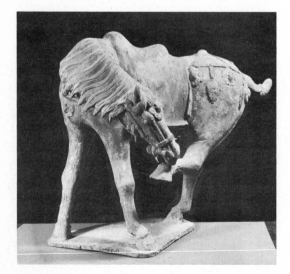

CERAMICS OF THE PAST

above A strongly modeled head, nearly life size, from a tomb figure. China, T'ang Dynasty, 618–906. Courtesy of the Art Institute of Chicago.

above Graceful court ladies from a Wei tomb. Loyang, China, ca. 500–530. Height 24 in. Courtesy of the Royal Ontario Museum, Toronto.

below, left The tomb figures also included amusing court dancers. China, T'ang Dynasty, 618–906. Courtesy of the Museum of Far Eastern Antiquities, Stockholm. **below, right** Tomb terra cotta of a Mohammedan Cloth Merchant. China, T'ang Dynasty, 618–906. Height 13 in. Courtesy of the Philadelphia Museum of Art.

A guardian beast roof finial, typical of tomb guardian sculpture. China, Sung Dynasty, 960 or earlier. Colored slip with lead glaze. Courtesy of the Museum of Far Eastern Antiquities, Stockholm.

The Sung Dynasty, 960 to 1280 A.D., was a period of conflicts with first the Northern Tartars and later the Mongols. The Mongols, under Jenghiz Khan and his successors, finally conquered China and adjoining territories in 1280. Nevertheless, there was a great flowering of Chinese culture and the Sung period is regarded as the classic era. The ceramic ware was characterized by strength and vitality, accentuated by a sensitive restraint. The stoneware body was finer and harder and ranged in color from white to grey to reddish-brown, depending upon the amount of iron present and the firing procedure (see reduction glazes in Chapter 6). Porcelains were very common, often with shallow incised designs. A few are so thin and the pattern so delicate that the piece must be held up to the light to reveal the design.

Colors were used sparingly, usually one or two colors in brown or black or shades of blue and green. The jadelike celadon and the ox-blood copper red glazes were also developed during the Sung Dynasty (see Chapter 6). Together with the porcelain body, these achievements will baffle the Middle Eastern and European potter for many centuries.

Stoneware bottle vase with white and black slips, incised lines under a transparent glaze. It is typical of the strength of the Sung ware and the appropriateness of form and decoration. Chih, China, ca. 1108. Courtesy of the Metropolitan Museum of Art.

CERAMICS OF THE PAST

Buff stoneware Tzu-Chou vase, covered with white slip and a brown brush decoration. The creamlike glaze has a fine crackle. China, Sung Dynasty, 960–1229. Courtesy of the Art Institute of Chicago.

Ceramics were no longer made for burial purposes but rather were produced for the enjoyment of everyday life. Many potteries produced superior work, and some worked only for the Imperial Court. The porcelain was now as equally esteemed as were the rare old bronzes and objects crafted in jade. Decoration attained a fluent and spontaneous freedom that echoes the best periods of Minoan art. Crackle glazes were used now on purpose, and the size of the crackle and its character was controlled to produce subtle decorative effects. The hardness and the integration between the stoneware body and glaze represents a unique development. No longer is the glaze film apt to chip off the softer and porous clay body. The viscous quality and crystalline structure of higher-fired glazes gave a new dimension to ceramics. The *temmoku* glaze, with its mottled rich browns and blacks and silky texture, is an example.

Porcelain bowl with carved and incised dragon decoration. China, Sung Dynasty, 960–1280. Celadon glaze. Courtesy of the Metropolitan Museum of Art.

It is no wonder then that the Sung ceramics would be admired and copied by succeeding generations of Chinese potters. Its influence was a predominant one on nearby Korea and Japan. Both countries developed individual characteristics such as the Korean *mishima* decoration, the fluid brush work of the Japanese Kenzans, and the cultivated yet primitive quality of the Japanese tea ceremony ware. Neverthless, the Chinese presence remained strong, and during the succeeding centuries it continued to influence its neighbors and eventually European ware as well.

The Mongol invasions from the north that ended the weakened Sung Dynasty in 1280 will occur several times again before modern times. During this considerable period, the Ming Dynasty, 1368 to 1644, and the Ch'ing, 1662 to 1796, were the most stable and of greatest ceramic importance. The work of the Sung period continued to be held in high regard, and quantities of stoneware and porcelain continued to be made in the older style. Very likely many pieces attributed to Sung potters in our museums were made during the Ming period.

left Stoneware jar with a deft, spontaneous brushwork that will be a great influence on later Japanese ceramics. China, Sung Dynasty, 960–1280. Courtesy of the Metropolitan Museum of Art. **right** A graceful stoneware bottle with inlaid *mishima* decoration. Korea, Korai period, 918–1392. Celadon glaze. Courtesy of the Metropolitan Museum of Art.

Stoneware tea bowl with a *temmoku* (hare's fur) feldspathic glaze. The high iron content produces a rich brown with a streaked, runny effect. China, Sung Dynasty, 960–1279. Courtesy of the Art Institute of Chicago.

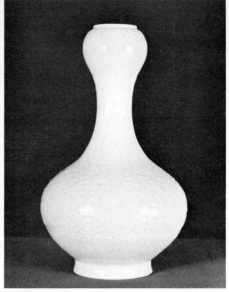

Ming porcelain jar decorated with cobalt underglaze colors. China, Hsuan Te period, 1426–1435. Courtesy of the Metropolitan Museum of Art.

Gourd-shaped vase, thin porcelain with pressed design. Sensitive yet lacking strength of Sung pieces. China, 1662–1722. Courtesy of the Art Institute of Chicago.

The Ming style might be compared to that of our own Baroque period. Both exhibit a great technical facility but with a tendency for over elaborated form and decoration. The subtle curves of the Sung forms became far more "S" shaped. The pieces illustrated represent the restrained style and not the flamboyant multicolored decorative designs that, like late Greek style, tended to float off the surface of the pot. These more ornate styles found much favor among the early Dutch, English, and French traders in the seventeenth and eighteenth centuries. This led to a great vogue in Europe for Chinese porcelains. The Dutch Delft ware was produced in imitation of the blue and white Ming ware. Forms became exaggerated, and decorations were derived from fabrics and paintings. European importers even had special designs made up, invariably gaudy in color and ill suited to the form for which they were created.

To the student of ceramics the Ch'ing Dynasty (1662 to 1796) reveals the characteristics of an artistically confused period. While some potters were creating sensitive forms with delicate pale blue and ox-blood glazes, other potteries turned out commercial ware in the poor taste of the Famille Rose enamel category. Then, during the nineteenth century, China was plagued with revolts; their rulers were ineffectual. Foreign intervention and trade further interrupted the traditional patterns of life. There is some question as to whether the unsurpassed ceramic tradition of China can withstand the twentieth century industrial and political storm as well as it did the invasions of the warring Mongols.

CERAMICS OF THE PAST

THE MIDDLE EAST AND LUSTERWARE

One of the fascinating aspects of ceramics is the obvious and extreme diversity found in the work of the various peoples of the world. In fact, we are generally surprised to find any similarities at all. We mentioned earlier the universality of the first pottery forms such as the rounded bottom and the corded decoration. Pottery sherds were found at a very early period in the Tigres-Euphrates river basins, and the earliest wheels were made slightly to the north in Iran in approximately 4000 B.C. Early slip-decorated ware, not unlike that of Egypt and Crete, was common. Egypt, due to her protecting deserts, and China, because of her immense size, were able to develop over the centuries a cultural continuity that allowed their art forms to develop distinctive styles. By contrast, the Middle East was little more than a cross roads of nomadic people and marauding armies. Among the more unique artistic developments of the Middle East, is the frequent use

Porcelain Kwan Yin figure (a Buddhist divinity), glazed. China, Ch'ing Dynasty, 1666–1722. Height 18½ in. Courtesy of the Art Institute of Chicago.

A copper-red glaze (*sang-de-boeuf*) on a classic vase form. The rich glaze makes further decoration superfluous. China, Ch'ing Dynasty, 1662–1722. Courtesy of the Metropolitan Museum of Art.

of glazed brick and tile. Lacking convenient stone for sculpture, the Mesopotamians used colorful glazed brick and tile in lieu of relief sculpture. A portion of the famous Lion Wall of Nebuchadnezzar II (605 to 562 B.C.) is illustrated. These tile reliefs representing lions and other beasts lined a processional street leading to the palace. Tin, as an agent to whiten a glaze, was used in a limited fashion in Assyria as early as 1100 B.C. Lead-fluxed glazes were common at this time although seldom used in Egypt where the alkaline fluxes were more available. Opaque glazes made possible color and decorative techniques not easily achieved with the older clay slip and transparent glaze methods.

All early cultures seem to go through a period of a mechanical-like, banded, and angular patterned decoration. In the Middle East, this style was accompanied by curvilineal design elements derived from leaves, vine tendrils, bird, and animal forms. Pottery from Susa, circa 3000 B.C., combined these angular patterns with exaggerated curved animal forms. Through the succeeding Babylonian, Assyrian, Persian, and Hellenistic empires the curvilinear motif grew and finally became the dominant design element. The birth of Mohammed (570 to 632 A.D.), and the rapid spread of the religious and political power of Islam extended this *arabesque* from distant India to Spain. The flowing curve and interlacing pattern was the major motif for ceramics as well as for fabrics and rugs. The Arabic script is of such decorative quality that it was often used, like oriental calligraphy, as a design. Islamic architecture, from the Taj Mahal in India to the Alhambra in Spain, would not be notable without the pointed dome and arch and the delicate floral tracery in marble and tile.

As early as the Han Dynasty, there was contact between China and Rome via caravan routes through the Middle East. The first translucent porcelain pieces imported to the Middle East were greeted with amazement and were highly treasured by the Islamic Caliphs. The thin white ware represented a challenge to the local potters. Without local kaolin deposits, his only solution was to use a cream colored earthenware and a lead-tin glaze. However, the Islamic potter was much too interested in his own decorative ideas to copy the Chinese designs for long. The opaque glaze they used was a perfect background for the intricate brush designs and was quicker and more fluent in execution than the earlier carved slip patterns.

Luster glazes had doubtless occurred accidently before in both Egypt and Mesopotamia. Luster refers to a mirror-like coating of metal on the surface of a glaze. An excess of metallic oxides in a glaze will often produce such a coating. The procedure is to glaze and decorate with coloring oxides. The piece is then fired and the luster decoration is later applied to specific areas and refired at a second and lower temperature (see Chapter 6 on luster glazes for details).

Portion of the Lion Wall of King Nebuchadnezzer, II (605–562 B.C.) in Babylon. Lead-tin glaze in white, tan, blue, and green hues on earthenware bricks. Courtesy of the Metropolitan Museum of Art.

The human figure was prohibited from being shown in religious art but was widely used in secular ceramic decoration. The delicate and flowing curvilinear style of the arabesque was naturally suited to the rich and elegant quality of the luster glaze. The earliest examples date from the ninth century, and the height of figural development is in Persia in the twelfth century. Major pottery centers were in Rhages, Rakka, and Sultanabad. All these declined after the Mongols under the Hulagre, the grandson of Jenghiz Khan, conquered Baghdad and the Middle East in 1258. Although the luster

Sultanabad ewer of buff earthenware, black brush decoration under turquoise glaze. Persia, thirteenth–fourteenth centuries. Courtesy of the Art Institute of Chicago, Mr. and Mrs. Martin A. Ryerson Collection.

opposite, left Rhages bowl decorated with golden luster. Persia, twelfth century. Courtesy of the Metropolitan Museum of Art, Rogers Fund, 1920. **opposite, right** Lusterware wall tile of a type used extensively on both religious and private buildings. Arabic script on border. Veramin, Persia, ca. 1265. Diameter 15″. Courtesy of the Metropolitan Museum of Art. **right** Pottery plate from Turkey, early seventeenth century. The stylized flowers have become stiff and lack the fluid brush work of earlier Islamic work. Courtesy of the Metropolitan Museum of Art, Rogers Fund, 1928.

decoration may be in a variety of hues, a light golden brown was the most popular. The alkaline-fluxed glaze continued to be used to obtain the unusual turquoise blues, usually combined with a brush decoration in black over a light ground.

The first century after the birth of Mohammed saw the great sweep of Islam across North Africa and into Spain, which was conquered by 712 A.D. With it came the Eastern Mediterranean culture that to this day makes Spain slightly different from the rest of Europe. Spain's most impressive buildings are still those from the Umayyad Dynasty, 765 to 1031. It was through Islamic Spain that the ceramic skills of the Middle East were carried into Europe. Valencia was an important pottery center and the Hispano-Moresque lusterware was the equal of the Persians. An extensive ceramic trade was developed with Italy, before the expulsion of the Moors in 1502 and the subsequent decline of this commerce.

ETRUSCAN, ROMAN, AND ITALIAN RENAISSANCE WARE

The Etruscans are thought to have come to Italy during the ninth century B.C. from an area that is present-day Syria and Southern Turkey. They prospered and eventually controlled an area in central Italy from slightly north of Rome to Bologna. Many cities that later became famous in the Renaissance, such as Pisa, Florence, Perugia, Orvieto, and others, were founded by the Etruscans. The year 474 B.C. marked the first time the Etruscans felt the growing power of the Roman state, which would gradually absorb them during the following 300 years.

Etruscan oinochoë in the typical buccero style. Italy, before 500 B.C. Courtesy of the Art Institute of Chicago, gift of P. D. Armour and C. L. Hutchinson.

The Etruscan ware of central Italy showed only Egyptian and Syrian influences during the eighth and seventh centuries B.C. Architectural reliefs and temple decorations were commonly made of ceramics as were sarcophagi with animated sculptural figures. By the sixth century B.C., Greek influences were felt, and many of their shapes were adapted to Etruscan purposes. The traditional *bucchero* ware of the Etruscans had a black sliplike glaze, much like the Greek black varnish, with impressed or relief decorations influenced by metal *repousse* work. Roman ware evolved from both Etruscan and Hellenistic Greek influences, although cruder in execution. In time it displayed all the ornate and tasteless features of the late Greek ware.

Urn in shape of a sarcophagus, showing influence of late Greek naturalism. Etruscan, third century B.C. Courtesy of the Metropolitan Museum of Art, purchased by subscription, 1896.

Etruscan ceremonial vase with figure of Satyr. The modeling reflects the more animated and realistic nature of Etruscan sculpture in contrast to the stylization of the Greek. This will also become a characteristic of Roman sculpture. Possibly from Orvieto, Central Italy, fourth century B.C. Courtesy of the Metropolitan Museum of Art, Rogers Fund, 1920.

A significant technical development in the Roman period was the extensive use of bisque-ware molds, undoubtedly influenced by metal casting procedures. Inasmuch as the designs were impressed in the mold, the need for applied clay ornament was eliminated. These innovations were spread by the numerous Roman colonies, and it is possible that the popularity of impressed decoration during the Medieval period in the southern Rhineland may be due to some such dormant influence.

Apparently there was little influence from Roman pottery upon early Renaissance ware. Such pottery, typically, had a red earthernware body covered with a lighter colored slip. The term *sgraffito* is of Italian origin and refers to lineal decoration that was commonly scratched through applied slip to reveal the contrasting clay color beneath. Lead glazes were used, which were rather runny in nature, with colorants of iron and copper that limited the glazes to hues of brownish-yellow and green. Like the eighth-century Islamic potter who was amazed by the sight of the thin Chinese porcelain, so also was the Italian potter impressed by the Hispano-Moresque lusterware. Naturally, the imported Spanish ware was copied; in time the new techniques were learned. It is said that the trading vessels from Spain stopped at the island of Mallorca (Majorca). In time this lead-tin–glazed ware came to be known as Majolica, supposedly due to this coincidence. The luster technique was learned but was not accompanied by the subtle decorative skill of the Hispano-Moresque potter. The Renaissance was interested in the more factual story of man, and painting and sculpture were the impor-

Hispano-Moresque lusterware plate. Valencia, Spain, sixteenth century. Courtesy of the Metropolitan Museum of Art, bequest of Mrs. H. O. Havemeyer, 1929. The H. O. Havemeyer Collection.

Majolica armory plate. Florence, Italy, ca. 1480. Earthenware, lead-tin glaze with overglaze decoration. Courtesy of the Metropolitan Museum of Art.

Majolica albarello, more of a portrait study than a decorated vase. Faenza, Italy, ca. 1475. Courtesy of the Metropolitan Museum of Art.

Madonna and Child with Scroll, terra cotta with lead-tin glaze. Luca della Robbia. Italy, fifteenth century. Courtesy of the Metropolitan Museum of Art.

CERAMICS OF THE PAST

tant arts. Soon the pottery was to become, as with the Greeks, a field on which to paint. There was no relationship between the design and the form that it decorated. The albarello illustrated is a restrained piece for the period. Later, whole paintings were copied on large plates that were intended to be hung as wall decorations.

It is rare when a culture interested in sculptural forms does not also produce ceramic sculpture since clay is universally used for study models. Most of the Renaissance sculptors whose work we know in bronze or marble also did madonnas and portraits in terra cotta that were eventually poly-chromed. Luca della Robbia, also an expert stone carver, was the major sculptor to work in terra cotta. Part of his success was doubtless due to his ability to successfully use the potter's lead-tin glaze on his pieces. The glaze fitted the body well and was of a soft off-white color somewhat like marble. Della Robbia seldom used any color other than a soft blue as a lunette background. His many followers, including members of his own family, were not as concerned about the sculptural form; as the baroque period approached, their altar pieces became gaudy displays of inappropriately applied color.

PRE-COLUMBIAN CERAMICS

It is currently assumed that the American Indians originally came from Asia, crossing the Bering straits in a series of migrations during a period of from 10,000 to 20,000 years ago. Wave after wave of these small bands of nomadic hunters gradually drifted southward seeking a more favorable climate. Pushing the earlier settlers in front of them, they eventually reached the southern most tip of South America.

Permanent settlements first developed in the warm fertile valleys of Mexico and Central and South America. Agriculture, based on indigenous plants—corn, potatoes, beans, tomatoes, squash—slowly grew from these centers. Cotton was used for cloth; in Peru, the wool of the llama was used. Jewelry was made of copper, gold, silver, and tin by casting, alloying, and plating. However, metal tools were rare and transport limited since the horse and donkey were not native to the New World.

The earliest settlements show pottery sherds similar to those of neolithic Europe. Decoration is of a banded, incised texture, not unlike a basket weave. They probably date as early as 1000 B.C., which, in comparison with

left Tarascon effigy jar. Michoacan, Mexico, ca. 800–1300. Burnished slip decoration, height 6 in. Permanent collection of International Business Machine Corporation. **center** Mohican bird-headed effigy bottle. Peru, ca. 100 B.C.–900 A.D. Burnished slip decoration, height 11½ in. Courtesy of the Museum of Primitive Art. **right** A double snake-headed vase. Tarascon culture, Michoacan, Mexico, ca. 800–1300. Burnished slip decoration, height 8 in. Permanent collection of International Business Machine Corporation.

A figurative pottery bowl. Central Mississippi Valley, ca. 1200–1400. Courtesy of the American Museum of Natural History.

the Old World, is rather recent. The small terra cotta figurines from Mexico shown earlier in this chapter indicate a world-wide similarity of interests and techniques. Since our knowledge of ancient cultures has been largely due to items included in burial sites, the more utilitarian pottery items are seldom in evidence. This is especially true of the New World where the ceramic items are of a more sculptural nature. With rare exceptions, such as in the cultures of Central Mexico, sculpture in stone is not frequent. The Mexican stone sculpture, although impressive, never developed the technical facility or diversity characteristic of Egypt or of Greece. The ceramics of the New World are more comparable with that of China where ceramic sculpture was of greater importance.

The Pre-Columbian culture was new and still influenced by animistic beliefs, and we therefore find much of their ceremonial pottery in human or animal form. Several examples are shown from the Mississippi Valley, in the North, from Central Mexico, and from Peru, further to the South. The important ceramic centers were located in Central Mexico and in the western coast of South America that is now Peru. In North America, considerable pottery was made by the Mound Builders in the Ohio, Indiana, Illinois, and Arkansas region. A much finer ware was made in the New Mexico-Arizona region, such as the Mimbres, which equals the skill and imagination of the ceramics further south. During the three thousand years of rather continuous settlements, these areas have experienced the rise and fall of numerous cultural groups, such as the Mayan, Toltec, Chimu, and so on. No effort will be made to distinguish these groups, except to indicate a few characteristics of interest.

It is but natural for man to have a sculptural interest in human representation. As we have seen, the oldest clay items are crudely modeled human figurines. The illustrations show a rapid growth in facility, but it should be obvious that the Indian has a very unclassical approach to his work. The elaborate headdress and the ceremonial costumes have undoubtedly influenced the pottery pieces. But this is a reflection of an over-all interest in the fantastic and make-believe. There is a great deal of humor reflected in the caricatures that are so free and easily modeled. The pottery of the Toltec culture from the west coast of Mexico, near Colima, is especially noteworthy for the true sculptural quality of smoothly flowing and well-integrated form. As in the Old World, there is a continual borrowing back and forth of design ideas between the art forms. The Zapotec piece shown with the hieratic headdress is reminiscent of the stone carvings of the period. In a similar manner, the designs of the Pueblo Indians reflect their basket techniques.

Effigy vessel of warrior with slingshot, with the flowing form and movement typical of the Colima. Mexico, ca. 300–1200. Height 14⅜ in. Courtesy of the Museum of Primitive Art.

opposite, left Pottery dog with burnished red slip in the rounded Colima style. Mexico, ca. 800–1000. In the Brooklyn Museum Collection. opposite, right Terra cotta female figure from Archaic period, 200 B.C.-300 A.D. Tarascon culture, Michoacan, Mexico, height 8 in. Permanent collection of International Business Machine Corporation. left Terra cotta figure more sophisticated than the preceding one, showing evidences of a burnished slip decoration and added texture. Jalisco, Mexico, ca. 800. Height 19¾ in. Courtesy of the Museum of Primitive Art.

above A terra cotta warrior from upper Cauca, Columbia, typical of the ceremonial dress of the half human-half demon. Courtesy of the American Museum of Natural History. right God of Fire, ceremonial funeral urn, derived from stone sculpture of the Zapotec. Oaxaca, Mexico, seventh century. Height 26 in. Permanent collection of International Business Machine Corporation.

Pre-Columbian Ceramics

It is extremely rare when a work from the past can evoke, after many centuries, a reaction in the beholder similar to that originally produced. The representations of ancient gods only provoke our curiosity, and the figures of the mighty warriors now have a theatrical make-believe quality. Perhaps, more successful than anything in this regard is the illustration of the Girl in the Swing shown on the opposite page. Certainly we have here, without sentimentality, a perfect evocation of the wonder and the excitement of childhood. The little head is modeled with strength and sensitivity; the flowing cloak and figure are simplified to the bare essentials. It is a perfect expression of the plastic and almost playful quality inherent in clay; it is a closer kin to the T'ang horses than anything we have so far studied.

The considerable ceramic achievements of the New World potter were achieved without two major developments, long used by the European and Asian potter: the spinning potter's wheel, and a true glossy glaze. Two-piece bisque molds were common for small objects, and larger pieces were made in two pieces and then joined. Most of the pottery was not heavy nor was it fired very high. The earliest pieces were smoked black with a corded decoration. Another technique was to incise designs on the polished black body. The development of better kilns made possible an oxidization fire permitting the use of colored clay slips. These slips were carefully prepared to give a fine surface that was further smoothed by burnishing.

Another New World potting center, somewhat further to the south than Colima, occupied the irrigated coastal region and some highland areas of what is now Peru. Numerous cultural groups lived in this and adjoining areas, but we will show only a few major examples. Sculpture in stone was rarely made in these areas with the result that the pottery became quite sculptural. It retained, nevertheless, a hollow form and a pottery feeling. These pieces have a smooth burnished surface, seldom textural. The earlier pieces such as those from the Chimu culture are nearly always jet black in color. The typical design is the stirrup bottle with a double neck or twin spouts. In this desert region, the water bottle became the most important pottery form. These were often in the shape of animals or of humans doing various tasks. Slip decoration was a highly developed skill, often derived from woven fabrics at which the Naxca peoples were unusually expert. The slips were in a wide range of hues in red, green, blue, yellow, black, and white. The burnished surface was not completely waterproof. Wax was employed to effect some of the color separations.

Girl in Swing, with a whistle attachment. Veracruz, Mexico, ca. 750. Terra cotta, height 9¾ in., slip decoration. Courtesy of the Museum of Primitive Art.

We tend to think of Indian life as harsh and vigorous, unrelieved by laughter. That they were more fun-loving than we might expect is suggested by the numerous whistling bottles. These are split- or double-chambered with orifices so constructed as to produce a whistle when the bottle was tilted or emptied (see illustration).

Pottery supplied the sole sculptural outlet for these people of ancient Peru. On the back of the portrait pot shown is the traditional hollow, looped handle and spout. The modeling is strong and the total effect impressive. This leads us to one of those strange anomalies of ceramics and art in general. Why is this portrait pot so acceptable? Most efforts at combining ceramic sculpture with a functional pottery form fail, due to attempts at excessive realism or emotional qualities of a sentimental or comic nature. For example, the Etruscan piece shown on page 29 has a disturbing incongruity about it. As we approach a certain degree of realism, a sort of wax world develops with an unpleasant living-dead sensation. The sculptured pot must have an identity of its own apart from the living world. All Peruvian pieces are not equally successful in maintaining this delicate balance. Some become caricatures like the English Toby pots. In the latter case, the jovial humor of the fat seated man and the details of the costume detract from the sculptural form. It becomes a bizarre curio that jumps from its surroundings.

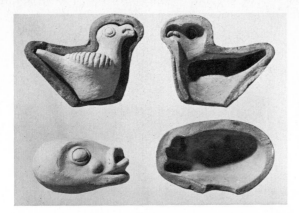

above, left Single and two-piece bisque molds. Peru. Courtesy of the American Museum of Natural History. above, right Nazca bowl with effective repeat design derived from a row of trophy heads. Peru, ca. 1000. Courtesy of the Art Institute of Chicago, Buckingham Fund. right Nazca stirrup pot with burnished slip design of feline goddess holding two trophy heads. Peru, ca. 1000. Courtesy of the Art Institute of Chicago, Buckingham Fund.

opposite, left Chimu puma stirrup pot with black burnished surface. Peru, ca. 1000. Courtesy of the Art Institute of Chicago, Buckingham Fund. opposite, right Mochica stirrup pot. Lacking a potter's wheel, the Indian potter tends toward more sculptural forms. Peru, ca. 1000. Courtesy of the Art Institute of Chicago, Buckingham Fund. left Mochica stirrup pot, more pottery-like in form with a warrior motif in lineal design. Peru, ca. 1000. Courtesy of the Art Institute of Chicago, Buckingham Fund.

39

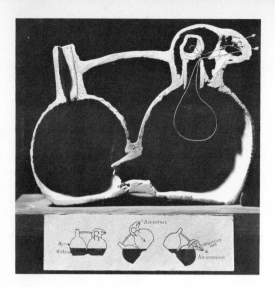

Cross section of a twin-chambered whistling bottle. Peru, late Chimu period, 1200–1400. Courtesy of the American Museum of Natural History.

The late Greek and Roman portrait vases are so obviously overdone as to lose their appeal. By contrast, the Mochica head has a monumental sculptural form that seems natural in spite of its bottle function. Yet, if a contemporary potter were to try such a piece the result would be ridiculous. The fact that the Chinese potters in past generations, were often able to successfully copy the styles and work of their forefathers is a reflection that the life of the potters had undergone little change and that cultural values remained largely the same. The many historical examples shown here are not intended as models but rather to suggest the possibilities of clay that man has discovered in past ages. The nature of life in recent generations has so changed that it is likely we shall never again have the unique regional qualities that has characterized world ceramics in the past.

Portrait face of a Mochica stirrup water bottle. Peru, ca. 1100. Courtesy of the Art Institute of Chicago.

Terra cotta horse, reminiscent of early Greek styles, but it may date much later. Morocco, North Africa. Height 4⅜ in. Courtesy of the Museum of Primitive Art.

AFRICAN CERAMICS

Cave paintings from the paleolithic ages have been found in the mountains south of the Sahara Desert. The existence of this great desert, however, tended to separate tropical Africa from the more temperate Mediterranean regions. Contacts were frequent between Egypt and Sudan, but other African trade was very rare until the fifteenth century.

The Moroccan piece shown is not unlike the early Greek figurines and may have in fact originated from a Greek colony in North Africa. Wood is the material commonly used for sculpture in Central Africa. Unfortunately, it does not survive long in a humid climate. The water buffalo head shown is evidently from a wooden prototype, since it displays the simple form usually associated with wood carvings done with primitive tools and none of the almost playful exuberance of form usually associated with ceramic sculpture.

As is true for all cultures, the early pottery was made by the women of the tribe. Neither the wheel nor glazes were used, and the ware seldom became an item of commerce. The gourd was a common container as evidenced by the sculptural pair from the Congo who sit on gourd shaped forms. Although a twentieth-century piece, the style of the figures are derived from the older wood sculpture.

The high point of African culture appears to have been centered along the southern coast of present day Nigeria. The ancient African kingdom of Benin is reputed to date from 1150 and to have continued until the nineteenth century. The Benin art was particularly noted for the bronze relief

African Ceramics

panels placed on doorways and buildings and the portrait heads of the ruling families. The finest work dates from 1500 to 1700, although bronzes were done at an earlier date. After contact with European naturalism, the quality of the sculpture deteriorated.

These bronzes are in the lost wax process and are of excellent workmanship. This has posed a problem for the archeologist as to whether the technique was of local development or the result of an old connection with the North during Greek or Roman times. Clay usually serves as a preliminary model for any bronze work, and it is but natural that terra cotta heads would be made. The portrait head illustrated has a plastic quality and a dignity of expression seldom equaled in any age.

right Water buffalo head, a totemistic piece perhaps derived from a wooden mask. Toso, West Africa, nineteenth century. Courtesy of the Museum of Primitive Art. **below** Pottery bottles, derived from gourd forms and older wood-carving techniques. Lower Congo, West Africa, perhaps early nineteenth century. Courtesy of the American Museum of Natural History.

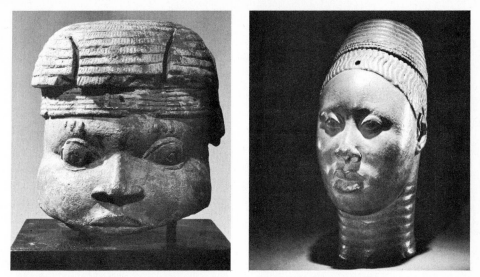

left Terra cotta head, in a style influenced by wood sculpture of the period. Beni, Nigeria, possibly nineteenth century or earlier. Height of fragment 8¼ in. Courtesy of the Museum of Primitive Art. **right** Cast of the Ife terra cotta head called, *Lajuwa*. Original in Nigeria and typical of the golden age of Benin art, ca. 1500–1700. Courtesy of the American Museum of Natural History.

LATER EUROPEAN CERAMICS

The early pottery in northern Europe followed the traditional pattern of black-smoked earthenware with corded and later incised and burnished decoration. The neolithic period was late, circa 2500-1500 B.C. Pottery development was slow, and it is likely that the common people used wooden ware and the wealthy few, metal vessels. From the Romans came the potter's wheel, and the Roman *terra sigillata* (a black sliplike glaze) was used for a period in southern France and Germany.

The absence in Europe of a long and vital ceramic tradition is possibly one reason why the industrialization of ceramics, which began in roughly 1750, produced so much pottery of atrocious design (see Chapter 10, Mass Production Methods). There were, however, several developments of interest before this period. For some centuries after the fall of the Roman Empire there was no glazed ware. The pottery, although crude, took on a more vigorous form that was less dominated by the embossed metal shapes that were often models of the pressed Roman vessels. Particularly pleasing are the tall pitchers and jugs from the fourteenth century made in England.

Simple slip decorations were now being used with clear lead glaze on a strong simple thrown form. As the potter became more adept at decoration, a new technique of slip trailing was introduced. In this method, a liquid clay slip is trailed onto the piece from a syringe-like container. It is a free hand performance that calls for considerable skill. Illustrated are two seventeenth century plates, quite dissimilar, done in this technique.

Another technical development was that of salt-glazed stoneware of the middle Rhine region in the early sixteenth century (see Chapter 6 on salt glaze). The shapes were the large beer tankards and jugs such as are still common today. Although thrown, the embossed and carved decorations gave an unpleasant metallic feeling to the form. For a time, salt-glazed ware was made elsewhere on the continent and in England, but never to the same extent as in the Rhineland.

After the development of stoneware, it was only a matter of time before porcelain could be made in Europe. Early in the eighteenth century, a red colored porcelain body was made in central Germany, by 1815, a German alchemist, Johann Böttger, succeeded in making a white porcelain body from a kaolin-like clay fluxed with alabaster.

The Middle Eastern and European potters had been trying to imitate the Chinese porcelain for nearly a thousand years. The early Islamic potter attempted to do this with his lead-tin glaze over a light earthenware body. During the Renaissance, the Italians, especially in Venice and Florence, mixed powdered glass with a white earthenware. This Medici Ware was not made extensively as the glassy material was quite brittle and warped badly in firing. A somewhat similar product was made a hundred years later by the French and called "soft paste" porcelain. The English then switched from their cream colored earthenware into the soft paste ware. Many experiments were tried during the eighteenth century in body and glaze formulation. By 1750, *bone china,* made of kaolin, cornwall stone (a feldspathic material), and fluxed with bone ash, became popular and is still made today in England.

Italian-style majolica spread into Europe after the Renaissance. While it all but ceased to be made in France, Germany, and England in favor of other bodies, it continued in Holland. This lead-tin glaze ware eventually became the famous blue and white Delft ware. The Dutch showed no interest in home manufacture of porcelain, due perhaps to their profitable import trade with Europe of Chinese and Japanese porcelains. It was largely left to German factories to develop porcelain ware.

The eighteenth and nineteenth centuries in Europe were a period of great

Iranian bowl with brown metallic lusterware decoration and flowing curvilineal motifs characteristic of Islamic art. Diameter 15 in. Rayy, Iran, ca. 1191. (Courtesy of the Art Institute of Chicago; Logan, Dalten, Pyerson collection)

A Peruvian single-spout bottle reflecting the tendency of the Nazca culture to combine potting with sculpture. The burnished leather-hard clay slips give the glossy finish. Ca. 200–500. (Courtesy of the Art Institute of Chicago; gift of Nathan Cummings). Color plate.

technical advances in ceramics and especially in production (see Chapter 10). This unfortunately, was not equally true of the quality of design. Fortunes had been made on the sale of imported porcelains. The ruling classes were living far beyond their incomes, and the new porcelain factory was looked upon as a source of new income. They were either owned solely by the ruling king or duke, or operated by his consent. The situation varied as to country, but the over-all result was to place design decisions into the hands of an entrepreneur and to relegate the potter to the lot of a hired hand.

above, left Delightful, fresh, and vigorous slip-trailed decoration on a large plate by Thomas Toft. England, ca. 1750. Courtesy of the Metropolitan Museum of Art, Rogers Fund, 1924. **above, right** Slipware dish with a calligraphic quality that will be lost in the industrialism of the succeeding centuries. England, seventeenth century. **left** English jug typical of the whimsy of the period. Grog was pressed into the wet clay and then salt glazed. Ca. 1740. Courtesy of the Metropolitan Museum of Art, gift of Carton Macy, 1934.

Hard-paste figurine in a rococo costume typical of the period. Nymphenburg, Germany, ca. 1760. Courtesy of the Metropolitan Museum of Art; gift of R. Thornton Wilson, 1950, in memory of Florence Ellsworth Wilson.

It is true, of course, that large workshops existed in China for centuries, but with the difference that they were working within a long tradition. The European factory consciously attempted to copy the oriental import ware that in turn had been made especially elaborate for the market. Soon Greek and Roman ware was copied, not only the pottery but the metal forms. Paintings and tapestries became the decorative source material. The life-sized classical sculpture was revamped into sentimental table-sized figurines. All and all it was a period unique in the industrious misuse and distortion of artistic values and concepts.

This sad phenomena is only mentioned because its influence is still potent on popular and official taste in America. The early colonial potters were not unlike their counterpart in Europe—they produced honest simple forms for everyday use. In time a ceramic tradition would have evolved in America were it not soon inundated by first the British and later the locally mass produced ware.

BIBLIOGRAPHY

Adams, Leonhard, *Primitive Art*. London: Penguin Books, Ltd., 1940.

Arias, P. E., *Greek Vase Painting*. New York: Harry Abrams, Inc., 1961.

Carter, Mrs. Dagny (Olsen), *China Magnificent*. New York: Reynal & Hitchcock, Inc., 1935.

Childs, V. Gordon, *New Light on the Most Ancient East*. London: Routledge and Kegan Paul, Ltd., 1935.

Cook, R. M., *Greek Painted Pottery*. London: Methuen & Co., Ltd., 1960.

Coulton, G. G., *Medieval Panorama*. London: Cambridge University Press, 1939.

Cox, Warren E., *Pottery and Porcelain, Vol. 1 & 2*. New York: Crown, 1944.

Digby, George W., *The Work of the Modern Potter in England*. London: J. Murray, 1952.

Fukukita, Yasunosuke, *Tea Cult of Japan*. Tokyo: Board of Tourist Industry, 1934.

Glatz, Gustane, *The Aegean Civilization*. New York: Knopf, 1925.

Goldscheider, Ludwig, *Etruscan Sculpture*. New York: Oxford University Press, 1941.

Hauser, Arnold, *The Social History of Art, Vol. 1 & 2*. New York: Knopf, 1951.

Hayes, William C., *Glazed Tiles*. New York: Metropolitan Museum of Art, 1937.

Hetherington, A. L., *Chinese Ceramic Glazes*. Los Angeles: Commonwealth Press, 1948.

Hobson, R. L., *Chinese Pottery and Porcelain*. London: Cassell, 1915.

Honey, William B., *German Porcelain*. London: Faber, 1947.

————, *The Art of the Potter*. New York: McGraw-Hill, 1944.

————, *The Ceramic Art of China*. London: Faber, 1945.

————, *European Ceramic Art*. London: Faber, 1949.

Lane, Arthur, *Early Islamic Pottery*. London: Faber, 1939.

Laufer, Berthold, *Beginnings of Porcelain in China*. 15:2, Chicago: Field Museum of Natural History, 1917.

Leach, Bernard, *A Potter's Book*. Hollywood-by-the-Sea, Fla.: Transatlantic Arts, Inc., 1951.

————, *A Potter in Japan*. London: Faber, 1960.

Lindberg, Gustaf, *Hsing-yao and Ting-yao*, Bulletin No. 25. Stockholm: The Museum of Far Eastern Antiquities, 1953.

Marquand, Allan, *Luca della Robbia*. Princeton, N. J.: Princeton University Press, 1914.

Munsterberg, Hugo, *The Ceramic Art of Japan*. Rutland, Vt.: Tuttle, 1964.

Noble, Joseph V., *The technique of Attic vase-painting. American Journal of Archaeology*, 64:4, Oct. 1960.

Petrie, Flinders, *The Making of Egypt*. London: The Sheldon Press, 1939.

Rackham, Bernard, N. S., *Medieval English Pottery*. New York: Van Nostrand, 1949.

Ramsey, J., *American Potters & Pottery*. Boston: Hale, Cushman, and Flint, 1939.

Raphael, Max, *Prehistoric Pottery and Civilization in Egypt*. New York: Phantom Books, Inc., 1947.

Savage, George, *Ceramics for the Collector*. New York: Macmillan, 1949.

Walters, H. B., *History of Ancient Pottery*. London: J. Murray, 1905.

CONTEMPORARY CERAMICS IN EUROPE AND JAPAN

CHAPTER 2

INTRODUCTION

The ceramics of the historical past were regional in nature, and local traditions were slow to change. Unless greatly superior, the occasionally imported item had little effect upon the accepted style of form and decoration. The situation today among studio potters is quite the reverse. Due to the increasing emphasis on individuality, the potter now tends to go in all directions, absorbing ideas from historical ceramics and particularly from other contemporary art mediums. Thus, it is quite possible for a potter to have more in common with his counterpart in another country than with the potter in the adjoining studio.

While much of the above situation is due to increased communications, travel, and trade, a large part of it is due to the demise of the small hand pottery. Very few of the potters whose work is illustrated here, either in the United States or abroad, have served a working apprenticeship in a pottery. Such training has a restraining effect on individuality and, at the very least, tends to channel ideas in traditional directions. The greater majority of the potters whose work is illustrated are graduates of either art or craft schools, but some have a very diversified background. A small number are even largely self-taught. The income situation varies from country to country. A few operate their own workshops. Some design for industry as well as making individual pieces. Quite a few have taught in the past or

A delicate porcelain bottle, brown with white interior. Sgraffito decoration adds a feminine touch. 8½ in. Lucie Rie, England. (Courtesy of the Craft Centre of Great Britain)

are presently teaching ceramics, either privately or at an established craft school. Many of these potters have, of course, worked for various periods in small workshops. This training is most valuable in developing a practical technique and an understanding of the economics of production and sales.

Any attempt to categorize the work of these varied personalities from the numerous European countries and Japan is bound to be somewhat incomplete. It would seem, however, that the same tendencies operating in the United States can be observed abroad. There is everywhere, for example, a group of what we might call *folk* potters. They are interested in the thrown form that emphasizes the natural qualities of the clay and the appropriateness of any decoration. Such decoration is usually limited to simple brush and scratched motifs done with the same deft freedom that characterizes the thrown form. Since he is a professional supplying primarily a local market, the folk potter prefers the functional form to the more decorative piece.

The term *decorative* covers a wide range of work. One might well argue that the decorative piece performs a very real function, and that this division of pottery is somewhat inaccurate. Nevertheless, there is a definite body of work in which the feeling and tensions of the thrown form are missing to the same degree that the impact of the decoration has become more important. It would seem that the universal pressure to do the unique and different has in recent years greatly expanded this area of ceramics. As any semblance to a pottery function disappears, the result becomes *ceramic sculpture*. The above developments are partially due, in Europe as in the United States, to the presence in the ceramic field of many whose initial training was in painting, design, or sculpture. The current American tendency toward the accidental effect in clay and glaze, borrowed perhaps from action painting, seems to be less prominent abroad where the controlled technique, although often unconventional, is still standard.

ENGLISH CERAMICS

England, as the chief innovator of the eighteenth-century industrialization of ceramics, has had a particularly long road to travel toward developing a viable craft movement. Commercial ceramics dominated the nineteenth-century market and formed the popular taste. The few small hand potteries remaining produced utilitarian flower pots, crocks, and the like for a local trade that was little disposed to see artistic values in any object lacking a mechanical perfection. A similar situation prevailed in the United States and in varying degrees throughout Europe.

A raku platter, done with an amazing blend of old English and Japanese techniques. Done prior to 1920, about 13½". Bernard Leach, England. (Courtesy of *Pottery Quarterly*)

The actions and philosophy of William Morris and his followers during the later nineteenth century were a part of a growing but largely inarticulate dissatisfaction with the low level of design brought about by industrialization. Meanwhile, both in France and England, isolated experiments were being carried out by potters such as Theodore Beck and William de Morgan. They were seeking to rediscover some of the old pottery skills that had been lost during the preceding centuries. Interest first centered on decorative techniques such as the lusterware of the Islamic potters, but later Oriental ware became the chief attraction as attempts were made to duplicate the Chinese copper reds and other lost or forgotten processes. Whereas the eighteenth century seemed only aware of the more ornate ware of the Ch'ing Dynasty, the nineteenth had an appreciation of the work of the classical Sung as well as the finer work of Korea and Japan. It is most ironic that while western industrialism was undermining an ancient Eastern way of life, we should in turn begin to adopt an Oriental esthetic philosophy. There is little doubt that Chinese and Japanese ceramics have been a most important influence upon present-day Western studio pottery.

The major trends of present day British ceramics had their origins in the years immediately after World War I. Of special importance in this development were William Staite Murray and Bernard Leach. Although they had much in common, they represented two divergent attitudes toward ceramics

A typical Leach vase, which emphasizes the qualities that throwing imparts to the form. The thin runny glazes do not obscure the combed decoration. Bernard Leach, England. (Courtesy of *Pottery Quarterly*)

A large, strongly-thrown covered jar by Michael Cardew. In recent years he has spent considerable time teaching in a small village in Nigeria. England. (Courtesy of *Pottery Quarterly*)

that continue to this day. Murray might be classified as an artist–potter interested in the one-of-a-kind piece; Leach could be said to believe in the cooperative workshop approach aimed at producing a moderately priced, functional ware with only an occasional "unique" piece.

The difference of opinion between Leach and Murray is quite understandable, even though both had formal art training. Unlike Murray, Leach went to Japan in his early twenties. Although trained as a painter, he soon became interested in pottery. His interest was great enough so that he served an apprenticeship of several years with a master potter, Ogata Kenzan. The workshop approach of anonymous craftsman cooperating to produce handmade objects had largely died out in Europe, although it was still current in Japan. Upon Leach's return in 1920, he set up a workshop in St. Ives. He was assisted in this effort by Shoji Hamada, a young Japanese potter who at this writing is still active and is perhaps Japan's most highly regarded potter. Indicative of their difficulties of selling handthrown ware is the revelation that pottery sent back to Japan represented an important item of sales during those first years at St. Ives. The workshop is still in operation, with Leach's son, David, in charge.

Murray, whose early training was at the Camberwell School of Arts, set up his own workshop after World War I. At first he experimented with glazes and firing techniques. He is reputed to have built the first oil-burning kiln of a size suitable for a studio workshop. Contacts at St. Ives with Hamada may have influenced Murray toward a looser style. His characteristic pieces are large bottle and vase forms, dynamic and freely thrown with a vigorous decoration. Like Leach's pottery, Murray's constituted a protest against traditional English values. Although Murray has left England for Africa, his influence has continued through the many students encountered during the years (1925 to 1939) that he taught at the Royal College of Art.

Impressed by the craft traditions of the east, it was but natural that Bernard Leach would feel an identity with the preindustrial English potter. Leach, along with several other English potters, found the medieval pottery particularly inspiring. Numerous experiments were made with salt glazing and slip trailing, combing, and decorative techniques common to the seventeenth century. This combination of both English and Oriental tradition

below Vase lacking the tensions of the Leach piece but interesting for its mat ash glaze, a subject of intensive research by the potter, Katherine Pleydell-Bouverie, England. **top, right** Bowl by Henry Hammond, plate by Roy Finch, and pitcher by Fishley Holland. The latter two are in the English slipware technique. **below, right** Thin porcelain bowls, with pressed and cut rim. Constance Dunn, England. (All pieces on this page courtesy of *Pottery Quarterly*)

has given much of the English work a national character and a feeling of continuity with the past. There are, of course, English potters, like Americans, who are desperately trying to eliminate any echo of the past in their work.

Leach has had a considerable influence upon American potters due to visits and lectures here, his several American apprentices, and his numerous publications. Although first published in 1939, his *A Potter's Book* is timeless and ought to be the first acquisition of any serious pottery student.

The position of the studio potter in the twentieth century is a difficult one. He obviously cannot compete with the machine. On the other hand, neither can the factory entirely supplant the craftsman. Bernard Leach has long been an advocate of the workshop system whereby a group of potters pool their efforts in order to effect economies in equipment, production, and sales. A large proportion of the work must be functional ware such as mugs, casseroles, sugar and creamers, and so on, which can find a ready retail market. This means that several potters will need to work for at least a portion of their time more or less duplicating a design made by one of the group. But such is the emphasis on individuality among today's potters that few are attracted to this solution.

Among the older, well-established potters who have studied at St. Ives are Michael Cardew, Katherine Pleydell-Bouverie, Nora Braden, Harry David, Dorothy Kemp, Margaret Leach (no relation) and, of course, David Leach. Among William Staite Murray's former students who are now prominent are Heber Mathews, Henry Hammond, Constance Dunn, and the late Sam Haile. Of course, there were in the period between the two wars other

Tea bowl shape with a runny hare's fur glaze. Murray Fieldhouse, England. (Courtesy of *Pottery Quarterly*)

Thin porcelain bowl, 10 in. in diameter with lined decoration typical of
Lucie Rie. England. (Courtesy of the Craft Centre of Great Britain)

important potters coming from either an art school or professional background such as Dora Billington, Charles Vyse, and from Austria in 1938,
Lucie Rie.

Since the war, a new generation of potters has developed, some of whose
work is illustrated here. Many are students of the previously mentioned
craftsmen; regardless of their training, all have been influenced by the
pioneering efforts of the 1920s. This has served to give contemporary
English pottery a certain homogenous quality that is, of course, bitterly
assailed by the younger avant-guard.

Sturdy vase with simple brushed oxide decoration. Janet Leach, England. (Courtesy of the
Craft Centre of Great Britain)

left Large vase with sgraffito decoration through dark glaze. James Tower, England. center Hand-built planter; unglazed with vitreous slip and oxide decoration, 18 in. David Ballantyne, England. right Earthenware vase, thrown and shaped with wax-resist and oxide decoration. Kenneth Clarke, England.

Ceramic sculpture construction of cut, thrown, and carved slab forms. Bryan Newman, England.

left Decorative plate with design emphasizing the effective contrast between smooth and cratered glaze surfaces. Rosemary Wren, England.

right Tall vases with distinctive comb and oxide decoration. Ian Auld, England.

left Austere slab vases relieved by cut, applied and stamped decoration. Ian Auld, England. (All pieces on this page courtesy of the Craft Centre of Great Britain)

End of the World, thrown by Adrick Westenenk, sgraffito decoration by Lies Cosyn, Holland. (All illustrations of Dutch ceramics courtesy of the Dutch Ceramic Society)

Earthenware bowl, engobe and sgraffito decoration. Form by Adrick Westenenk, decoration by Lies Cosyn, Holland.

The Gypsy Caravan, sgraffito through opaque glaze to expose dark slip below. Adrick Westenenk, Holland.

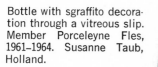

Bottle with sgraffito decoration through a vitreous slip. Member Porceleyne Fles, 1961–1964. Susanne Taub, Holland.

DUTCH CERAMICS

Historically, the Dutch have always engaged in trade with the Far East. Prior to the large scale importation of porcelains from China and Japan, Holland had developed, under the influence of Italian majolica, their famous blue and white Delft ware. Although originally inspired by the blue on white decorations of the Ming Dynasty, the Italian example of over-all pictorial effects became a prominent feature of the blue Delft ware. The success of faience during the seventeenth and eighteenth centuries led the Dutch to largely ignore the development of stoneware and porcelain that at this period engaged the attention of the English and especially the Germans. The valuable import trade of oriental porcelains also deterred its local manufacture.

Handsome earthenware vase with sgraffito decoration through glaze. Member Porceleyne Fles, 1957–1963. Adrick Westenenk, Holland. (Courtesy of the Dutch Ceramic Society)

Blind Court Musician, earthenware sculpture with greenish-black engobe. Member Porceleyne Fles, 1956–1962. Lies Cosyn, Holland.

To this day, the familiar blue and white Delft ware has continued to be produced in Holland but with a greater industrial sterility. This brief historical background is included because it in no way prophesies the rise of a vital group of young potters during the late 1950s. After Frans and Marguerite Wildenhain and Dirk Hubers, who were prominent in the period between the two wars, left for the United States, there existed a vacuum of creative pottery talents except for the more traditional pottery of the Zaalberg family. An important factor in this revival in the 1950s was the establishment of the Experimental Group at the Porceleyne Fles at Delft in 1956. Patterned after studio groups in many Scandinavian factories, it provides studio facilities and a salary to young potters making individual one-of-a-kind pieces. This pottery is exhibited and sold by the factory and may on occasion serve as a design prototype for factory production. Theo Dobbelmann, a noted sculptor, glaze chemist, and teacher at both the Art Academy and Craft School in Amsterdam, has served as Director of this project since its inception.

The major characteristic of the work of the Porceleyne Fles group is the decoration. Tastefully done, it usually is a linear sgrafitto technique over an engobe. The forms are simple and adapted to a decorative treatment. A workshop procedure is followed, and after the piece is thrown it may be decorated by a second party. The majority of this group, primarily girls, are former students of the School for Applied Arts where the emphasis has been more on decoration and less on the dynamics of the thrown form.

above Covered jar with pear-wood lid; earthenware with wax-resist and oxide decoration. Sonja Landweer, Holland. **left** Forceful stoneware jar; cut sides and underglaze decoration in iron and cobalt, 10 in. Jan de Rooden, Holland. **right** Bulbous stoneware bottle, reduced, with runny glaze; iron and cobalt colorants. 9½ in. Johnny Rolf (Mrs. Jan de Rooden), Holland.

Earthenware built with fluid flowing quality, vitreous engobe of greenish blue and black. Member Porceleyne Fles 1961–1965. Maryke van Vlaardinger, Holland.

A second and more varied group are the six Amsterdam potters whose work is also illustrated. At the time of this writing, all were in their early thirties. Their background follows no common pattern, and several have had professional training in other areas. Ceramics was not the first interest of those attending art school, but for all it became an overwhelming fascination. A majority received workshop training either in Holland, Scandinavia, or England; for several, self-training has been the key to their individual style. All presently have their own workshops and produce individual, one-of-a-kind pieces. English potters have had a considerable influence on most of the Amsterdam group. Also of importance are the existence of fine private and public collections of Oriental ceramics in the major Dutch cities.

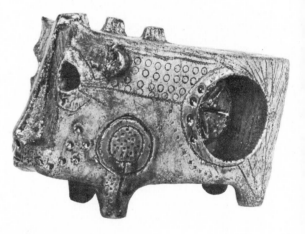

above Dish with transparent cornwall glaze over dark colorants, reduced, 12½ in. Jan de Rooden, Holland. (Photo Trits Weeda) **right** *The Coach Beast*, typical of Hands de Jong's fantastic animals. Earthernware, thin lead glaze with colorants in incised areas, height 10 in. Hans de Jong, Holland. (Photo Th. J. Marks, Jr.) **below** Slab planter, reduced stoneware with iron and cobalt colorants under glaze, height 9 in. Johnny Rolf, Holland. (Photo Trits Weeda)

above, left Forceful jar shape, stoneware, barium mat glaze with iron and manganese, height 8 in. **above, right** A "tulip holder," doubtlessly of great interest to the Dutch. Height 20 in. brown-black mat glaze. Both pieces by Jan van der Vaart, Holland.

below *The Politicians*. Very inventive construction, amusing to all but the type depicted. Hans de Jong, Holland.

In contrast to his earlier work in a cubist design, Pierre Caille's latest work is plastic with an imagery of strong emotional content. Brussels, Belgium. (Illustrations on these pages courtesy of the ceramist Pierre Caille)

BELGIUM

Historically, Belgium ceramics has been dominated by French styles. The French potter in turn has continually been in the shadow of the arts of painting and sculpture. The soft paste and porcelain factories of the eighteenth and nineteenth centuries regarded the pottery form primarily as a space for pictorial decoration in a Louis XIV style. The French stoneware potteries, which to this day produce a functional ware of a simple honest character, have never received public acceptance as having any merit other than utility. The much publicized pottery of Picasso has little relationship to pottery values. Like the Italian Renaissance plate, Picasso's also has a hole in the foot rim for hanging and must be judged as a painting and only incidentally as a ceramic work.

The Belgium ceramist, Pierre Caille, whose work is illustrated, has been working in ceramic sculpture since the late 1930s. He has maintained an interest in the figure ranging from early cubistic constructions to his present more plastic pieces. Like Hans de Jong, the Dutch ceramist who studied in France, Pierre Caille has more Mediterranean feeling in his work than evidenced by the potters so far illustrated. Although at times his work has consisted of unrecognizable animals and birds, Pierre Caille's major interest appears not to be the abstraction of the form but rather the psychological impact of his images. The recent examples are somewhat reminiscent of the contemporary French painter, Bernard Buffet.

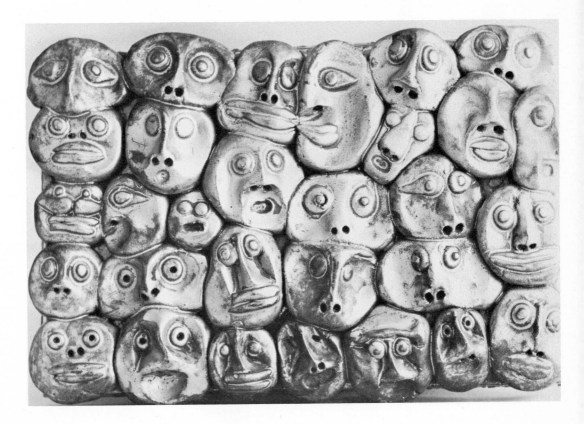

Belgium

ITALY

The pictorial tradition of Italy has been mentioned before in connection with Renaissance majolica. To this day, the highly decorated majolica ware has remained an Italian favorite. Save for dinnerware, few stoneware temperature ceramics are made. Ceramics is the most widely distributed craft in Italy, in contrast to glass, which is largely centered in Murano. Although slight local variations exist, the majolica technique persists, colorful and over-elaborate in form and decoration. Industrialization is less pronounced in Italy than in northern Europe, but much of the uninspired hand-crafted pottery turned out for the tourist trade is no less injurious to public taste.

More related to contemporary trends in other countries is the work of Guido Gambone, whose work has gradually changed from whimsical assembled pottery figures and animals to the more recent rigid architectural forms. Equally known outside of Italy is the work of Giovan Battista Valentini whose pots are generally stark in form with a rich textural surface. Carlo Zauli's work is characterized by strong simple forms, thick glazes with a minimum of decoration. The bottles of Nino Caruso, however, are most unpot-like, resembling rather a strangely disjointed animal. Typical of Italian ceramists, he is interested in form of a plastic sculptural nature. Since Italy is a virtual museum of 2500 years of sculptural activity, this concern is no surprise.

below Although this pottery figure bottle by Guido Gambone has the sculptural quality of Peruvian ware, the result is light hearted and amusing. **left** Somewhat related to the work of Gambone is the work of Salvatore Meli, whose illustrated pottery shows much of the exuberant quality of Italian ceramics.

In this light, the fact that Italian pottery seldom exhibits the tensions derived from a thrown form is no more unusual than that this feature should be predominant in Oriental ceramics. Included in the illustrations are several examples of the differing directions taken by Italian ceramic sculpture. The sculptural tradition in Italian ceramics is an old one with high points early in Etruscan times and later during the Renaissance.

below In contrast to the previous pieces, the two bowls by Gian Baltista Valentini and the single bowl by Carlo Zauli would seem to come from a different age as they reflect a restraint not characteristic of the Italian potter. **right** The work of Nino Caruso (top) and Leoncillo Leonardi (below) evolves from a philosophy alien to the traditional values of either pottery or sculpture. The emphasis is upon abstract sculptural form and the exciting textural and manipulative qualities of clay itself. (Illustrations on these pages courtesy of the International Ceramic Museum at Faenza)

right *Centauro e Ninfa* is an old classical theme. This piece has a flowing plastic quality that is Picasso-like and effective. **below** A strong and colorful wall plaque, majolica technique. Both pieces by Germano Belletti, Italy. (Courtesy of *La Ceramica*)

right *Lettrice* is an interesting piece in its construction, although the rubber-like arms are disturbing. Majolica. Alda Ajo, Italy. **far right** It is difficult to judge this figure apart from the weathered post on which the ceramic crucifix is mounted. Enrico Casmassi, Italy. (Both pieces courtesy of *La Ceramica*)

CONTEMPORARY CERAMICS IN EUROPE AND JAPAN

GERMAN CERAMICS

The Rhineland in the vicinity of Cologne has long been a center of German ceramic activity. It was here in the early fifteenth century that salt-glazed stoneware was first produced. This ware is still produced but is not of the unique quality of that of the sixteenth and seventeenth centuries. As mentioned before, porcelain was first produced early in the eighteenth century at Meissen. Other factories were started later at Dresden, Vienna, and elsewhere in Europe. Coinciding with the industrialization of production, this new porcelain industry was in no sense an outgrowth of local pottery traditions. Rather, it was strictly a business enterprise designed to profit from the popularity of the imported Chinese porcelains.

Copying as they did the Chinese form and decoration with added Italian and French Rococo influence, these porcelain factories hardly represented a German tradition. As elsewhere in Europe, this immense production has had little to offer the contemporary studio potter in the way of inspiration. It is perhaps fallacious to assume that there is a similarity between the German ceramics shown and the seventeenth century salt ware. Nevertheless, the forms of both are relatively solid with little feeling of the thrown form. Impressed decoration has been an old German favorite, going back to Roman times.

Oval bottle with stamped pattern and a mottled mat red-brown and copper glaze. Karl Scheid, Germany. (Illustrations of German ceramics are through the courtesy of the Rat für Formgebung)

Stoneware bottle with a zinc crystalline mat glaze, height 6 in. Design and glaze by Hubert Greimert, Germany.

It is significant that Klaus Schultze, whose work is in an avant-guard sculptural vein, is presently living in France. Walter Popp, although now teaching at the Hochschule für Bildende Kunste at Kassel, is largely self-taught and was originally a photographer. Possibly as a result of this, his shapes are less traditional than the others presented. Several of the illustrated pieces are by faculty members of the famous ceramic school at Höhr-Grenzhausen, near Cologne, in the old salt-glaze region. Their program would seem strange in an American school since ceramic design and the techniques of throwing are taught to two separate groups. After graduation, the students will become either throwers for small factories or designers for industry. This procedure explains in part the formality of design and lack of spontaneously applied decoration; some pieces have been designed, decorated, and glazed by one person but thrown by another. A similar situation prevails in Sweden in several of the factories where the design staff have skilled throwers to execute their designs. Later, applied decorations and glazes are executed by the designer. As a result, perhaps more than normal effort has gone into glaze formulation. Glazes in Germany and several Scandinavian countries are particularly rich in texture and color and are perfectly applied. This, of course, develops a certain tightness that is objectionable to the workshop potter who feels that a slight irregularity of glaze is a more natural expression of the medium.

CONTEMPORARY CERAMICS IN EUROPE AND JAPAN

below Textural, sculptural form, constructed in sections, height approximately 6½ feet. Klaus Schultze, Germany.

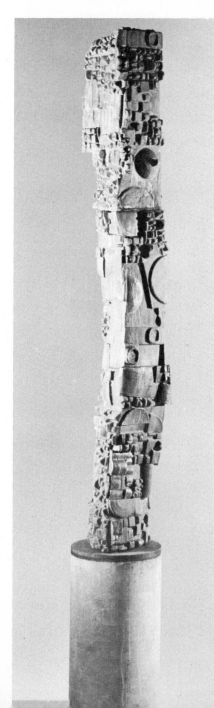

above Stoneware bottle, reduced body, unglazed except for dipped sections, 3 shades of blue. **right** Stoneware bottle, reduced, dark sections, blue and black, height 7 in. **below, left** Assembled cylinders, partially glazed in white, black and blue, height 14 in. **below, right** Stoneware bottle with opaque glaze, iron brown and green decoration, height 12 in. (All pieces on this page by Walter Popp, Germany)

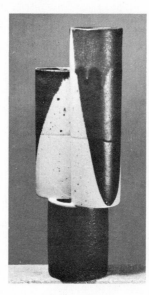

left Austere vase with a casual decoration formed by a crackled glaze splashed over the dark mat, height, 7 in. Karl Scheid, Germany.
center Stoneware bottle with zinc crystalline brown-green glaze. Design and glaze by Hubert Greimert. Thrown by a member of Professor Greimert's master class at the Höhr Grenzhausen Ceramic School, Germany.
right Restrained vase forms with mat iron-rutile glazes. Large vase, height 20 in. Heiner Balzar, Germany.

below Multicolored assemblage of tubular ceramic sections, height 5½ feet. Klaus Schultze, Germany.

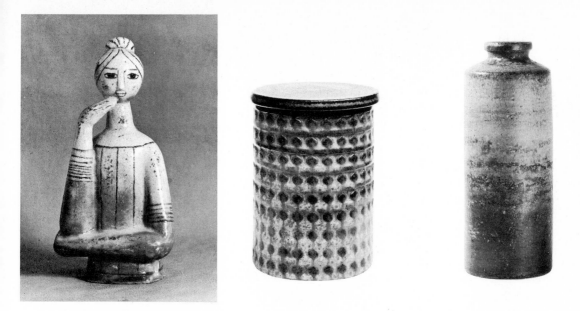

left Decorative bust with brushed linear accents, crackle glaze, height 16 in. Stephan and Ida Erdos, Germany. **center** Covered jar with pressed decoration. Iron brown on the thinner glazed areas, height 6 in. Ursula Scheid, Germany. **right** Simple stoneware vase depending on body color and texture under mat glaze for its appeal. Heinz H. Engler, Germany.

left Subtle decorative patterns in tans, browns and greens. **right** Stoneware teapot with scratched engobe decoration. Hildegard Storr-Britz, director of ceramic decoration at Höhr-Grenzhausen, Germany.

SCANDINAVIAN CERAMICS

The term *modern design* has been associated with Scandinavia for so many years, that this area is of special interest to most craftsmen. Contrary to popular opinion, Scandinavian design was not an outgrowth of peasant style handicrafts; industrialization was less injurious here than in many areas of Europe. Historically, the great masses of people have used the most simple and functional of products. The peasant sat on a stool, rough bench, or pile of skins. For the wealthy few, however, furniture had to be elaborate and ostentatious. Anyone who has sat in an Italian Renaissance chair knows that it is a back breaker, however impressive. The styles in succeeding centuries in France and England were in this respect little different. Such items in the decorative arts of all categories, forced bastard flowers at best, formed the models of the new industries of the nineteenth century.

Scandinavian design in the last century was little different than elsewhere in Europe except for being slightly more provincial in the copying of fashionable foreign styles. There is doubtless more than one reason for the surprising contemporary developments. The Art Nouveau movement at the turn of the century, although illogical, shook up old attitudes. Architects, craftsmen, and painters alike reevaluated their goals. Social institutions and economic conditions were changing, and for the first time middle and even lower class needs were considered. The German Bauhaus movement was unlike other movements in France and Italy in that the emphasis was on machine-type production and intended for a mass market. The renown of the Bauhaus in the United States is partly due to our industrial society, which makes such a philosophy logical, as well as the accidents of history, which forced the major Bauhaus innovators to the States and into influential teaching positions.

A fundamental factor in Scandinavia was the development during the late nineteenth and early twentieth centuries of a socialist concept of society. A demand slowly arose for better designed products for the average person. Interested parties were not only those of political persuasion but also designers, teachers, industrialists, government and labor officials, as well as the performing artist. This pressure led to the employment by many factories during the 1920s and 1930s of designers with training in the traditional fine arts. Although not knowledgeable in production techniques, they

Typical of Scandinavian emphasis on function, stoneware teapot, yellow-brown glaze, in teakstand, height 15 in. Saxbo, designer Kirsten Weeke, Denmark. (Illustrations of Danish ceramics are through the courtesy of *Den Permanente.*)

were a fresh inspiration. The five present Scandinavian craft schools, originally formed by their national design societies, provide both industry and small workshops with graduates trained both in design and practical techniques. It is true that postwar prosperity and the export market have led to certain frills in design, but the basic concept of practical and economic yet attractive design remains. Although simplified and overstated, this explanation is more valid than that which would have the streamlined modern design descend from the rather fussy traditional crafts.

The four Scandinavian countries have many cultural similarities but do not compromise a monolithic society. Three share a language that is roughly similar, but Finland has its own very ancient and unique language. However, long and close ties with Sweden over the centuries has given Finland a cultural identity with this Nordic grouping. The present day design importance of Scandinavia is even stranger when one realizes that the population of the largest country, Sweden, is less than that of New York City. Because of the differences that do exist among them, each country will be covered separately.

Denmark

Lying closest to central Europe, Denmark has been long subject to influences from Germany, France and England. The forerunner of the present Royal Copenhagen factory was established early in the eighteenth century to produce first a Delft faience and later a German type of porcelain. The foreign influences remained quite strong until the 1920s when trained artists instead of just copyists joined the factory staffs. Axel Salto was perhaps the most influential of this early group. At present, the Bing and Grondahl factory also has an active studio group producing one-of-a-kind pieces as well as designs for production.

The small workshops of Denmark have made an equal if not greater contribution to the present level of design. There are a number of active individual potters as well as workshops with a dozen or more potters that make small production runs of a generally handmade quality. Especially noteworthy is the Saxbo pottery under the direction of Natalie Krebs, a noted glaze chemist. The Saxbo stoneware, fired at cone 12 (about 1300°C, 2400°F), a round beehive coal burning kiln, is famous in Europe for the

above Stoneware vases of groggy clay, partially unglazed. Helle Allpass, Denmark. **below** Severe bottle forms with an angular emphasis. Finn Lynggaard, Denmark.

CONTEMPORARY CERAMICS IN EUROPE AND JAPAN

above, left Stoneware pieces at the Saxbo pottery showing the present emphasis on textured forms. Design Eva Staehr Nielsen, glaze Nathalie Krebs, Denmark. **above, right** Stoneware dish with a Japanese-like brush decoration. Niels Refsgaard, Denmark. **opposite** Stoneware vase with pressed decoration and a transparent crackled glaze. Niels Refsgaard, Denmark.

variety and perfection of its mat glazes. The emphasis of Danish ceramics has gradually moved from the rounded glazed form of the thirties to one that is stamped and incised. At present, the interest is in a coarser body that is left partially unglazed for greater contrast. However, it would appear that the Danish potters are less experimental and are more interested in a functional ware than many of the Swedish or Finnish potters.

Stoneware forms with mottled grey, brown and green mat glazes. Conny Walther, Denmark.

Brown and white production ovenware. Stig
Lindberg, Gustavsberg Studios, Sweden.

Sweden

As in Denmark, there are in Sweden a number of individual potters and
small workshops. But perhaps equally as significant in the Swedish ceramic
picture is the work done by the design studio members of two of the largest
factories in Sweden, Rörstrand and Gustavsberg. Rörstrand was founded
early in the eighteenth century and Gustavsberg a century later. Like the
Danish factories, the German and English influence was strong. Wilhelm
Käge in the 1920s at Gustavsberg and Gunnar Nyland at Rörstrand in the
thirties were responsible for developing new concepts of design related in
part to similar efforts in other applied arts. These designers were originally
trained as painters and sculptors and needed a thrower to execute their
designs. Incised decoration, glazing, and so on are done usually by the
designer. The second generation of designers had a greater familiarity with
clay. And it is likely that the third generation now graduating from the
craft school rather than the art academy will execute the entire design.

There is no set pattern for the Scandinavian ceramic designer employed
by industry. A large sized factory will have five or six. A few will design
only for production. Others will make one-of-a-kind pieces serving a dual
purpose as prestige items for the factory to exhibit as well as developing
ideas and prototypes for production. The philosophy is different from that
of Bernard Leach and the craft traditions of the Far East. The dynamics of
the thrown form and the tensions imparted to it are little in evidence as the
critical experimentation is more with decoration than with form.

Scandinavian Ceramics

Unique stoneware pieces with slip glazes in reds and browns. Carl-Harry Stålhane, Rörstrand Studios, Sweden.

The position of the Scandinavian designer is quite unlike the situation in America. For example, in a Scandinavian furniture store a tag on the item will identify the designer and the cabinetmaker. Not being anonymous, the designer receives individual credit but also has a social responsibility. While sales and production factors are as important as elsewhere, the Scandinavian designer has a greater voice in the decision as to what will eventually be produced.

The Scandinavian craft school is also quite unlike our own. With the exception of Sweden, which has a school in both Stockholm and Göteborg, each country has a craft school located in their capital city. Most were formed in the mid-nineteenth century by the national design societies in an effort to fill the gap caused by the demise of the centuries-old craft guilds. At present, the schools are largely supported by the city and national governments. Enrollment is quite limited as the purpose is only to supply the design needs of the country. The hobby aspect of ceramics is developing in the more prosperous European countries but nowhere to the extent that we find in the States, and teachers are not needed for the public schools since nonacademic courses are rarely taught.

left Decorative production pieces in Faience. Designed by Marianne Westman, Rörstrand Studios. above Earthenware luncheon sets, red, white, and green. Designed by Stig Lindberg, Gustavsberg Studios, Sweden.

Decorative bird with body of a groggy stoneware. Sylvia Leuchovius, Rörstrand Studios, Sweden.

Porcelain dinnerware designed by Sylvia Leuchovius, Rörstrand Studios, Sweden.

Stoneware vases and figures by Lisa Larsson, Gustavsberg Studios, Sweden.

Another feature of the Scandinavian craft school is its close contact with industry. Many of the instructors are practicing designers and craftsmen who teach on a part-time basis. For example, Kurt Ekholm, the director of the Göteborg school, was formerly with the Arabia factory in Finland. Stig Lindberg, protégé of Wilhelm Käge, and for several years head of the design group at Gustavsberg, is director of the ceramic program at the Konstfackskolan in Stockholm. The change from the idealism of the school to the demands of the business world is shocking for all students. To cushion this transition, a few factories provide summer employment to selected students or studio space and employment on a probationary basis. The Swedish ceramics illustrated include the work of individual workshop potters as well as production models and one-of-a-kind pieces from factory design staffs. From the variety of work shown, it does not appear that the industry studio need be as inhibiting as claimed by most studio potters.

Decorative dish (or wall plaque) by Sylvia Leuchovius, Rörstrand Studios, Sweden.

Plate with incised design completed with engobes and oxides. Transparent over glaze. Hertha Bengtson, Rörstrand Studios, Sweden.

Wall tiles with cut through designs. Karin Bjorquist, Gustavsberg Studios, Sweden.

above Stoneware sculpture, assembled sections, glazed and textured, Stig Lindberg. below Stoneware vases, pressed and carved decoration. Britt Louise Sundell-Nemes, Gustavsberg Studios, Sweden.

Large vase with incised decoration and multi-colored slip glazes. Fired several times. Carl-Harry Stålhane, Rörstrand Studios, Sweden.

Large stoneware vase, iron glaze with applied clay and stamped decoration, height 28 in. Stig Lindberg, Gustavsberg Studios, Sweden.

left Stoneware coffee pot, salt glazed, Gerte Moller, Sweden. **above** Covered jars, with decorative incised and stained designs. Hertha Bengtson, Rörstrand Studios, Sweden.

Stoneware vase and bowl, salt glazed, yellow to brown, Tom Moller, Stockholm. (Photo Bengt Carlen; courtesy of *Form*)

Stoneware vases, cobalt colorant, partially dip glazed. Karin Bjorquist, Gustavsberg Studios, Sweden.

opposite Hertha Hillfon decorating a sculptural form in her garden studio in a Stockholm suburb. Sweden. (All pieces by Hertha Hillfon are courtesy of the ceramist)

CONTEMPORARY CERAMICS IN EUROPE AND JAPAN

left Portion of figure, lead glazed in vivid hues. **center** Sculptural construction with an exploding movement, clay and engobes, unglazed. **right** Clay sculpture of an open quality free from traditional three-dimensional concepts. All pieces by Hertha Hillfon, Sweden.

Vigorously thrown stoneware vase with mat dark blue, grey, and copper glaze. Anja Jaatinen, Arabia Studios, Finland. (Illustrations of Finnish Ceramics are through the courtesy of the Finnish Society for Crafts and Design)

Finland

Although possessing an ancient culture related to the Hungary of prehistory, Finland is relatively new as a nation. Independence from Russia resulted from an uprising at the time of the Russian Revolution. Although a province of Russia for one hundred years, Finland was less influenced by this source than by the Swedish, to whom Finland had been joined culturally since the twelfth century. The rather rapid emergence of Finland as a leader in contemporary design can only be explained as an outpouring of spirit and energy released by nationhood after centuries of foreign control.

Unlike Denmark, whose neolithic pottery dates from 2500 B.C., the ceramic traditions of Finland are quite recent. The Finnish peasant traditionally used wooden bowls and the wealthy landowner, vessels of metal or imported faience or china. Save for a few small earthenware potteries near the Russian border, the entire ceramic life of Finland is centered in the Arabia factory, located on the outskirts of Helsinki. Founded by the Rörstrand interests of Sweden in 1874, it passed into Finnish ownership in 1916.

Wall decoration for dry grasses and the like. Unglazed, textured surface. Faces painted in center rings add further touch of whimsy. Francesca Lindh, Arabia Studios, Finland.

Although having large production of all types of ceramic ware ranging from firebrick, sanitary ware, and dinnerware, Arabia is best noted internationally through its studios for individual potters. In addition to a staff of four or five designing for factory production, there are studios for about ten potters on the spacious eighth floor of a relatively new factory wing. In addition to potters, several of this group have a major interest in decorative wall reliefs and sculpture. The dominance of Arabia is in part due to the lack of a native ceramic tradition, the waste of the war years, and the cost of equipment, plus the geographic disadvantage of being on the edge of European trade routes.

While there have been numerous non-Finnish members of the art studio group, a majority are graduates of the Ateneum, the craft school in Helsinki, and studied with the late Elsa Elenius. More recently Kyllikki Salmenhaara, a noted Arabia potter, is teaching at this school. A number of the major

Stoneware vases and bowl characterized by the random designs developed by the poured glazes of iron and black and grey white. Liisa Hallamaa, Arabia Studios, Finland.

Stoneware bottle and bowl with effective contrast by brushed and dipped iron oxides over base glaze. Anja Jaatinen, Arabia Studios, Finland.

Handled stoneware vases of groggy clay, with the expanding quality of a thrown piece. Francesca Lindh, Arabia Studios, Finland.

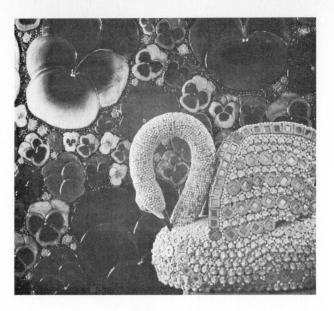

Swan constructed of ceramic mosaics against floral background panel, which is also formed from numerous colorful tiles. Birger Kaipiainen, Arabia Studios, Finland.

Finnish designers of this generation have taught at the Ateneum that, despite inadequate facilities, is most successful. Kaj Franck, for example, art director at Arabia during the 1950s and one of Finland's most versatile designers, now spends a considerable portion of his time at the Ateneum.

Several examples of a few of the Arabia potters are illustrated here. In general they exhibit an interest in the tensions of the thrown form or in the textural qualities of clay. The fascination of mat glazes that once characterized Scandinavian work is now missing. The work of Birger Kaipiainen is truly unique and as it is a mosaic art more related to painting.

Cylinder vases with applied clay texture accented by contrasting glazes. Toini Muona, Arabia Studios, Finland.

Pitcher and animal container, bright faience decoration. Rolf Hansen, Norway. (Illustrations of Norwegian ceramics courtesy of Norwegian Society of Arts and Crafts and Industrial Design)

Norway

With a small population divided by mountainous areas and an economy dominated by fishing and shipping interests, the growth of modern design has been slower in Norway than in the neighboring countries of Sweden and Denmark. Although long established, the present Norwegian factories have not supported a creative design program to the same extent as her neighbors. There are, however, a number of small workshops and individual potters.

The isolation caused by mountain and sea served to preserve peasant art traditions for a longer period than in industrial Europe. Certain crafts were able to combine the new with the traditional. For example, the elaborate ski sweaters needed little change in design to become "modern." Color and pattern has always seemed to interest the Norwegians, perhaps as a result of the long, colorless winters. A few years ago, when all Scandinavian glass was predominately heavy and clear, Norwegian glass was multicolored. Ten years ago, Oslo's shops had only bright faience and sgraffito decorated earthenware. Today the studio potters are working at higher temperatures. The pieces illustrated are primarily stoneware. The shapes are simple and depend greatly upon the incised and pressed decoration for their effectiveness. With few exceptions, the pieces seem to be designed rather than thrown, a characteristic of most contemporary Scandinavian ceramics.

Vases of dark groggy clay with scratched design through the opaque glaze. Rolf Hansen, Norway.

Squared, low stoneware vase, sgraffito decoration on the raw glaze, height 5 in. Erik Pløen, Norway.

Matching pitcher, mug, and bowl with groggy unglazed exterior and incised decoration. Erik Pløen, Norway. (Photos by Kjell Munch)

Rough-textured teapots, un-glazed outside, of simple, functional design. Richard Dubourgh, Norway.

Vase forms with applied and incised decoration that seems a bit overdone. Dagny and Finn Hald, Norway.

left, top Casserole with stamped decoration. Grey-green glaze. Rolf Hansen, Norway. **left, bottom** Vase with roller-applied pressed decoration. Erik Pløen, Norway. **above** Stoneware vase of groggy clay, sgraffito and wax-resist decoration. Erik Pløen, Norway. (Photo Kjell Munch)

Haniwa warrior figure. Earthenware, unglazed with simple but expressive modeling. Ca. 500, Japan. (Courtesy of the Museum of Primitive Art)

JAPANESE CERAMICS

The influence of Oriental ceramics upon the West has been very considerable for several centuries. Until recent years, however, our opinions of the ceramic art of Japan was largely conditioned by the elaborately decorated Imari and Satsuma ware that was exported in large quantities to Europe during the seventeenth and eighteenth centuries. Our present taste has become more appreciative of work not made for this export market.

During the prehistoric period, which lasted from about 5000 B.C. to 100 B.C., Japan was inhabited by a Caucasian people whose descendants are the nearly extinct Ainu aborigines in the far northern islands. The pottery of this Jomon period is typical of all neolithic ware, being low fired, unglazed, with a rounded or pointed base and modeled and cord decorations. During the second century B.C. the southern island, Kyushu, was invaded from Korea, the closest contact with mainland China. Succeeding waves of Mongol invaders pressed northward, and by 500 A.D. the major area of the Japanese islands had been overrun. With them came a more advanced pottery technique. This Yayoi ware was wheel thrown, higher fired, and had a burnished

Shoji Hamada, a major influence among Japanese potters, decorating a slab jar. (Illustrations of Japanese ceramics are the courtesy of the Japanese Embassy, Dr. Hugo Munsterberg and Allen Landgren)

Contemporary tea bowl in traditional Edo style with a thick crackled glaze, 6½ in. diameter. Guro Kamiguchi, Japan.

Shino style tea bowl with a coarse body that has colored the glaze crackle in areas, 4 in. diameter. Toyoza Arakawa, Japan.

slip or shallow, incised decoration. Most popular in recent years have been the Haniwa sculptures of warriors and horses, circa 500 A.D. To our age, trying to live down neoclassic traditions, these simple tubular figures have a fresh, unaffected charm. They were made in large numbers to encircle burial mounds and probably evolved, as did the Chinese Wei and T'ang clay sculpture, through efforts to provide a substitute for the burial of actual guards and horses.

Although a slight Chinese influence is evident in the Yayoi period, after the introduction of Buddhism via Korea in 552 A.D., the Chinese influence became a predominant aspect in all cultural areas of Japanese life. The T'ang, Sung, and later the Ming ceramics were highly regarded and frequently copied. Nevertheless, distinctive Japanese tendencies were evident. Pottery making is widespread in Japan; in addition to the major centers at Seto and Kyoto, potteries operate in most districts with considerable local variations in style. The local Kyushu potteries still retain Korean characteristics.

Unique to Japan and perhaps fundamental to its present-day esthetic is the Zen Buddhist philosophy and its development in the *tea ceremony*. The present ritual doubtless grew from the priestly meditation while having a tea break. From a Buddhist ceremony in the fourteenth century, it became popular with first the aristocracy, then the war lords, and finally the general populous. It is held in a small room, which is bare except for a single wall

Shallow molded dish with trailed glaze decoration. Shoji Hamada, Japan.

Although the brush work is free and contemporary, the form reflects strong Sung influences. Stoneware with red iron glaze. Shoji Hamada, Japan.

scroll or flower arrangement. The major utensils, tea bowls, water container, covered jar for tea, and so on, are all ceramic, a factor that greatly encouraged the Japanese potter during the fifteenth and sixteenth centuries. At first, only Chinese pieces were used, often rare Sung bowls. The essence of the ceremony is its simplicity and lack of ostentation. One was expected to comment upon the beauty of the pottery as well as the flavor of the tea. It was only natural that in time the tea masters would be attracted to the ordinary ware of the day, thrown and decorated with a careless skill. The Raku ware with its coarse body and irregularity became especially popular. Old pieces were sought after and fantastic prices were paid for pieces rather crudely made. It reminds one somewhat of the tulip craze that swept seventeenth century Holland. At that time, the financial speculation was such that the otherwise solid burghers mortgaged their homes for the price of a few rare bulbs.

Through the centuries, even while several elaborate and decorative styles developed and export trade flourished, there continued an interest and appreciation for the simple ware of the tea ceremony. Industrialization, in spite of its late arrival in Japan, has had the same disastrous effects as in Europe. A large proportion of ceramic production is for export and is done in foreign styling. When possible, factory copies were made of the popular Chinese and Japanese ware of traditional design. But the worst aspect of industrialization for the workshop potter was the tremendous decline in the local market for everyday wares.

At present, somewhat of a revival is occurring in the handcrafts. Part is undoubtedly due to better economic conditions; when so much fine work from the past can be seen, it is obvious to most Japanese that the mass-produced article lacks the quality of vitality. Much credit for arousing this interest is due to the late Dr. Soetsu Yanagi, who founded the Japanese Craft Society, its Folk Museum, and its numerous retail outlets for handcrafts. Unlike the situation in America, the newspapers are cooperative and the large department stores hold many craft shows.

But like America there is a difference of opinion as to the direction of ceramics among the potters. The late Rosanjin Kitaoji, active until 1960, was a major potter working in the traditional styles influenced by the early tea ware in the styles of Shino, Oribe, and Kenzan, as well as Chinese Ming porcelains. Among those also interested in various older tea styles are Toyozo Arakawa, Kokuro Kata, Mineo Kato, and Toyo Kaneshige, some of whose work is shown.

above, left Porcelain plate decorated in a traditional overglaze style. Colors are red, green, yellow, and black, 14 in. diameter. Kitaoji Rosanjin, Japan. **above, right** Stoneware dish decorated in a contemporary Seto style. Mineo Kato, Japan. **opposite** Porcelain jar in a personal decorative style. Red base with delicate pattern in gold and silver, height 7½ in. Kenkichi Tomimoto, Japan.

Pressed and molded jar with reduced iron and copper-red decoration. Height 13¼ in. Kanjiro Kawai, Japan.

As a young man, the late Kenkichi Tomimoto (1886 to 1963) and Bernard Leach studied together with Ogata Kenzan. He was the sixth in a line of followers of the famous first Kenzan (1660 to 1743). It was he who developed a personal style uniquely Japanese and is perhaps regarded as Japan's greatest potter. Creating original forms, decorated with the poetic brush work more common to the scroll painter, Kenzan's work simulated a wide circle of potters whose combined efforts during the middle Edo period, 1703 to 1800, is regarded by many as the high point of Japanese ceramics.

Onda folk art teapot from village in southern Kyushu, Japan.

Onda covered jar, White slip, trailed glaze decoration, green, black, and brown, done in typical folk-art tradition. Height 24 in. Japan.

Although Tomimoto's early work was in the folk craft traditions, he later changed and produced highly decorated porcelain wares of a very individual character. Potting is a very personal affair, some can work within a tradition, others cannot.

Shoji Hamada is undoubtedly the most recognized potter in Japan today and is the major exponent of the folk pottery tradition. He does not even sign his pieces! As a young potter, he accompanied Leach to England in 1920, and together they built a kiln at St. Ives and started potting, combining their eastern training with an examination of medieval English pottery and seventeenth century slipware.

After several years, Hamada returned to Japan and in 1924 settled in Mashiko, a small pottery and farming village in the foothills about eighty miles north of Tokyo. Together with Yanagi, Hamada and his friend Kanjiro Kawai, a Kyoto potter, provided the major impetus for the present folk art (*Mingei*) movement. Other potters have moved to Mashiko and at present there are fifty kilns with about four hundred workers. There are other smaller centers of hand pottery in Japan including such remote workshops

Double vase with slip-trailed decoration in the experimental western style. Height 15 in. Osamu Suzuki, Japan.

above and to the right Work by Totaro Sakuma, Skimaoka Tatsuzo, and Hamada taken in craft shop in Mashiko. **below** Digging clay in local hills at Mashiko, Japan.

Abstract sculptural form with decorative marblized body and glazed accents. Height 24 in. Yoshimichi Fujimoto, Japan.

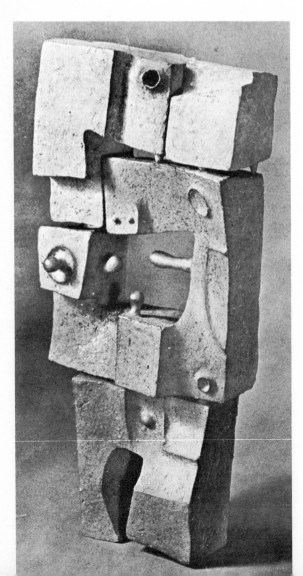

Sculptural assemblage akin to the works of Arp, Noguchi, and Brancusi. Height 20 in. Kazuo Yagi, Japan.

as those found in Onda in Kyushu. Typical of several villages in the area, Onda has a communal kiln; all materials are local, wood for fuel, clay, ash glazes, and so on. The Onda ware is primarily made for the local market and has strong functional shapes showing a Korean influence.

The dilemma of the contemporary potter is perhaps more strongly defined in Japan than elsewhere. Unlike Europe and the United States, the folk art potter producing a functional ware of a high artistic quality still flourishes. But many Japanese potters have turned to mass production design as in Scandinavia. A few attempt a very personalized style and are influenced by painting and sculpture and are thus more akin to the potter in the States. It will be most instructive to observe the situation as it unfolds in Japan in succeeding years. Can the crafts exist in an industrial society? Is it possible for age-old traditions of craftsmanship and good taste to survive the mediocracy that seems to be the other side of the coin labeled materialism?

CHAPTER 3 CERAMIC DESIGN _____

INTRODUCTION

The term ceramic design would imply that there is a concept of design unique to ceramics. This is true only to the extent that the clay, forming methods, and, in some cases, functionalism, will impose limitations. An almost universal belief among artists is that there exists certain basic design principles that are applicable to such seemingly diverse fields as architecture, painting, ceramics, and sculpture.

Before trying to identify these general principles, we should realize that our personal attitudes are often a determining factor in whether we can have a meaningful experience somewhat akin to that which motivated the artist. For example, very few of us can view a painting without seeing it through the experiences of our own background. We tend to arbitrarily reject anything that does not conform to these highly personal notions. It is only natural that we should have fond and nostalgic memories from the past. Everyone has favorite melodies or even types of scenery that are fraught, with associations of personal experiences in such a manner that they always evoke a positive, pleasurable reaction. Unfortunately, some individuals, because of extreme emotional involvement, cannot ever be objective.

Stoneware vase with the exploding tactile treatment of the upper form in sharp contrast to the uniform texture of the base. Height 30 in. Carl E. Paak, U.S.A.

One of the most valuable aspects of foreign travel (not at tourist hotels and the like) is that the traveler is placed in a new and strange environment. He begins to see the common, everyday aspects of life in a fresh light, which in some cases leads to a re-evaluation of ideas heretofore uncritically accepted. The efforts of the recent Pop and Op Art groups were primarily shock treatments aimed at forcing the viewer to look with a new eye. These movements have been greatly influenced by advertising techniques that are basically similar in that they try to shock the viewer and gain his attention by one device or another. The ceramic field has its own variation of the avant guard that, for lack of a better title, is sometimes called the *No-Pot*. It is a curious hybrid, neither pottery nor sculpture.

Prior to the war, ceramic and craft exhibits were a rarity. There was only the Ceramic National Exhibition at Syracuse and a few regional craft groups who could find a suitable exhibition area. But in recent years, local museums and community art organizations have multiplied at such a rate that craft exhibits of one type or another occur in every moderate-sized city. As public galleries have expanded their activities, they have taken over exhibition events formerly conducted solely by craft-guild types of groups. It is perhaps only natural that professional gallery staffs in time come to regard ceramic art objects not as accouterments of everyday life but rather as items created especially for exhibition purposes. There is little doubt that a significant proportion of the work seen in the average ceramic exhibit today is not intended for the local buying public but rather for the purpose of attracting the attention of an exhibition jury. The complexion of the jury is always a dilemma for the gallery director or exhibition committee. Shall it consist of professionals in the field, a popular critic, or a talented amateur? Is the jury to receive some general instructions? Does the gallery want a representative cross-section or does it lean toward either conservative or avant guard extremes.

We have thus far touched on a miscellany of seemingly unrelated subjects. They all, however, constitute hurdles faced by the student who is seeking some scale of values with which to guide and judge his own work. First, it is necessary for him to realize that the selection of ceramic art found on his mother's what-not shelf and so highly cherished is most likely to be a hodge-podge of popular commercial ceramics of poor design. Taste, accepted art forms, or whatever term is used, will vary from generation to generation. All values are relative—each generation must write its own version of history to correspond to its own beliefs. Man has been modeling clay objects for over 20,000 years, and to miss or avoid the stimulation of this immense and varied storehouse is very shortsighted. Museums, libraries, and contemporary galleries should be the object of the student's curiosity. Unfortunately, official esthetics as evidenced in installations in historical museums are apt to be a generation or two behind contemporary interests. The student must not feel therefore, that displays in the entrance foyer are necessarily superior to those stuck away in an ill-lighted basement case. In a similar fashion, he ought to realize that current exhibitions must be viewed critically for they are apt to be biased in one direction or another. It is a most unsettling experience when the student realizes that there are no ready-made guides to artistic judgments. Cultural backgrounds, even religious factors, exert such great influences that we cannot and should not expect rigid conformity or consistent judgment. But there are, nevertheless, certain broad design elements that ought to underlie rational criticism of our own work and the work of others.

BASIC DESIGN FACTORS

Our entire knowledge of the world and our continuing reaction to it is based on physical stimulation to specialized nerve cells located in our eyes, ears, and so on. Most of the stimuli with which we are concerned are visual ones. It is true that in ceramics the physical touch of a silky glaze or a rough texture is an added sensory factor, but so coordinated is the nervous system that we can practically recall the feel of an object by its visual appearance.

The vigorous incised and slip decoration, revealed by the salt glaze, attracts our attention. Later we see the curve of the lip echoed in the throwing rings. Richard Leach, U.S.A.

A unique piece, featuring an almost geometric form of rough groggy clay contrasted with the smoothness of the inner glazed surface. Ruth Duckworth, an English potter now living in the United States.

When viewing paintings, sculpture, or ceramics, the eye is first caught by shape or form, intense color or sharp contrast of chromatic value or texture. Without this initial point of contact, we would only give the piece a passing glance. Viewing an inconspicuous object without distinguishing features leads to a feeling of frustration or boredom. The eyes must, it seems, come to focus on a localized area. This may be a factor related to our sense of equilibrium.

The enjoyment we have in viewing an art object is relative to the length of time our eyes can be tricked, as it were, into observing it. Whether man has some innate tendency to organize data or the physical eye relaxes when sensations slightly repetitive occur is not known. But the eye very definitely seeks out repetition of the first stimulation whether it be form or color. If they are too identical, interest wanes. The design problem then is to repeat with subtle variations the predominant motif. This motif may be a simple shape or a more complex form involving pattern, color, and texture. In time, the eye gets tired of this game and seeks relief itself much as we rest our eyes by glancing away from a page of fine print. But before this happens, we must introduce a contrasting theme in our composition. For example, angular and flat surfaces will react against the round and bulbous, warm colors versus the cool, and soft forms contrast with rough textures.

This explanation, rather briefly expressed, of the physical phenomena of viewing an art object may seem at first glance to be too simple, but further examination may prove it to be a useful method with which to evaluate the formal aspects of your own work and that of others. This analysis consists of three basic questions.

1. Does the object have a center of interest, a focus to which our eye is attracted?
2. Is this focal element repeated with subtle variations in other areas of the composition so as to lead our eye to explore it?
3. Is a counter motif employed to make the major theme of greater interest due to the continual interaction between the major and minor elements?

It is the author's belief that this simple theory accounts for the basic components of design in the visual arts. It is perhaps also valid in the field of music and dance. Since these factors are based upon physical sensory reactions, they remain constant regardless of the cultural overtones. Style or fashion usually appeals only to our desire for novelty. Art must rest upon a design structure to become more than a passing fad.

The formal design of a work of art is not by any means the totality of an art experience. As mentioned earlier, what the viewer brings to the work in the way of personal experience is often as significant as the work itself. The presence of a strong bias of a religious, moral, or even of a socio-economic nature may serve to negate any possibility of meaningful rapport. These considerations may not apply as strongly in ceramics as in painting and sculpture, which historically have had stronger religious and social overtones. Tradition is essentially the sum of the values and experiences of our forefathers. It is a valuable heritage but not necessarily as sacrosanct as some would have it. The greatest asset any student can have, regardless of his field, is a curious mind, unimpaired by prejudice.

FACTORS INVOLVED IN CERAMIC DESIGN

Every art form and each material used in its creation has certain advantages and limitations. Each generation will try these limitations and will occasionally succeed in going beyond previous efforts. Speaking of the crafts specifically, the various media have unique qualities derived jointly from the material and the tool. A valid design theory must stress the full development of these qualities. Stated briefly, this means that a ceramic piece should look as though it were made of clay and not metal, glass, or wood. This is equally true of the other materials. To fail to exploit the full potential of the material, or to misuse it, is to limit our possible aesthetic enjoyment as well. For example, it is the nature of wood to be sawed and planed into thin sections that are later glued or otherwise fastened into numerous useful containers. It may also be carved, but always in relationship to its grain. In both solid and laminated forms, it is an ideal material for furniture. But wooden articles that are painted, stained, and highly varnished, tend to lose the unique characteristics that make it so enjoyable and that distinguish it from other materials.

Clay is an extremely versatile material. Coupled with the added possibilities of color and surface effects of the glaze, it tempts one to go beyond its normal limitations. Therefore, we habitually find ceramic designs that do imitate those of metal, glass, or wood and that would be more successful in these materials. The unusual material of our time is also the most recent, plastics. Since it is a liquid in the raw state and can be extruded in such a variety of forms before hardening, it really has no recognized character. But the basic problem of plastics is that the experimental model is generally made of plaster and the final mold of metal. How can this process do other than reflect the character of these materials to the loss of what are still the largely unknown potentials of plastics. Mention might be made in passing that this is the problem of most commercial ceramics, the design of which passes from paper to plaster models without development in clay. The resulting products only superficially reflect the qualities of the material. It is unfortunate that industrial design today tends to stress the drafting board in place of an apprenticeship in the crafts. In fairness, it must be stated that most commercial ware is practical and much cheaper than any craftwork could hope to be.

The plastic quality of clay is clearly revealed in this freely-thrown and decorated stoneware bottle. Robert Eckels, U.S.A. (Photo Thomas Kinney)

Ceramics has traditionally been divided into two fields, one consisting of functional wares and the other of more decorative or completely sculptural pieces. Since the plastic clay is one of the easiest methods of making studies in form, it has been used by untold generations of sculptors. The immediacy of expression, its durability, plus the wealth of color and glaze have given ceramic sculpture an advantage over other three-dimensional mediums. But the technical problems involved have limited its widespread use to certain cultural periods that saw the close cooperation or the combination of the skilled craftsman and the sculptor. Chinese T'ang ceramics are a prime example of such a fortuitous development in the field of ceramic sculpture.

The ceramic industry in America is in an unfortunate situation. The commercial dinnerware and tile companies are hard pressed by competition from other materials such as glass and plastics, as well as by foreign imports. In such a situation they are loath to make the investment in the design staffs that might be their best solution. On the other hand, most ceramic students look at industry with horror and have no interest in the technical and design problems to be solved in developing dinnerware patterns or accessory pieces for production.

It is roughly two hundred years since we have had many potteries whose output reflected the range of possibilities inherent in clay. This has been a period of great achievement in production techniques and in factory growth. It is unfortunate that during this time the authority for basic design decisions should have gravitated toward the technical and sales managements.

There are very few potteries to my knowledge who employ creative producing potters on their design staffs. Nor is there a move on the part of our schools to recognize this problem. With few exceptions, teachers of ceramics in our colleges have no contact or interest in the commercial area. Their background is generally in the fine arts and not the craft school or industry. I wonder if the recent trend toward the sculptural piece rather than functional ware is related in part to a subconscious desire to find accommodation in an atmosphere orientated more to the fine art avant guard than to the traditional crafts.

Straddling, as he does, two divergent fields, it is especially necessary for the student ceramist to have a clear idea of his objectives. In functional ceramics, there is no excuse for pitchers that do not pour properly, likewise handles must balance and be comfortable to grasp. And so on down the line—the piece must fill its need as perfectly as possible. Once in a Swedish railway diner, I noticed the unusual coffee cup design that had a series of steps on the inside. Later I accidently met the designer and learned

A most functional teapot, simple yet vigorous in form. The reed handle integrates perfectly with the form. Donald E. Frith, U.S.A.

of his trials in developing this nonsloshing coffee cup. Seldom does one have so specific a problem. Fortunately, form has infinite possibilities and clay and glazes such variety that one should be able to combine function with one's own very personal idea of beauty.

Ceramic sculpture, on the other hand, places no restraining hand on the potter. Our problem here is to exploit the potential of clay and glaze in purely sculptural form. Even a commission allows one a tremendous variety of directions. Disregarding subject matter, our only concern need be the development of a composition within the basic design principles discussed earlier in this chapter. Concepts and working habits carried over from other materials may at first inhibit our expression. If, for example, one has had considerable experience in the traditional sculptural techniques, such as stone carving, it is most difficult to conceive of form in other than a very rounded and solid manner. On the other hand, students whose three dimensional experience is largely limited to pottery tend to make ceramic sculpture in a manner reminiscent of an assemblage of pot sections with a lot of applied texture. In neither case is the full sculptural potential of ceramics realized. It is hard to know in what category to place the No-Pot. I must confess that after making a score or two of sugar and creamers, which are a bread-and-butter item, I get a bit bored and often make a slab piece or two. These tend to be quite potlike in character, but they are hardly functional and definitely have strong sculptural qualities. Can it be that our current cultural inclination to favor whatever is new and different places a temporary positive value on such minor experiments as the No-Pot?

POTTERY FORM AND DECORATION

How are the rather generalized design principles previously discussed related to the very real and definite problem faced by every student—that of form and decoration. The mastery of technique, although sometimes frustrating, is far easier to achieve. While trying to establish a few helpful guidelines, the author realizes that none will be true in all cases and that countless examples may be found among historical and contemporary ceramics to refute one or another of the comments that follow. For example, I have always maintained that even slightly realistic figures on a pot are out of place and destroy the unity of the form. Yet, the Peruvian portrait pots, which are nothing if not realistic, seem most normal and not objectionable. Is there any explanation of this reaction other than that there are various cultural factors that subtly impinge upon the aesthetics of each

Salt glazed pitcher with a simple contour flowing from base to lip. Flared top draws our attention. Throwing ridges and pulled handle emphasize the rounded form. Angelo Garzio, U.S.A.

generation, leading it to accept, reject, or ignore certain possibilities in content and formal design? It is said that skillful art forgeries are seldom detected until a generation or two later when the unconscious mannerisms of the period have become dated and stand out as subtle anachronisms. The diversity of expression in contemporary ceramics illustrated in this text points out the dilemma of the student. We have no craft traditions. We have no apprentice potters who learn, in a very natural and easy way, a feeling for design along with the necessary skills. Instead we have a great freedom to experiment, with perhaps not too much emphasis on technique, plus the encouraging historical and contemporary examples that can be seen in numerous museums and books. We can benefit from this rich heritage only if we can appreciate its varied and unique qualities. In no other way than by analysis and understanding will it truly become a part of our own background.

Form

Whether conceived of as either a mass or a silhouette, form must be the dominant element. This is our focus of attention. To water down its impact by frivolous treatment of the lip, elaborate handles, or by a flashy decoration gives the viewer a sensation of uncertainty, leading to indifference. On the other hand, the basic form, however simple in outline, must not be static in concept. The sphere, in spite of its symmetry, remains a dynamic form. But the elongated pot with its greatest diameter in the center, creates a feeling of monotony because of its equal division. A similar reaction occurs in sculpture or painting when the focus of attention is too centrally located. A more interesting proportion develops in a thrown piece if the base and the top diameter are not too equal.

Since the ceramist is involved with the pot physically as well as visually, his concept of form is quite different from the layman who is apt to think of it as an outline. Throwing a pottery form is not unlike blowing glass in that it is a process of the stretching and pulling of a hollow form. This feeling of flow and motion is one of the unique features of clay and should be reflected in the final design. It is not natural to the throwing process nor structurally sound to have abrupt angular changes in the form. The movement should flow from base to lip, with changes in direction but not enough to divide the piece into sections and so destroy the unity of the whole. Handles, covers, and knobs should flow into the form and should not appear as welded or glued appendages. To give the maximum impact, the contour

Stoneware bottle with sgraffito and slip decoration repeating the dominant motif of the vessel form. Height 30 in. Lyle N. Perkins, U.S.A.

of the form must not be like a smudged charcoal drawing but decisively straight or curved. Subtlety must never be confused with ambiguity nor invention with merely the quaint or the different.

Variation

Variation of the major theme is generally accomplished by having slight repetitions of the basic form appear in the shape of the handles, a knob, the rim, and occasionally even the foot. The various types of decoration, ranging from deep carving to brushed slip and stains, can also effectively echo the character of the form. In the case of a bowl, the throwing rings do this automatically. In developing the variations of the major theme, we are apt to become a little forced and perhaps overdo it. In each case, the simplest method should be used, for pottery is not basically an occupation of ornamentation. We must learn to do all the operations with efficiency of time and effort. For example, on a predominantly vertical form, a simple scratched texture is often enough to reinforce the original impression and lengthen our appreciation.

Counter Motif

The counter motif must not be so powerful that our attention is drawn too quickly from the major form. This is a real problem since we often work for a time undecided as to which is our major or minor motif. Our goal here is to find a contrasting element in both the basic form and decoration that relate one to the other and at the same time serve as a foil to the major theme and its variations. Glaze effects and color may play an important part in sustaining interest in the form and decoration.

Naturally, when we speak of such compositional efforts, we do not have a tea cup in mind but rather a large ceramic piece, a sculptural form, or a mural. We must not feel, however, that design is only for the show piece.

Stoneware bottle with numerous variations of a circular motif. Applied, scratched, and stain elements in contrast. Height 21 in. Nan McKinnell, U.S.A.

If we are to become competent potters, we must consider each piece as a problem in design. In a simple bowl, the angle of the foot or the flare of the lip can make all the difference. A pot need not be large and elaborately decorated to be a fine work. We all ought to pay more attention to the subtleties and variations possible in a basic, simple shape.

Stoneware vase, although strong and expressive it relies only upon a simple applied-
and scratched-clay decoration, brown and
yellow slips over a slightly deformed sphere.
Frans Wildenhain, U.S.A.

CHAPTER 4

CLAY AND CLAY BODIES

Most persons confuse clay with soil, and this is quite understandable as they are related. A garden soil is a combination of clay, sand, and humus (partially decayed vegetable matter). Compared with other materials in the earth, this layer of soil is extremely thin, usually only a few inches thick and seldom over a foot. There are, of course, great areas without soil such as most desert and mountainous regions. Between the soil proper and the rocky mantle of the earth, there is a subsoil that may vary from a few inches to hundreds of feet in thickness. The subsoil may be composed of clay, sand, or gravelly mineral deposits in either a pure or mixed form.

After the fiery formation of the earth, it first cooled for billions of years before water vapor and an atmosphere were formed. The slow march of the seasons began. Erosion from wind and water and contractions from heat and ice slowly crumbled the rock that comprised the earth's surface. The initial composition of this rock varied from place to place. Minerals that were slightly water soluble or softer broke down much quicker. The miracle of plant and later animal life hastened this process as the organic acids contributed to their decomposing action. In certain locations, the movement and melting of ice cover during the glacial ages had considerable effect on the mixing and breakdown of minerals composing the surface rock.

The composition of pure clay is $Al_2O_3 \cdot 2SiO_2 \cdot 2H_2O$. For the most part, these kaolin particles resulted from the decomposition of granite, feldspathic, or pegmatite rocks. Impurities or variations in this basic formula account for the differing characteristics of the numerous clay types. A unique quality of clay and one most valuable is its *plasticity*. Unless a clay will hold its shape while being formed, it is useless. This quality is dependent upon the fineness of particle size. A fine grain of sand is $\frac{1}{500}$ inch in diameter. Even this is huge compared with a clay particle that is only 0.7 microns in diameter and 0.05 in thickness. (A micron is about $\frac{1}{25,000}$ inch.) The softer and more soluble components of the granite-type rocks decomposed and left the alumina silica clay particles. The natural structure of the clay particle is a flat, shingle-like shape that tends to slide together and to give support one to another whether wet or dry. By comparison, even the finest ground minerals have large granular crystals with no ability to adhere.

CLAY TYPES

All clays may be first grouped into either a *sedimentary* or a *residual* category. The sedimentary clays are those that by action of wind or running water have been transported far from the site of the original parent rock. This action was apt to occur only to the clay particles of the finest size. Therefore, the sedimentary clays are the more plastic of the two types. The *residual* clays are those that remained more or less at the site of the original rock formation. As a rule, they are the less plastic type and contain many of the larger sized particles.

Kaolin

Kaolin is the pure clay mentioned earlier. Although never used alone as a body, it serves a standard with which to compare other clays. It is pure white in color and can be fired to an extremely high temperature. It serves as a source of alumina and silica in glazes and as an important ingredient in high-fired white ware and porcelain bodies. The types of kaolin available is but indicative of the difficulties in classifying clays. The major commercial deposits are in the southeastern states. North Carolina produces a residual type kaolin. The deposits in South Carolina and Georgia are of the sedimentary type. However, the Florida deposits are even more plastic and are termed ball kaolin.

Ball Clay

Ball clay is similar chemically to kaolin after being fired. Prior to firing, the color is dark grey from the presence of organic material. Although weathered from a granite type rock similar to kaolin, the ball clay particles were deposited in swampy areas where the organic acids and gaseous compounds released from decaying vegetation served to break the clay particles down into even a finer size than the sedimentary kaolins.

CLAY AND CLAY BODIES

Ball clay imparts increased plasticity and dry strength when used as a body component. If 10 to 20 percent is added to the clay body, it greatly improves the throwing qualities of a body. Like kaolin, it has a high maturing temperature. Ball clay may be used as a glaze source of alumina and silica as well as a binding agent. However, such glazes tend to form gas leading to glaze defects if stored for long. The glaze may be dried out and reused, or a few drops of formaldehyde may be added to discourage fermentation. The principal United States sources of ball clay are in Tennessee and Kentucky.

Stoneware Clays

Stoneware clays are of particular interest to the potter as they are generally plastic and fire in a range from cones 6 to 10. (See appendix for temperature charts giving cone equivalents in degrees F and C. Cones indicated in the text refer to the Orton series. Please note that the Seger cones have a slightly different range.) Depending upon the atmospheric conditions of the firing, the color will range from buff to grey. Stoneware clays are found in scattered deposits ranging from New York and New Jersey westward to Illinois and Missouri and on the Pacific coast. These stoneware clays vary in composition; in comparison with kaolin, they contain impurities, such as calcium, feldspar, and iron that lower the maturing temperatures and impart color to the clay. It is very seldom today that a single clay is used as a throwing body. To the major clay, which may be either a stoneware or fireclay, additions of ball clay, flint, feldspar, and even earthenware are added to obtain desired plasticity, firing temperature, color, and texture.

Fireclay

Fireclay is a refractory type clay commonly used for insulating brick, hard firebrick, and kiln furniture. Its physical characteristics vary, with some fireclays having a fine plastic quality while others being coarse and granular and unsuitable for throwing. Fireclays generally contain some iron as an impurity but seldom calcium or feldspar. The more plastic varieties may, like some stoneware clays, be found adjacent to coal veins. Fireclays may be high in either flint or alumina and as such have special industrial uses. Fireclays of one type or another are found in most states, the exceptions being a few mountain states and states on the southeast and northeast coasts.

Earthenware Clays

Earthernware clays constitute a group of low-firing clays (cones 08 to 02) of interest to the beginning potter. The presence of numerous fluxes, or iron impurities, limits its commercial use to building bricks and drain tile. Earthenware clays of one type or another can be found in every state although commercial deposits are more abundant in the lower Great Lakes area. Many such clays, available commercially, are of a shale type. Shale deposits consist of clays laid down in prehistoric lake beds. Time, chemical reactions, and pressure from overlying material have served to cement these clay particles into shale, a hard stratified material half way between a clay and a rock. Considerable shale clays are mined and ground into a powdered form similar to ordinary clay. Small lumps will be troublesome if not screened out, as they will absorb moisture and expand and rupture in the body much like a piece of plaster. Unlike stoneware bodies, which are nearly vitreous, the average earthenware body has a porosity ranging from 5 to 15 percent. Due to the various fluxes it contains, earthenware cannot be made vitreous, it deforms and often bloats and blisters at temperatures over 2100°F (1150°C).

Some earthenware clays are of glacial origin and therefore are quite varied in composition. They frequently contain soluble sulfates that are drawn to the surface during drying. When fired, a whitish film appears on the surface. This defect may be eliminated by the addition of 2 percent barium carbonate to the clay body.

Slip Clay

Slip clays are those clays occuring naturally, which contain sufficient fluxes to function as a glaze without further additions. Although the author has heard of slip clays with a white and even a blue color, all those that he has personally used have ranged from a tan, to a brick red, to brown black in color. Most such slip clays fire in a range from cones 6 to 10. The best known commercial slip clay is Albany, mined in small pits near Albany, New York. There are many small deposits of glacial clays scattered through the northern states that will make satisfactory slip glazes with little or no additions. Slip glazes are easy to apply, and they usually have a long firing range and few surface defects.

Bentonite

Bentonite is an unusual clay that is used in small amounts by the potter as a plasticizer. Deposits are found in most of the western mountain states and in several southern gulf states. It has the finest particle size of any clay known. Bentonite was formed in prehistoric ages from the air-borne dust of volcanic eruptions. It is largely silica in composition. One to 3 percent may be used in a nonclay glaze to assist adhesion without noticeably changing the glaze. When used in nonplastic, or short clays, one part is about equal to five parts of ball clay. It should be mixed dry as it gets quite gummy when mixed alone with water.

CLAY BODIES

An *earthenware* or *stoneware* clay that is completely satisfactory in all respects seldom occurs in nature. It may not be plastic enough, nor have the right color, nor fire at the desired temperature. Even clays from the same bed will vary slightly in chemical and physical qualities.

In making up a clay body, we generally start with a clay that is available at a reasonable price and that has no great faults, such as an excessive amount of sand or grit. No clay should be considered unless it is moderately plastic. The plasticity may be improved by additions of ball clay or bentonite. In rare cases, a clay may be so fine that it will not dry out easily without cracking. In this case, a less plastic clay, a silica sand or fine grog (a coarse, crushed, fired clay), may be added to *open up* and make the clay body more porous so it will dry uniformly. This latter treatment is often necessary to make an extremely fine or *fat clay* throw and stand up better.

Occasionally, a clay will lack sufficient fluxes to fire hard enough at the desired temperature. We seldom add a refined flux but usually use inexpensive materials containing fluxes, such as feldspar, talc, dolomite, nepheline syenite, bone ash, and so on. If color is no objection, iron oxide may be used. Often a lower-fired clay may be economically used. This has the advantage of not cutting down on the plasticity that additions of all of the above items will do.

If, on the other hand, our body deforms, we must either begin again with a different clay or add clays that are higher in alumina or in silica and alumina. Generally, this would mean additions of a plastic Florida kaolin or a plastic fireclay of a high maturity.

Whiteware and Porcelain

Whiteware and porcelain bodies are generally used only for commercial ware, which are mechanically reproduced in plaster molds, since the hand potter prefers the reduction effects of his grey or reddish stoneware in addition to its plastic qualities. (See Chapter 10.) The porcelain bodies are compounded principally from kaolin, feldspar, and flint. If more plasticity is desired, some ball is used, resulting in greater shrinkage. For a throwing body, the ball clay may amount to 25 percent. (See the appendix for suggested clay bodies.) Chemically, there is little difference between a stoneware and a porcelain body save the presence of small quantities of iron and other impurities that color the stoneware and fireclays used. Bone china is similar to porcelain with the exception that bone ash has been added to the body as a flux to increase translucency and to reduce the temperature needed for maturity to about 2275°F (1250°C). Like porcelain, bone china is very hard, white, and translucent when thin. Its greatest fault is a tendency to warp in firing.

The term *chinaware* is used rather loosely to designate a white body usually fired between cones 4 to 8. Some types such as restaurant china, are very hard and durable. However, they should not be confused with the even harder and more translucent porcelain bodies fired from cones 10 to 16. The white body in the cone 4 range often uses nepheline syenite in place of feldspar. White earthenware clay is not too common. The low-fired white bodies commonly used for gift ware pottery contain large amounts of talc to reduce their firing temperatures to cones 08 to 04 (1750° to 1950°F, 955° to 1065°C).

TESTS FOR CLAY BODIES

Before any amount of new clay or clay body is used or purchased a few simple tests should be made.

Plasticity

Plasticity is a must for a throwing clay. A standard, simple test has been to loop a pencil-sized roll of the plastic clay around one's finger. If this coil cracks excessively, it will probably not throw well. The only satisfactory test, however, is to throw several pieces. In comparing bodies, all ought to have been aged for an equal period. Three weeks in a plastic state is usually sufficient for a clay to improve appreciably in throwing qualities. This is due to the complete wetting of the finest particles as well as the slight chemical breakdown that occurs because of the organic matter contained in all clays. The increase of plasticity by aging is more pronounced in acid than alkaline clays. If it is necessary to use an alkaline body, a small amount of vinegar in the throwing water will prove helpful.

Wedging, a process by which the clay is kneaded by hand to remove air pockets, has a considerable effect in increasing plasticity. In a coarse clay, the realignment of particles by the wedging action may also be a factor.

Water of plasticity refers to the amount of water needed to make a dry powdered clay into a physical state so it can be kneaded together and will hold its shape, that is, the consistency of a throwing clay. The finer the particle size of the clay, the more water it will absorb and therefore the more plastic the clay.

Porosity

Porosity of the fired body is directly related to the hardness and the vitrification of the clay. Most bodies used by the hand potter may be fired with a variation of at least 50°F (10°C) without proving unsuitable. As a general rule, we might state that most bodies will fall within the following porosity ranges: earthenware 4 to 10 percent, stoneware 1 to 6 percent, and for porcelain 0 to 3 percent. (See Chapter 9 on firing of clay bodies.) A higher firing will reduce the porosity, but normally a specific firing temperature will have been already chosen. We have indicated in the previous pages how adjustments are made to the body to increase or decrease fluxing action. In making the porosity test, an unglazed fired clay sample is weighed. After soaking overnight in water, the sample is wiped clean of surface water and weighed a second time. The percentage gain in weight will be the porosity of the clay body.

Shrinkage

Shrinkage of the clay body occurs first as the clay form dries in the air and secondly as the firing occurs in the kiln through the bisque (a low preliminary firing) and up to the glaze temperature. The more plastic clays will always shrink the most. The test is most simple; first, a plastic clay slab is rolled out and either cut or marked to a measure; after completely drying, a second measurement is taken; and after firing, a third. Clay shrinkage rates generally range from 5 to 12 percent in the drying category, with about an additional 8 to 12 percent shrinkage during firings. Thus, we can plan on having at least a total shrinkage of 13 percent with an extreme of 24 percent. Generally, however, the shrinkage from wet clay to the glazed ware will be between 15 to 20 percent.

Because of shrinkage strains placed upon large sculptural forms, it is necessary to use a grog up to 30 percent of the body. Since this material is already fired, little further change occurs in it. There is also a tendency in drying for the clay to pull away slightly from the grog and thus open up air channels that facilitates the drying out of thicker portions that would otherwise crack. The normal shrinkage rates previously referred to are those of plastic-type throwing clays. Special whiteware bodies using spodumene ($Li_2O \cdot Al_2O_3 \cdot 4SiO_2$) in place of the feldspar and using only small amounts of clay have a greatly reduced shrinkage and can even be compounded to develop a slight expansion in firing. Wollastonite, $CaSiO_3$, as a replacement for silica and flux in a body will also decrease firing shrinkage and increase thermal shock.

QUARTZ INVERSION

A major problem related to the successful compounding of ceramic bodies is that of quartz inversion. During the firing of a ceramic body, silica changes its crystalline structure several times with a rapid expansion in size. This is especially true of free silica that is in excess and is not in a chemical bond with other body components.

The coarse type of quartz called macrocrystalline flint is preferred as a body ingredient over the fine cryptocrystalline flint, which tends to develop more readily into the unstable cristobalite. Silica expansions in a clay body occur as alpha cristobalite changes into beta cristobalite between 428°F and 527°F (220° and 275°C). Further silica expansions occur at 1063°F (575°C) as alpha quartz changes into beta quartz; a critical 15 percent change develops at about 1600°F (870°C), as quartz converts into the tridymite form of silica. At about 1850°F (1010°C), tough interlocking mullite crystals composed of alumina and silica begin to form, which gives the fired body its major strength. However, the free or extra silica not so combined continues to be a source of trouble as in cooling it reverses the actions with subsequent contractions. This quartz inversion is one of the reasons why a slow cycle of firing as well as slow cooling is so necessary. For oven ware and even tableware, minimum thermal expansions are essential. The soft, porous, and thinly glazed Mexican ware conducts heat so slowly that there is no problem. But the hard and dense stoneware body must be perfectly compounded to serve as oven ware. Occasionally, a thick glaze that is poorly adjusted to the body is at fault in body failures.

Fortunately there are several minerals containing silica in a more stable form. A combination of pyrophyllite and talc substituted for part of the feldspar will reduce thermal expansion and glaze crazing—crazing is a network of cracks in the glaze layer that usually occurs if the glaze and clay body have uneven expansion and contraction rates during firing and cooling. If present, spodumene, $Li_2O \cdot Al_2O_3 \cdot 4SiO_2$, changes from alpha to beta spodumene between 1600 and 1700°F with an expansion that is irreversible. Petalite, $Li_3O \cdot Al_2O_3 \cdot 8SiO_2$, reacts in a similar manner to form a body with limited thermal expansions and a resulting resistance to heat shocks. It may be substituted for silica in the body formula. In a high-fired body, petalite would be preferred to spodumene. Wollastonite, $CaSiO_3$, where it can be used, also reduces firing shrinkage and aids in developing a tougher body that is more resistant to heat shock.

CLAY PROSPECTING AND PREPARATION

There are few sections of the country in which a suitable pottery clay cannot be found. Digging and preparing one's own clay is seldom an economic proposition, but it can be rewarding in other ways. If one is teaching in a summer camp, a hike can easily be turned into a prospecting trip with greater interest to all. In commercial clay mining, the soil over burden is removed by power shovels and the entire operation is quite mechanized. For the few hundred pounds of clay we wish to obtain, we will depend upon the accidents of nature to reveal the clay bed. A river bank, a road cut, or even a building excavation will often reveal a deep bed of clay that is free of surface contamination. If the clay located contains too much sand or gravel it may not be worth the trouble. A few tree roots will not disqualify a clay but any admixture of surface soil or humus will.

On the first trip out, it is advisable to take samples of a few pounds from several locations. These samples should be dried and then pounded into a coarse powder after which they should be soaked in water. Passing the clay slip through a 30-mesh seive ought to be sufficient to remove coarse impurities. If the clay proves too sandy, one can allow these heavier particles to settle for a few minutes after stirring and then pour off the thinner slip. This slip is then poured into drying bats and tested as described earlier.

In most localities, this surface clay is apt to be of an earthenware type. The samples should also be tested as slip glazes. It is surprising how many pockets of glacial clay work nicely as glazes, either alone or with a small amount of added flux. In some areas, the river-bank clay may be of a stoneware or fireclay type. All in all, clay prospecting may be profitable, but it is mostly fun. In this day of the super processed item, starting out from scratch gives one a rare feeling of satisfaction.

FORMING METHODS

CHAPTER 5

FORMING METHODS _____

POTTERY

Several techniques are illustrated in this chapter for the purposes of introduction and reference. Actual instruction in the workshop is most necessary. Throwing on the wheel is perhaps the most difficult problem faced by the beginning ceramist. The illustrations present a method of throwing, not *the* method. The physical characteristics of the potter, the type of wheel, plus the size of the pot and the character of the clay may well call for a variation in technique from that which is shown.

Skill in throwing is essential for the potter. It even plays an important role in the determination of the basic form that the pot will take. Obviously, a poor thrower is limited in his choice of shapes, and even these will lack freedom and vitality. While an industrial designer need not become an expert, this skill is a necessity for the studio potter for both design and economic reasons. Before throwing, the clay must be:
1. wedged perfectly, with neither air pockets nor any lumps
2. plastic, but neither sticky nor too stiff
3. aged, by storing at least three weeks in a moist state
(See page 135, Problems in Throwing, for further suggestions.)

Stoneware teapot and cup with triangular decoration formed by dip glazing. Reduction at Cone 10 causes mottled spots to form in a greenish-blue mat glaze. Angelo Garzio, U.S.A.

Throwing on the Wheel

Centering

1. Place the clay ball on a freshly moistened bat.
2. While the wheel is turning, force the clay down with the right hand.
3. With elbows braced at the sides, center the clay with the hands.
4. When the clay has been centered perfectly, open the ball with the thumbs.
5. Pressing the hands downwards and outwards, open the ball into a thick bowl shape.

FORMING METHODS

The Bowl Shape

From the basic clay form thrown on the opposite page, any number of shapes may be made. The bowl presents the fewest problems. The opened ball must be perfectly centered. Throwing should be done quickly lest the clay become too wet. The clay should not be pulled too thin where it flares up from the bat. The concave form must be maintained as any flatness of the curve will cause the piece to sag. Any unevenness in the outer rim may be trimmed with a needle. Moisten the rim and use a soft leather to finish it.

The Cylinder

1. The low cylinder must be perfectly centered.
2. Whenever possible, join the hands for better control.
3. If the top is uneven, cut it off with a needle.
4. The walls may be thickened and pulled up slightly by necking.
5. Even pressure forces the clay wall upward.

FORMING METHODS

The Bottle Form

1. The cylinder shown on the opposite page is flared out by pressure from the inside.
2. The top is necked in and thickened.
3. Then the top is pulled up and thinned out.
4. This process is repeated until the desired shape or height is reached.
5. Finally, the lip is finished with a soft leather.

The following illustrations show a slightly different technique from the previous ones. In the first photo, a rib (a flat oval of hardwood) is used to thin out the wall and smooth the surface. Since the pressure is concentrated, it creates less torque and less water is needed than when working with the fingers alone. Use of the knuckle is common in the preliminary shaping of a form and when throwing larger pieces. The cut away photos illustrate how the clay is both thinned out and pulled up by the forming process.

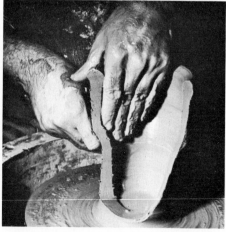

FORMING METHODS

Problems in Throwing

The previous illustrations have shown several throwing techniques that make the process appear deceptively easy. In throwing, the clay ball must first be perfectly centered into a low beehive form. In spite of the softness of the clay, a considerable amount of pressure must be exerted. Water must be added only to reduce friction and to prevent the clay from peeling off on one's fingers. Too much water will soften the clay and cause it to sag.

Only when the ball is perfectly centered should one attempt to open the clay with even pressure from both thumbs. Until this can be done with assurance, the student should not waste his time proceeding further. If the ball is opened without being centered on the wheel head, it cannot help but have one thick side and one thin. If the difference is slight, a skilled potter can pull up the thick side and come out with an even pot; the beginner will have a piece whose opposing sides grow progressively more uneven.

The first project ought to be a series of cylinders. Every thrown shape is based upon the cylinder; until the student can throw this basic form, he cannot hope to have much success in potting. In pulling the cylinder upwards, the elbows should be braced at the sides when possible and the thumbs should be joined for support. This upward motion ought not to be so rapid as to cause deep ridges in the wall that will eventually lead to irregular thicknesses in the body or an uneven top. Instead, move the hands up slowly, leaving the finger ridges about three-eighths of an inch apart.

Normally, the palms of the hands are only used in centering or for necking in a form that has flared out too far. The finger tips are used for throwing small and average-sized forms. They are more sensitive in detecting the action of the clay and create a minimum friction drag and torque.

In throwing larger forms, the fist is clenched and the knuckle of the index finger is used for greater pressure. Occasionally, an elephant-ear sponge is used to prevent the finger tips from digging in too deeply while applying a heavy pressure. The use of ribs is another means of increasing pressure and compacting the clay without excessive friction. The throwing ridges seem appropriate for the stoneware body, but a final shaping with a flexible rib is often more suitable for the finer textured porcelain body.

As a series of cylinders was thrown to learn the technique of that form, so it must be for all other shapes. A dozen or more bowls or teapots must be made to get the feel of things and achieve the most desirable flow of

Thrown stoneware bottles in a shape that needs little decoration. Forms such as these are generally thrown in two or more sections. They are carefully measured and thrown so as to join top to top or bottom to bottom. This is to maintain a similar moisture content. The surfaces are scratched and joined with slip. Depending upon the form and the condition of the clay, additional shaping is occasionally possible after joining. Lyle Perkins, U.S.A.

form. In repeating a form, the student will be amazed to find that he will eventually throw a similar shape using less clay with each attempt. This will happen even with an experienced potter. The proportions of the basic cylinder must be adjusted according to the final form. As the operations are repeated, the most logical sequence will evolve. As a result, the form will be thrown quicker and with a dryer and thinner wall. Equally important is the fact that design will develop in a more natural manner, evolving from the material and the technique. It is very likely that the original concept will change in the process. Beginning students seldom profit from drawing forms as they have no feeling for the clay. It is not likely that those who throw a different form each trial will learn much in the way of the needed techniques.

Throwing Aids

While large bowls need to be thrown on a plaster bat and later trimmed, most pieces may be more conveniently thrown on a metal head and cut off with a twisted wire. A hinged, adjustable pointer, as illustrated, is a handy guide for throwing sets. Small pieces, such as the egg cup shown, are best thrown off the hump (a 50-pound ball of clay). In this case, a groove is cut into which one end of a string is placed. Revolving slowly, the string cuts through the pot at its base.

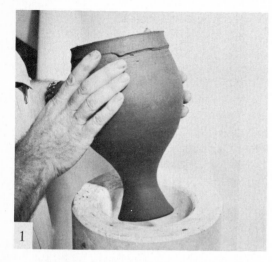

Trimming the Bottle

The foot is difficult to trim conveniently unless the bottle has a large and stable rim. If the object is small, a wide-mouthed glass jar, centered on the wheel head and held in place with clay lumps, can serve as a turning chuck. For trimming larger pieces, keep in the studio several plaster cylinders of assorted sizes that will fit the wheel heads. With such equipment on hand, trimming the foot of a long-necked bottle or jar is a simple operation.

Drying Problems

After trimming, place the bowls and other objects on a flat shelf in an *upside-down* position, if possible, to equalize the drying rates. Before placing the objects on the drying shelf, wrap the handles of pitchers and similar objects with damp paper towels. If the handles dry first, they will crack off when the drying shrinkage takes place in the body proper.

Trimming the Bowl

1. While the bowl is on the bat, excess clay can be trimmed away.
2. An old hacksaw blade (with its teeth ground off) cuts off the bowl from the bat.
3. Turn the bowl upside down. While it is held in place by soft clay lumps, the excess clay can be trimmed away.
4. The center section is cut out.
5. Making a good foot rim is the final touch to any pot.

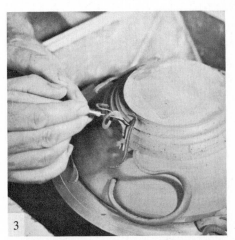

Large stoneware plate with a rich glaze of feldspar
fluxed by barium carbonate with a copper colorant.
Kyllikki Salmenhaara, Finland. Color plate.

The Pitcher

1. The lip is shaped from the soft clay.
2. The handle is pulled from a lump of stiff clay.
3. Formed with plenty of water, the handle takes the natural shape of the fingers.
4. The handle is attached as soon as the pitcher is firm enough to work with.
5. The finger marks where the handle is joined make a natural decoration.

Detail of mural showing varied glaze and textural effects. Curved wall 12 by 100 feet. Frans Wildenhain, Straesenburgh Laboratories, Rochester, N.Y. Color plate.

The Teapot

The teapot presents a number of interesting problems to the potter. The relationship, from the point of view of design, between the various parts must be envisaged before throwing begins. The lid must be so flanged that it will not fall out. The handle should balance well and should be designed so that it will not become too hot. The spout must pour properly, and its strainer should be large enough and located low enough so that it will not become clogged with tea leaves.

1. The bowl of the teapot should be thrown with a thick enough lip to allow for an inner rim.

2. The lip and rim are finished with a soft leather.

3. Measurements for the lid must be accurate. Both parts should be thrown with clay of identical moisture content.

4. The lid is thrown upside down with a deep flange.
5. Immediately after trimming, a knob is thrown on the lid.
6. The knob and lid may either harmonize with the vessel form or emerge as a contrasting element.
7. The base of the spout should be large enough to allow for considerable trimming.
8. The thrown handle is quite functional and relates well with the spout.

FORMING METHODS

9. It is essential that the various parts of the teapot be of the same moisture content before they are joined.

10. The spout and handle are cut to fit the vessel. A thick slip is coated on both surfaces before joining.

11. The strainer holes should be large enough not to clog with glaze. The volume of the holes should be equal to or slightly larger than the spout opening.

12. After joining, the teapot should be placed in a damp box for a day or two to allow any unevenness in the moisture content to equalize.

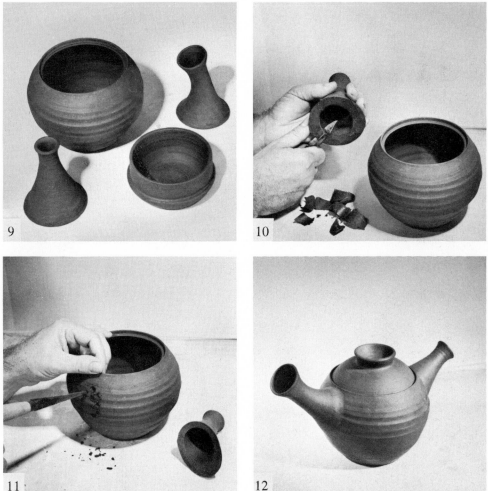

The Coiled Pot

Coiling is a pottery technique that goes back to the misty reaches of time. It requires no equipment other than the clay and is ideal both for teaching in the public school and the beginning pottery student. For the advanced potter, it is foolish to coil forms that can be more easily made on the wheel. On the other hand, asymmetrical shapes, unless the potter distorts wheel pieces, can only be made by slab or coiling methods. Likewise, groggy clay, which can be thrown only with difficulty, is ideal for coiling.

1. A round pad is used as a base and a wad of clay is squeezed into a rope. In rolling the coil, the entire hand from heel to finger tips is used. Rolling begins at the ends, and works towards the middle.
2. The coil circles the base pad and in three or four turns forms the wall of the pot.
3. The coils are joined together inside and out, with an up-and-down wiping motion of the finger.
4. Another series of coils is added. The inside must be finished as work progresses.
5. The outside form is refined with a flexible metal scraper.

FORMING METHODS

The Slab Pot

As illustrated on the following pages, there are many nonsymmetrical shapes that can be conveniently made by the slab method. The clay is rolled out on a plaster slab, allowed to dry slightly, then the sections are joined by roughing the surface and applying slip. A variety of interesting forms, unlike thrown pieces, are thus possible. Frequently the two techniques are combined.

Hand-built form with subtle asymmetry. Groggy stoneware clay, height 15 in. Ruth Duckworth, English potter now residing in the United States.

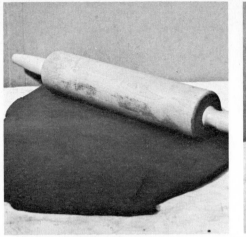

FORMING METHODS

Hand-built textured bottles constructed by the slab method.

Thick Coil and Paddle

Historically, large pots have been made by the thick coil and paddle method. The illustrations show a relatively small piece since the coils can be as thick as one's arm. A curved block of wood is used inside and a flat paddle compresses the clay. The initial form should be narrow, as the beating stretches the clay. It is possible to pull the form in but not to the small extent as on the wheel. The clay should be slightly drier than that used for throwing. If a closed form is desired, extra coils may be added and finished off as illustrated. Occasionally, combination techniques may be used; for example, a heavy base may be thrown, coils added and paddled, and then the whole finished off on a slow wheel with a rib.

Square stoneware casserole, wax-resist decoration, 10 by 8 in. Stephen Polchert, U.S.A.

FORMING METHODS

Slab-built stoneware planter with form and texture developed by paddling. Cone 10, reduced, diameter, 18 in. Louis Raynor, U.S.A.

CERAMIC SCULPTURE

From the brief survey of historical ceramics in the first chapter, it is obvious that the ceramics of the past were as varied as they are today. The major esthetic contribution of the twentieth century has been the development of nonrepresentational art. Ceramic sculpture has felt this influence no less than painting and other forms of sculpture. The displacement of figurative imagery by abstract form, color, and movement has resulted in a greater exploitation of the unique qualities of a particular material whether it be paint or clay. The ceramic sculptor is fortunate to have a material capable of easy manipulation and yet durable and weather resistant.

Forming Techniques

The basic techniques of forming ceramic sculpture are little different from those needed to make a coiled or slab pot. However, ground fireclay grog must be used in the body to reduce shrinkage and to avoid drying problems. Drying and firing cracks may also develop if the over-all wall thickness is not uniform. Sheets of plastic make it convenient to maintain and equalize moisture while working on a large piece.

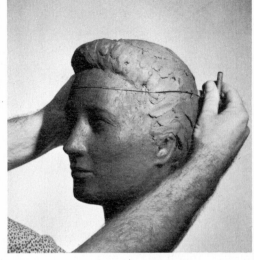

left Hollow figure constructed by combined slab and tube methods. Supporting stilts were needed but no cracks occurred in drying or firing. Height 30 in. **above** A head, modeled solid, showing top section being cut off preparatory to hollowing out interior.

Large forms will need supporting partitions to avoid sagging during both construction and firing. Unfired clay stilts may be needed to support protruding forms. These are superior to shelf supports since they will shrink with the body during firing. Elongated forms may be fashioned from assembled tubelike sections formed over a broomstick. Such forms must have a continuous air passage with an open end to avoid an explosion from expanding moisture during firing.

While a modified slab and coil procedure is the most common, it is possible to model a simple form as a solid and later, with a fine wire or knife, cut the piece into two or more sections. After the center portion is hollowed out, the sections are luted together with slip to form a single hollow mass. Occasionally a tapered core is used as an armature for a simple vertical form. However, it must be removed before any appreciable shrinkage occurs.

Stoneware figure, neither bird nor human, emphasizing pure form and texture with the subject matter of minor importance. Height 35 in. Dirk Hubers, U.S.A.

Ceramic Sculpture

The inevitable clay shrinkage excludes the use of the traditional armature of the clay modeler. It is, of course, possible to use this clay modeling method and then make a piece mold in plaster over the clay study. Small objects may be slip cast and larger projects assembled from sections of plastic clay pressed into the plaster mold. Although these methods are widely used for commercial duplication, they are seldom considered for serious use by most ceramic sculptors. The major drawback of this procedure is that the form must be overly simple and can have no undercuts. The texture and the finer detail do not reproduce well. Furthermore, any indirect process has an inhibiting effect on the spontaneity and immediacy of the execution so desired by today's sculptor.

Any cracks that develop, however fine, in either drying or firing will be enlarged by subsequent firings. Therefore, it is desirable to plan for only a single fire. The salt glaze, although requiring a special kiln, has much in its favor as a glaze for sculpture. The glaze, formed by reaction of the volatile salt and the silica in the body, achieves a greater feeling of unity with the body and less of an applied coating on the surface. The use of a glossy, colorful glaze on sculpture should be avoided as it detracts from the form. A more subtle and richer effect is obtained by rubbing coloring oxides plus small amounts of flux or glaze into the body. Even when an over-all glaze is used, it is customary to sponge it down so the clay color and textural areas show through in contrast to the glossy character of the glaze.

Sculptural Pots

As other container materials developed in recent years, it was but natural that ceramics assumed a more decorative function. Historically, the pottery form was functionally derived, and sculpture was frankly imitative of animal or human life. These dividing lines no longer exist. Shown here are several illustrations that indicate some of the current and rather divergent tendencies. These pieces are basically related to a hollow pottery form but suggest the visual world in a more or less abstract sense.

Related more to trends in painting than either sculpture or pottery, are those pots that have been deliberately made so as to be unlike the normal pottery or sculptural form. In doing so, the significance of the form must necessarily be sacrificed. Intentional design or decoration would destroy the accidental effect desired. In certain respects this development is related to the collage that was used in the early twentieth century by some academically trained painters to break away from the tyranny of their training and the almost unconscious manner in which it directed their eye and hand.

left Thrown and pinched forms, obviously a bottle and yet subtlely suggestive of the human figure. Stoneware. Frans Wildenhain, U.S.A.

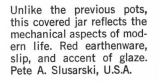

right Stoneware fountain derived from bulb and leaf forms, 48 in. high with dark terra sigillata glaze. William D. Parry, U.S.A. (Courtesy of Mel Richman Collection of Contemporary Ceramics)

Bottle forms implying a human couple. Hand-built stoneware, 34 in. high with metal overlay. Lyle N. Perkins, U.S.A.

Unlike the previous pots, this covered jar reflects the mechanical aspects of modern life. Red earthenware, slip, and accent of glaze. Pete A. Slusarski, U.S.A.

The tactile qualities of clay and the viscous and the runny nature of the glazes become the major emphasis in this construction, rather than the more traditional values of either pottery or sculpture. Rudy Autio, U.S.A.

Seen in this respect, the careless jointing of clay, even the cracks and excess running of a thick glaze becomes a positive achievement. The qualities of clay, glaze, and color are values in themselves instead of a means to an end. These experiments have much to offer the more traditional potter. Far too many pots are lifeless in form, decoration, and glaze and could well stand the infusion of vitality that comes from a new approach.

Stoneware vase with a salt glaze, which does not obscure the textural qualities of the clay so important in this piece. Iron stain with a carborundum and silica paste. Cone 9. Irv Taran, U.S.A.

Sculpture

Due to the versatile nature of clay, it has often been influenced by the sculptural form of other materials. Historically, Luca della Robbia comes to mind as his work is definitely imitative of marble. But, it is also likely that clay, which is so widely used as a sketch material by the sculptor, has equally influenced the form of other materials.

A simple cross form, most effective, that gains its appeal from the accidental quality of its rocklike texture and fissures, 66 in. John Mason, U.S.A. Collection of the Art Institute of Chicago.

An open form, like a skyscraper superstructure, in which the empty spaces become an important factor in the composition. Dirk Hubers, U.S.A.

Psalm 98 Let the floods clap their hands and the hills be joyful together. The textured stoneware shapes with veins of slip and variegated glazes convincingly suggest eternal qualities in nature, 24 in. long. William D. Parry, U.S.A.

The pieces illustrated feature a wide variety of techniques as well as conflicting concepts. For example, one can conceive of sculpture in an open manner in which the voids, the negative spaces, play as important a role as the positive form; the form may be treated as a solid or treated in numerous variations of these two extremes. In all these contemporary efforts, however, we see the same influences at play as observed in the previous pottery forms: that is, an emphasis on the unique qualities of clay and a desire to have a symbolic rather than an actual reference to the living world.

Big Warriors, 1. Although the cat-headed Homeric warriors are striking, the rich texture, the incised decoration, and the contrasts of clay and glaze are of as equal importance as the concept. Stoneware, 20 in. Kenneth M. Green, U.S.A. Collection of Carl Freeman. (Photo Leo Irrera)

An unusual set of door panels, the rocklike texture contrasting with delicacy of the floral plantings. Mat surfaces in tan and brown. 84 by 60 in. Sterling Holloway residence by John Mason, U.S.A.

Ceramic relief, 24 by 41 in. The actual cutting of the tiles was a major element in the development of this design. Clyde Burt, U.S.A.

Architectural Ceramics

Contemporary architecture, with its emphasis on the rectangular and the plain, unadorned surface, was satisfactory only as a point of departure from the eclectic hodgepodge of the nineteenth century. The need to introduce variety and contrast is evident in the more recent use of textured bricks and sculptural units in cast concrete. But architects and potters have been slow to join forces. No material has quite the decorative and structural qualities of the ceramic mural. The surface may be of smooth and minute mosaic-like tiles or of massive, deeply carved slabs. The color never fades; if properly applied, the ceramic sections will outlast practically all building materials.

The so-called murals made from small commercial tiles are rather discouraging and usually succeed in only reminding one of a bathroom floor. The lack of interesting variety in architectural decoration is disappointing. The designer must, therefore, either execute the entire project or do it in conjunction with an experienced potter.

The illustrations indicate a few of the possibilities of using ceramics as a wall decoration. The use of flat tile shapes with slip and glaze decoration and with textures in low relief is most suitable for interior locations where it functions much as a painting. Larger compositions must utilize deeper textures and greater contrast in shape and color in order to be effective. For the potter whose approach is often tactile and restrained as regards glaze and design, the change to the demands of the mural may be most difficult to make. The small sketch or segment will not enlarge satisfactorily unless conceived on a bolder scale that, depending upon location, may have to carry fifty or more feet.

Detail from frieze prior to installation, showing the strong contrasts of shape, value, and texture that contributes so greatly to its effectiveness. Frans Wildenhain, U.S.A.

Ceramic Sculpture

CHAPTER 6 **CERAMIC GLAZES** _____

SIMPLE FORMULATION

A ceramic glaze and its formulation ought not to be the great mystery that it appears to be to countless pottery students. Basically, a glaze is nothing more than a thin glasslike coating that is fused to the clay surface of the pot by the heat of the kiln. While some glaze compositions may be quite complicated and use a variety of chemical compounds, a glaze need not be complex for its necessary elements are only three in number.

THE ESSENTIAL GLAZE INGREDIENT IS SILICA, commonly called flint. It is also known as quartz in its pure crystalline state. Were it not that the melting point of silica is so high, about 3100°F (1700°C), this single material would suffice to form a glaze. By contrast, most earthenware clays mature at about 2000°F (1093°C) and will seriously deform if fired higher. Stoneware and porcelain bodies have a maturity in a range of 2250° to 2400°F (1238° to 1315°C).

THE TERM FLUX is given to those compounds that have the effect of lowering the melting point of the glaze. Fortunately, many chemicals with a low melting point will readily combine with silica to form a glassy crystal. The common materials used as fluxes in low-fired glazes are of two types: the _lead oxides_ (lead carbonate, red lead, galena, and litharge) and the _alkaline compounds_ (borax, colemanite, soda ash, boric acid, and bicarbonate of soda). Although these two basic types of low-fired fluxes have roughly

Stoneware vase with double glaze, wax and scratched decoration. The exciting surface is caused by a more fluid underglaze breaking through. Colors are rust, tan and orange, height 12 in. Maija Grotell, U.S.A.

comparable fluxing power, their effects upon glaze colorants and many of their other qualities are different. (See characteristics of ceramic chemicals in Chapter 8.)

A REFRACTORY ELEMENT is desirable to form a stronger glaze that will better withstand the wear of normal use. The glaze produced solely by a mixture of silica and either lead or borax compounds is soft and rather runny and therefore suitable only for the low-temperature glazes. We add a third ingredient to the glaze, *alumina,* to gain more substance. Silica and alumina unite to form tough, needle-like mullite crystals making a bond more resistant to abrasion and shock. The glaze now consists of its three necessary components: silica, the *glass former*; a flux, which *lowers the fusion point* of the silica; and alumina, a *refractory element* that gives increased toughness and hardness to the glaze and allows a higher maturing temperature.

It is not economically practical to use refined and pure oxides to make up our glazes. The compounds used by the potter are usually those minerals that are found abundantly in nature in a relatively pure state. Therefore, our simple low-fire glaze will be made from kaolin ($Al_2O_3 \cdot 2SiO_2 \cdot 2H_2O$), potash feldspar ($K_2O \cdot Al_2O_3 \cdot 6SiO_2$), and with either red lead (Pb_3O_4) or borax ($Na_2O \cdot 2B_2O_3 \cdot 10H_2$) as the flux.

The silica content will be provided by both the clay (kaolin) and the feldspar. Alumina is likewise a constituent of both the kaolin and feldspar. The feldspars are minerals that contain alumina, silica, and varying amounts of potash, sodium, and calcium. The predominate flux gives its name to the compound, such as soda feldspar. Potash feldspar, the more common type, is slightly cheaper and fires harder and a trifle higher than the soda feldspar. Feldspar should be considered only in a minor way as a flux in the low-fire range since it is an important source of silica and alumina. In addition to aiding the fusion of the glaze ingredients, the flux also combines with the silica contained in the clay body of the pot to form a bond uniting the body and glaze. This union becomes stronger as the temperature increases. Occasionally, a porous clay will absorb so much flux that the glaze will become thin and rough and require adjustments to either glaze or body.

LOW-FIRE GLAZE TESTS should be made by the beginning student with varying proportions of feldspar, kaolin, and lead and then fired to cone 04 in order to gain an understanding of the qualities imparted to the glaze by the silica, alumina, and the flux. Earthenware tiles ¼-inch thick and 2 by 3 inches are satisfactory. These should be bisque fired to about cone 08. The glaze samples should always be fired upright to detect any runny tendency in the glaze. The bottom $\frac{1}{4}$ inch of the tile is left unglazed should this fluidity be present. A suggested starting point for an 04 glaze test is 3 parts red lead, 3 parts feldspar, and 4 parts kaolin. Unless the scales are extremely accurate, a total sample of 100 grams is advisable. After weighing, the ingredients are ground in a mortar with water added until a creamy consistency is obtained. Modern ceramic materials are finely ground, so only a few minutes mixing is needed for a small sample. The glaze is brushed on the clean, dust free tile. Several thin coatings are applied. Experience is the only judge as to thickness. Cracks will occur if the layer is too heavy. Make succeeding tests, leaving the feldspar constant, and decrease the kaolin by half, and add a like amount to the red lead until the clay content is down to 1 part. The clay also functions as a binder to hold the other nonplastic ingredients together; if no clay is present, methocel or other binders must be added.

The fired samples will show a gradual change from a claylike white coating to one that becomes more fluid and glassy as the lead combines with the silica. Finally, a point is reached where the glaze runs excessively. This may be retarded by substituting additional feldspar for some of the lead. Keep the total at ten so valid comparisons may be easily made. At different firing temperatures the proportions needed of flux, alumina, and silica will vary. As the temperature goes above 2050°F (1230°C), the low-fired fluxes mentioned previously must be gradually replaced by calcium carbonate (whiting), the principal high-fire flux. At temperatures above 2100°F (1150°C), the lead and alkaline fluxes run excessively and are only used in minute quantities. A glaze may have a different crystalline surface structure due to slight variations in the proportion of alumina to silica. A slight excess of alumina will produce a mat instead of a glassy surface. However, either an excess of or too little silica will result in a rough surface. This is a material easily added to the glaze in its pure form if necessary.

After we have been able to produce successful tests with our three basic compounds and understand their function, then we can try some of the many other ceramic materials with which we can vary our glaze to produce slightly different effects. Some of these are nepheline syenite, spodumene, lepidolite, and cornwall stone. Firing at slightly lower temperatures are cryolite, dolomite, and talc. Additions of these compounds may extend the firing range of our glaze, eliminate crazing (small cracks that occur in the cooling glaze surface due to uneven contraction) if it occurs, and vary color and surface qualities. Consult Chapter 8 on ceramic chemicals for more specific details on these materials. Barium carbonate additions will develop mat glazes in cases where increasing the alumina content is not convenient. Zinc oxide may be added to the glaze in small quantities to obtain more fluxing action and reduce surface defects. It is essential that the glaze and the body cool and contract at the same rate after firing. If the body is weak and underfired, a contracting glaze may cause it to crack. It is the uneven contractions that are responsible for crazing. If sufficient tensions exist, the glaze will eventually craze, although this action may not occur for days or even years. Expansions due to moisture collecting in a porous body may have a similar effect. (See Chapter 7 on glaze defects.) On a decorative piece, these tiny hairline cracks may be pleasing and add to the interest of the total design. If intentional, these effects are called crackle glazes to distinguish them from the unexpected and undesirable crazed glaze.

Elimination of crazing is necessary in all functional ware to prevent seepage of moisture and to avoid odors from trapped food particles. Changes may be made in body materials to increase or reduce contraction and thereby adjust it to the glaze. The addition of silica to either body or glaze is one method used to prevent crazing. The crystal formation developed by excess silica in the body usually increases its contraction, whereas in the glaze's glassy state the silica is more likely to develop an expansion. Generally, however, a potter has developed a satisfactory body with desired plasticity, vitrification, and so forth. Experimental glazes are normally adjusted to fit the body. Another solution to this problem may be found in the observation that mat glazes seldom if ever craze. Suppose we have a bright shiny glaze that crazes badly. By holding the flux and silica constant and then adding slightly greater amounts of alumina, a change should gradually occur towards a bright, uncrazed surface and then a semimat and finally a mat surface. If this change does not occur, the silica content may be too high in proportion to the flux. Limit formulas have been worked out at great length giving permissible ratios of silica and alumina to the flux related to the production of bright or mat surfaces. Because of the many variables involved, such ratios are of greater value as a means of understanding the general problem rather than as a specific guide. Among the variables are the fluxing power and contraction rates of the bases. It is often possible to make exchanges in the bases to reduce crazing. For examples, boric oxide and colemanite have lower expansion rates than borax or soda ash and lepidolite less than the feldspars.

HIGH-FIRE GLAZE TESTS differ from the previous tests only in the substitution of calcium carbonate ($CaCO_3$), commonly called whiting, for the low-melting lead and alkaline compounds. Our tiles must be made from a stoneware or porcelain body. A suggested starting point for a cone 6–8 glaze would be 4 parts of kaolin, 4 of potash feldspar, and 2 of whiting. The first test will be white and claylike in character. Make succeeding tests holding the whiting constant, gradually increase the amount of feldspar and decrease the proportion of the more refractory kaolin. As the kaolin is lessened, the test glazes will become smoother and glassier in character. Depending upon the temperature, a satisfactory glaze should be reached at the point the kaolin content is in the vicinity of 10 to 20 percent. In the process of this substitution, we have lowered the fusion point of our glaze by the additions of the active flux, potash, which is contained in the feldspar. Only in the higher temperature ranges can the feldspar ($K_2O \cdot Al_2O_3 \cdot 6SiO_2$) be considered a flux since it is also a major source in our glaze of alumina and silica.

A satisfactory stoneware glaze can be developed using only feldspar, kaolin, and whiting. As mentioned earlier, however, it may be desirable to add small amounts of other chemicals to obtain a greater firing range, achieve a better adjustment to the body, provide a more varied color range, and develop a surface free from minor defects. Flint can be easily added to supply additional silica, if needed. The student should attempt to vary his basic glaze so as to produce a glossy surface, a mat surface, and one that is fairly opaque (without the use of an opacifier such as tin oxide). Try substitutions of some of the feldspar-like materials with different fluxes such as lepidolite or nepheline syenite. Often small amounts of another flux will result in a great improvement in a glaze. Other suggested additions are zinc oxide, talc, and barium carbonate. (See Chapter 8 for more detailed information on these and other chemicals including colorants that will be used in further tests.)

GLAZE TYPES

In the beginning of this chapter, we stressed the simplicity of glaze formulation and indeed it is so (see also the first glaze in Chapter 1). A functional and satisfactory glaze can be made from only a few materials. Several glazes, however, use rather uncommon ingredients or require special firing techniques. Refer to the glaze recipes included in the appendix for a clarification of the general descriptions of the glazes that follow.

Low-fire Glazes

Low-fire glazes may be grouped into two distinct categories distinguished by the major flux used.

Lead glazes comprise the largest group, firing from cones 016 to 02, which is between 1450° to 2050°F (790° to 1120°C). These glazes take their names from the flux used, primarily oxides of the lead compounds. The most common flux is lead carbonate ($2PbCO_3 \cdot Pb(OH)_2$) and red lead (Pb_3O_4). Lead is a very active flux, melting at about 950°F (510°C), flowing uniformly, and giving a bright, glossy surface. Used alone, it may comprise 50 percent of the glaze batch; it is often combined with other fluxes. It is a common practice to use more than one flux, since each one has slightly different qualities; in combination they tend to encourage a lower melting point and a more complex and intimate reaction than can be obtained from a single flux. Lead has the disadvantage of being very poisonous and requires careful handling to avoid breathing the dust or getting particles in the mouth. For this reason, lead is often converted into the nontoxic silicate form by fritting. Fritting is a procedure by which a flux and silica are melted and later ground to form a glaze addition that is both nontoxic and insoluble in water. Vessels glazed with lead should not be used to store liquids containing large percentages of acid fruit juices. Lead glazes fired in gas kilns using manufactured gas will often blister unless they are fired in a muffle chamber. The blistering is caused by the sulphur contained in all manufactured gas. Natural gas or propane are free from these sulphur impurities.

Alkaline glazes have a firing range similar to the lead glazes (cones 016 to 02) and use the alkaline type of fluxes such as borax, colemanite, and soda ash. Alkaline fluxes encourage certain color effects, particularly the turquoise-blues that lead glazes cannot produce. The alkaline fluxes, because of their extreme solubility, should never be used on raw ware. When absorbed into the clay, the expansions and contractions that alkaline compounds undergo during firing and cooling will cause the body to crack.

A very soft bisque should not be glazed either, as it will absorb a portion of the flux leaving an incomplete and usually a rough-textured glaze upon firing. Because of their solubility and their tendency to get lumpy in the glaze solution, the alkaline compounds (such as borax) are often fritted into the nonsoluble silicate form. In general, the alkaline glazes have a smooth glossy surface similar to those in the lead group.

High-fire Glazes

High-fire glazes are generally compounded to fire in a range from cone 6 to 14, which is from 2250° to 2500°F (1230° to 1370°C). Because of the extreme temperature, the common low-fire fluxes such as lead and borax are replaced by calcium carbonate, which has a higher melting point of about 1500°F (816°C). Glazes are compounded to fit the maturity of the clay body. Since earthenware can seldom be fired much over 2000°F (1093°C) nor stoneware much below 2300°F (1260°C), we have a gap between these temperatures at which little work is fired by the average studio potter. There are numerous commercial bodies compounded between cones 02 and 6 in the dinnerware, artware, and tile lines. As seen in the appendix, glazes for these temperatures must contain both high- and low-fire fluxes to adjust within these limits.

Porcelain and stoneware glazes are identical except in cases where adjustments must be made to accommodate a difference in firing shrinkage. Because feldspar is a major ingredient in such glazes, the term *feldspathic glaze* is often given to stoneware glazes. Due to the high temperature, the union of glaze and body is very complete. The interlocking mullite crystals prevent detection of the line of junction that is easily seen between the glassy glaze coating and the porous earthenware body. The feldspathic glazes are very hard (they cannot be scratched by steel) and are resistant to most acids, the exceptions being hydrofluoric, phosphoric, and hot sulphuric acids. The surfaces may be either mat or smooth but never with quite the excessive gloss of the low-fired glazes.

Ash Glazes

Ash glazes represent, perhaps, the oldest glazes used by man. At present they have no commercial use but may be of interest to the studio potter. The ash used may be from any wood, grass, or straw. Depending upon the specific source, the chemical composition may vary considerably; it is generally very high in silica, with some alumina and calcium, fair amounts of fluxes such as potash, soda, and magnesia, plus iron and small quantities of numerous other compounds. Because of the high silica content, the ash can seldom be used in low-fire glazes in amounts over 15 to 20 percent. This is seldom sufficient to make much change in the basic glaze. A suggested starting point for a stoneware ash glaze test would be 40 parts ash, 40 parts feldspar and 20 parts whiting. Fireplace ashes ought to be collected in a fairly large amount and then mixed thoroughly to insure uniformity. The general practice is to first run the dry ash through a very coarse sieve to remove unburned particles. The ash is then soaked in water that is decanted and changed several times to remove the soluble portions. The ash is then screened through 60–100-mesh sieve and dried. Care must be taken during the first washing, as the liquid will be caustic and can blister the hands.

Frit Glazes

Frit glazes may be little different chemically from the two low-fire types mentioned before. Fritting is a process that renders the raw-glaze materials either nontoxic or nonsoluble. Lead or alkaline fluxes (borax or soda ash) are melted in a frit kiln with silica or silica and a small amount of alumina. When the glaze becomes liquid, a plug is pulled in the bottom of the frit furnace and the contents discharge into a container filled with water. The fractured glaze particles are then ground to the necessary fineness. Small amounts may be made in the studio using a crucible. One disadvantage to studio manufacture is the extremely long grinding time necessary to pulverize the frit in a ball mill to an adequate fineness.

Many different types of frit glazes are on the market. Frit composition is complicated as the nontoxic or nonsoluble elements must be completely absorbed within a satisfactory firing range and without creating later adjustment problems. A frit glaze is seldom a complete glaze for several reasons. Since it is usually colorless, opacifiers or colorants have to be added later. The frit has little adherence quality so a small amount of a plastic clay or bentonite is usually necessary. Adjustments for the final firing ranges also have to be made. Frits have a great use commercially where large amounts of standard glazes are used. For the studio potter, frits are of most value in eliminating the lumpy character of borax needed in crystalline, copper reds, and similar glazes.

Crackle Glazes

Crackle glazes cannot be characterized by their composition as they are merely the result of tensions developed when a glaze and a body expand and contract at different rates. In most glazes, save perhaps the mats, a crackle can be made to develop in the glaze. The simplest way is to substitute similar acting fluxes for others having a different contraction rate. Of course, the reverse is true if a noncrackling glaze is desired. A crackle is a network of fine cracks on the surface of a glaze and must be used on a light body to be seen effectively. To strengthen the effect, a coloring oxide or strong black tea is often applied to the crackled area. The Chinese were able to achieve, by successive firings, a network of both large and fine crackles, each stained with a different coloring oxide. On certain shapes, a crackle in the glaze can have an interesting decorative quality. It is more practical on the vitreous stoneware or porcelain body because a crackle on a porous earthenware body will allow the liquids to seep through and make it unsatisfactory for holding food.

Stoneware bowl with crackled celadon interior glaze banded by a red-brown mat. Cone 10 reduction. Irwin Whitaker, U.S.A.

Mat Glazes

Mat glazes are generally formed either by adding an excess of alumina or by substituting barium carbonate for some of the flux in the glaze. Therefore, they are usually called *alumina mats* or *barium mats*. A mat glaze should not be confused with a thin, rough, or underfired glaze. It should be smooth to the touch but should have neither gloss nor transparency. The mat effects sometimes observed on an underfired glaze are due to incompletely dissolved particles, whereas a true mat develops a different surface crystalline structure. An unusually long cooling time will encourage the formation of mat textures. To test for a true mat, cool the glaze quickly to see if it will develop a shine. A mat surface caused by the incomplete fusion of particles will continue to have a mat surface regardless of the cooling time. This type of mat surface is generally a bit rough to the touch and lacks the smoothness of the true mat. Mats can be calculated for all temperatures. I particularly like them in the low-fired ranges since typical lead and borax glazes are so shiny that their glare tends to kill all decoration and form. Mat glazes are related to the crystalline group since both depend upon the surface structure of the glaze for their effects. Therefore, occasional mats are also made with iron, zinc, and titanium (rutile) when properly compounded and cooled slowly.

Reduction Glazes

Reduction glazes are those that are especially compounded to develop their particular color characteristics only if fired in a kiln capable of maintaining a reduction atmosphere during certain portions of the firing cycle. The normal kiln firing is an oxidizing fire. An electric kiln always has an oxidizing fire since there is nothing in the kiln atmosphere to consume the oxygen, which is always present. To reduce the atmosphere in a gas or oil kiln, the draft is usually cut back to lessen the air intake resulting in an incomplete combustion that releases carbon into the kiln interior. In a muffle kiln, some of the muffles will have to be removed to allow the combustion gases to enter the kiln chamber. Carbon has a great affinity for oxygen when heated and will steal it from the iron and copper-coloring oxides in the glaze. It was in this manner that the Chinese produced their famous copper reds (sang-de-boeuf) and celadons. When either copper or iron oxide is deprived of its oxygen, it remains suspended in the glaze as the pure colloidal metal. Thus the normal green copper glaze becomes a beautiful ruby red with occasional blue or purple tints. The iron oxide loses its usual brownish-red tone and takes on a variety of soft gray-green hues. Because of its likeness to jade, which had religious symbolism for the ancient Chinese, celadons of remarkable quality were developed there. In a small muffle kiln, a reduction can occur if pine splinters or moth balls are inserted into the peep hole. The usual reduction fire starts out with an oxidizing fire, and reduction does not begin until just prior to the melting of the first elements of the glaze. After the reduction cycle, the firing must return to oxidization in order to develop a surface free from pin holes and other defects. (See Chapter 9 on kiln operation.) A so-called artificial reduction can be achieved by using a small amount of silicon carbide (carborundum), about one-half of one percent, in the glaze. The effects are a little different from the standard reduction as the color is concentrated in little spots around the silicon carbide particles. But it has an advantage in that it can be used in an electric kiln, since the elements are in no way affected. The firing range of copper red and celadon reduction glazes are quite wide, from about cone 08 up into the porcelain range.

Crystalline Glazes

Crystalline glazes are of two types: one has large crystal clusters embedded in or on the surface of the glaze; the second type, called adventurine, has single crystals, often small, suspended in the glaze, which catch and reflect the light. These are an interesting group of glazes technically, but they need to be very carefully related to the pot shape. The jewel-like

Porcelain bottle with flower-like blue and brown crystals. Zinc crystalline glaze with cobalt and manganese, height 8¾ in. (See Appendix for formula.) Marc Hansen, U.S.A. (Photo Douglas Lyttle)

effects seem to float off the surface of all but the most simple and reserved forms. The crystalline formation is encouraged by additions of zinc and iron or by titanium (rutile). Borax and soda may also be used, but not lead. Possible firing ranges are wide and, as with mat formations, the rate of cooling is most important. In order to allow the crystals to develop properly, the temperature of the kiln should be allowed to drop only about one hundred degrees Fahrenheit (38°C) after maturity, and then they must be held at this level for several hours before slowly cooling off. Crystalline glazes are very runny so a pedestle of insulating brick should be cut to the foot size and placed under the ware. If fired high, the piece may be placed in a shallow bisque bowl that will collect the excess glaze.

Bristol Glazes

Bristol glazes are very similar, in most respects, to the typical porcelain glaze, except that a relatively large amount of zinc oxide is added. In most cases, this tends to lower the melting point and to add a certain opacity to the glaze. Most Bristols fall into the cone 5 to 9 range, although formulas have been successfully developed for cones 3 to 14. The most common use of the Bristol glaze is for architectural tile and bricks. Since a large amount of clay is normally used, the ware is generally given a single firing, and there is no problem of shrinkage. However, by calcining part of the clay, the glaze can be fitted to double firings. The commercial single fire usually takes 50 to 60 hours not only because of the thickness of the ware being fired but also because of the extremely viscous nature of the Bristol glaze.

It is this quality of the glaze that makes it valuable to the studio potter. Interesting effects may be achieved by using the Bristol glaze over a more fluid glaze that breaks through in spots. A perfect glaze coating must be developed during the glazing operation because the viscosity of the glaze prevents any cracks that may occur from healing. Moreover, the edges of the cracks will pull further apart and bead up. In general, the Bristol glazes are shiny but they can be matted by increasing the amount of calcia while reducing the silica content.

Luster Glazes

Luster glazes usually consist of a thin metallic coating, decorative in nature, fired on top of a lead-tin glaze. This coating is achieved by applying a solution of pine resin, bismuth nitrate, and a metallic salt dissolved in oil of lavender over a fired glaze. This is fired at a low red heat, sufficiently hot to fuse the metal and burn off the resin but lower than the melting point of the original glaze. A variety of reds, yellows, browns and silvery-white lusters as well as nacreous and iridescent sheens are possible. The metals normally used are lead and zinc acetates; copper, manganese, and cobalt sulfates; uranium nitrate; and silver and gold compounds. Bismuth is generally used as a flux. Until 1529 A.D., bismuth was thought to be an impure form of silver and therefore the silver mentioned in old records probably was a silver-bismuth compound. (See also preparation of lusters in Chapter 8 for the historical method.)

Usually the luster is not an over-all coating, but rather it is applied in the form of a design in conjunction with colored slips or stains. This is especially true of Islamic pottery, which, because of religious edicts against representational painting, developed an unusual type of intricate and interlocking decorative motif during the ninth to fourteenth centuries.

Salt Glazes

Salt glazes have staged a revival in recent years after a long period of neglect by the studio potter. From the twelfth to the midnineteenth century, such glazes were common in Europe and later in Colonial America. Commercial uses are largely limited to stoneware crocks, glazed sewer pipe, hollow building brick, and similar products. The salt glaze procedure is a simple one. The ware in the kiln is fired to its body-maturing temperature

Collection of bottles with typically reserved Scandinavian form. Rich mat glazes with incised decoration. Stig Lindberg, Gustavsberg Studios, Sweden. Color plate.

Salt-glazed vase with slip decoration. In this glaze, all glaze color and surface quality is dependent upon the oxides and silica contained in the body and the slip. Richard Leach, U.S.A.

at which time common salt (sodium chloride) is thrown into the firebox or through ports entering the kiln chamber. The sodium combines with the silica in the clay to form a glassy silicate. The studio must be well ventilated at this point as deadly chlorine gas is also released at the moment of salting. Occasionally, additional silica may be added to the clay to form a better glaze coating. By reducing conditions (incomplete combustion to introduce carbon into the kiln atmosphere) buff or red clays can be glazed either brown or black. Other colors can be obtained only by using colored slips or body stains. The disadvantage of the salt glaze, other than its limited color effects, is that it coats the entire interior of the kiln. This generally renders the kiln unsuitable for other types of glaze firing. The firing range of salt glazes is wide, from cones 02 to 12, but the most common firings are from cones 5 to 8. (See Chapter 9 for more specifics on the salting techniques.)

Slip Glazes

Slip glazes are made from raw natural clays that contain sufficient fluxes to function as glazes without further preparation except for washing and sieving. In actual practice, additions are often made to enable the slip glaze to fit the body or to modify the maturing temperature. But in general these changes are minor ones. The so-called black varnish of the Greeks and the terra sigillata of the Romans are slip glazes formed by decanting off the finer particles of a liquid slip made from the red clay body. Reduction forms the black color by converting the red iron oxide into black and magnetic iron oxides. A later oxidizing fire converts the iron in the more porous clay body back to its red form while leaving the black iron sealed in the denser slip. This Greek glaze was not a true glaze as a glassy state did not develop. It is half way between a slip and a glaze and was not completely waterproof. Slip glazes were commonly used by the early American stoneware potteries that produced such utilitarian objects as storage crocks, bowls, mugs, and pitchers. Albany slip clay is the only commercial slip clay widely used. It fires a brown-black at cones 8 to 10. The addition of 2 percent of cobalt to Albany slip will give a beautiful semigloss jet black. Wrenshall slip, mined near Duluth, Minnesota, fires out to a pale yellow at cones 6 to 10 with the peculiar streaked effect characteristic of rutile. There are many slip clay deposits that are not recognized as such. Frequently earthenware clays turn out to be slip clays when fired high enough. Occasionally, additional flux in small amounts is all that is needed. Most slip clays fire in a range from cones 6 to 12. The slip-clay fluxes are generally the alkaline earth compounds plus iron oxide in varying amounts. A high iron content serves, also, to give a color ranging from tan to a dark brown.

A word of caution: Inasmuch as slip clays are generally mined in small pits, their composition will vary slightly. Each new shipment of material should be tested before being used in quantity. Some Albany slip I have used has been so lacking in the usual brown colorant that the resulting glaze was a pale semi-transparent tan. Studio potters should pay more attention to this group of glazes. Slip clays are easy to apply, adhere well, and fire with few, if any, defects. The composition, chemically, is most durable and since additions are few, much time can be saved in glaze preparation.

Raku Glazes

Raku glazes are low-fired glazes used on bodies containing a high proportion of grog. The ware is associated with the Japanese tea ceremony and with Zen Buddhism. The Raku tea bowls, usually hand built and irregular, fit in perfectly with the Zen emphasis on nature and the simple unaffected way of living.

The firing procedure is an essential part of the Raku technique. The clay body used is generally a stoneware containing up to 30 percent grog. The grog and the firing procedures tend to limit the form and size of the ware. Simple bowl shapes are the most common. As the glaze temperature only reaches 1750°F (955°C), the glaze may contain up to 60 percent lead or colemanite. The ware is bisqued (given a low preliminary firing) and then glazed. The firing is most unusual and somewhat of a dramatic event. In Japan small charcoal burning kilns are used, usually outside, and often contain only a single pot. The glazed piece must be perfectly dry and is often placed on top of the kiln to insure that all the moisture has evaporated.

Raku piece in typical asymmetrical form with accidental effects of smoking. White engobe and iron decoration. Paul Soldner, U.S.A.

When the kiln has reached glaze temperature and the bricked up door is opened, the pot is quickly placed into the chamber with a pair of tongs. Because of the high grog content and porous nature of the body this sudden heat change has no effect. Firing proceeds and in a few minutes the pot begins to glow. (Most kilns in the United States are fired with a single gas burner and have a capacity for several pieces, and insulating bricks may be easily bolted together to form top cover.) Depending upon the character of the kiln, the glaze should begin to melt and develop a liquid shine in 10 to 15 minutes. Before running occurs, the pots are quickly removed with the tongs. The tong marks on the glazed surface are regarded as a decoration. Generally the glowing pot is placed in a covered metal container filled with sawdust that gives a smoked and accidental quality to the glaze. After a few minutes of smoking, the ware may be immediately doused in a bucket of water. If, however, the pot has a closed form or is in varied thicknesses, cooling in the open air for several minutes before dousing is necessary to avoid cracking.

The Raku body remains soft and porous and the glaze is not waterproof. Nevertheless, Raku has become quite popular in recent years. The glaze effects are most varied, and while accidental, have unusual qualities. The speed of the firings, the flame, and the smoke give it all the quality of a "happening." The oxides used in Raku decoration tend to develop a luster when reduced leading to some fantastic color combinations. A deep crackle generally occurs, which is in keeping with the rather simple form that characterizes pots made of a coarse body.

CHAPTER 7 DECORATION AND GLAZING _____

DECORATION

There can be no doubt that throwing the form is the more critical operation in pottery making, but the techniques of glazing and decoration must not be overlooked. As the final operation, they can be the deciding factors in the success or failure of the pot. Throwing must be done with freedom and ease and be expressive of the fluid plastic quality of clay. The trimming and refining of the thrown form must not destroy this spontaneous quality. The throwing ridges left on the surface of the piece may well prove to be a more suitable decorative device than one laboriously contrived.

The decision as to what decorating technique he will use should be made by the potter as shortly after the piece is thrown as is possible; there are certain types of decoration that must be done while the clay is still plastic. The character of the thrown form will usually determine the type of decoration that is most suitable. For example, a delicate brush decoration is obviously out of place on a vigorously thrown piece of heavily grogged clay. It is equally essential that the decoration only compliment and not overwhelm the form. Practice is necessary in order that the execution can be fresh and fluid. It is well known that a drawing done with a certain vitality of stroke is always more pleasing as well as more convincing than the labored but more correct drawing, which does not hold our interest since it lacks life and spirit.

Covered jar of Kansas stoneware with iron
slip, wax and sgraffito decoration. Cone 8
reduction, height 10 in. Sheldon Carey,
U.S.A.

The character of clay is revealed in this bottle in the throwing ridges by the freely applied clay of the top section. Uneven glaze, stoneware, height 12 in. Robert Eckels, U.S.A.

Clay in a Plastic State

Immediately after being cut off from the wheel, the pot may be pressed or pinched to change either its shape or surface. The accompanying illustrations show a few of the many possibilities for surface decoration of the clay while it is still in the soft plastic state. These include scratching, incising, or cutting away with a tool. Additional clay may be added to form raised designs. Impressions may be made with various tools, even a cord, a serrated roller, or with stamps of ceramic or other materials.

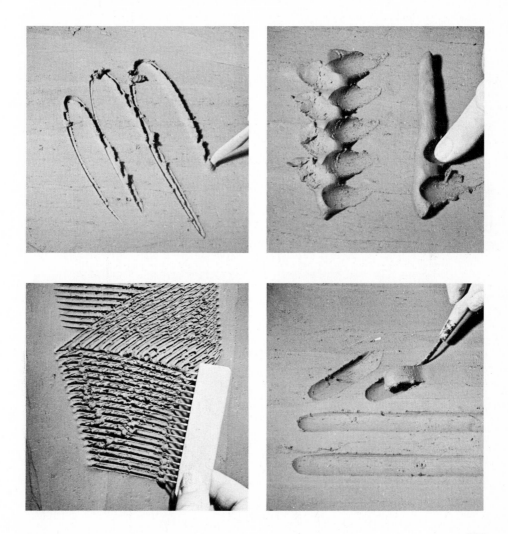

DECORATION AND GLAZING

Stoneware planter of slab construction with freely applied decoration in plastic clay. Height 12 in., length 15 in. Dorothy W. Perkins, U.S.A.

Large thrown bottle with applied clay sections and incised design. Diameter 18 in. Clyde E. Burt, U.S.A.

Stoneware bottle, thrown but with pinched sides and cut decoration. Glaze 70 percent volcanic ash reduced at Cone 8. 9½ in. Sheldon Carey, U.S.A.

Leather-hard Clay

The term *leather hard* refers to the clay body that has dried slightly so that it can be handled without deforming or suffering other injuries. However, it contains sufficient moisture so that handles and knobs can be readily joined and clay slips can be applied without caking off. Carving and incising are more conveniently done at this stage as the clay does not stick to the tool and cuts cleanly.

SGRAFFITO refers to a design obtained by scratching through a layer of clay slip to expose the contrasting color of the clay body beneath. Care must be taken that the slip is not too dry or it will flake off. If it is too wet, the incision will be smudged.

MISHIMA is a decorative device of Korean origin. It entails the filling of an incised area or line with a plastic clay of a contrasting color. When partially dried, the surface is scraped flush revealing the design. A slip glaze may also be effectively used.

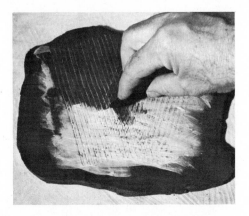

SLIP TRAILING, using a syringe in the manner of cake decoration, must be done before the ware has dried too much. The piece should stay a day in a damp room after the design has been applied. Raised glaze decoration may be applied in a similar fashion. This technique was popular in colonial America and at an earlier date in England. (See Chapter 1.)

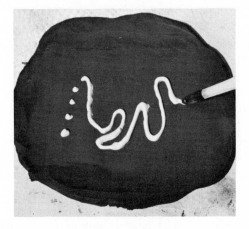

Clay in the Dry State

Decoration on a clay surface that has dried is limited to brush application of engobes, coloring oxides, and stains. An *engobe* is clay slip to which feldspar, flint, and a flux are generally added. This has the effect of reducing the shrinkage of the engobe as well as increasing adhesion when fired. (See engobe in Appendix.)

COLORING OXIDES should be applied to the dry clay in much the same way as one would paint a watercolor. Too thick an application will flake off either before or after the bisque and will result in an uneven surface and poor glaze adhesion.

WAX-RESIST decoration is generally used in conjunction with coloring oxides. The wax may be a hot paraffin or beeswax or one of the more convenient water-soluble wax emulsions now on the market that need not be heated. The wax design repels the applied stain, which may then serve as a background color. Incised lines through the wax will absorb color thus allowing a lineal type of decoration that is difficult to achieve by other methods.

GLAZES may be applied to some clays and fired in a single firing. The operation must be done quickly to prevent uneven moisture absorption from causing cracks. Occasionally adjustments will need to be made to a standard glaze that is intended for a single firing due to the greater shrinkage of the clay body. Overglaze decoration may be used on the raw glazed ware in the usual manner.

Clay in the Bisque State

The possibilities of decoration become much more limited after the pottery has gone through the bisque firing.

AN ENGOBE decoration may be brushed on provided the clay content is low enough to reduce shrinkage and that sufficient fluxes are present to bind the engobe to the body when fired. By far the more convenient method is to apply such decoration at the leather-hard stage.

SGRAFFITO decoration may be applied to this kind of engobe or to a glaze. In order to execute the lineal design with clarity, the glaze or slip coating must not be too heavy. If it is too dry, the surface coating will flake off and leave a ragged incision. The purpose is, of course, to reveal the contrasting color of the clay beneath.

above Low vase form with a simple brush decoration of oxides over the glaze. Warren MacKenzie, U.S.A. **left** Flat stoneware bottle from separately thrown sections. Sgraffito decoration on glaze. Robert Sperry, U.S.A.

COLOR OXIDES OR STAINS may be used as a brush decoration or as an over-all colorant either on the bisque body or on the glazed surface. Designs incised into plastic clay are generally brushed with oxides prior to glazing in order to be more effective. As a rule, brush decoration with oxides is more effective over the glaze. Underglaze designs on the bisque may be obscured by an uneven glaze or damaged during its application.

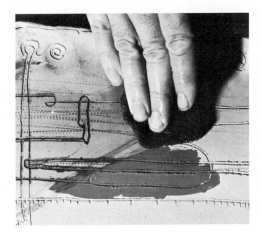

Decoration

Stoneware casserole with overglaze decoration with wax and oxides. James McKinnell, U.S.A.

WAX-RESIST decoration is very frequently used both under and over a glaze and in combination with stain and sgraffito decoration. It has a tendency, however, to ball up when used on a sprayed glaze. A binder may be necessary even in a dipped glaze to provide a stronger decorating surface.

GLAZING

GLAZING IN THE RAW-CLAY STATE has been mentioned briefly in the section on decoration. There are definite advantages to this method. By eliminating the normal bisque fire, there are savings not only in the labor needed for the extra stacking, unloading, and operation of the kiln but also in the fuel or power needed for the extra firing. A single firing also promotes a better union between the body and the glaze. There are several disadvantages, however, to the single glaze fire, of which the fragile nature of the raw, dry clay vessel is primary. Not only is it apt to be broken in handling but the expansions caused by the moisture absorbed into the dry clay may also cause the vessel to crack. In general, only when the body of a piece is rather thick and uniform can the glaze be poured safely. Other pieces should be sprayed since the glaze, with its troublesome moisture content, can then be applied at a slower rate. One additional precaution must be taken in glazing raw ware. As mentioned before, alkaline fluxes must first be fritted before they can be safely used on raw ware. These compounds have a high coefficient of thermal expansion. When they are absorbed into the outer portion of the clay, their expansion and contraction rate during firing and cooling is so great in contrast to the remainder of the body that they will cause it to crack.

GLAZING IN THE BISQUE STATE is the most common procedure. Normally the bisque ware is fired to about cone 010 or 1650°F (900°C). At this stage, the bisque is hard enough to be handled safely yet porous enough to absorb the glaze readily. A bisque fired too low tends to absorb too much glaze; if fired too high, it is especially difficult to glaze as the glaze tends to run off. An exception to the normal bisque firings are the high-fired chinawares. Such pieces, like thin teacups, which are fragile and tend to warp, are often placed in the kiln with supporting fireclay rings inside their lips, or they are stacked upside down and then fired to their maximum temperature. Later these chinaware pieces are glazed and fired on their own foot rims at a lower temperature where warpage losses are much less.

How to Glaze

GLAZING is a process that can be described only rather inadequately. Before the actual glazing operation takes place, however, there are a few precautions that must be observed. If the bisque ware is not to be glazed immediately upon its removal from the glaze kiln, it should be stored, if possible, where dust and soot will not settle on it. The bisque ware should not be handled excessively especially if the hands are oily with perspiration, which will prevent the glaze from adhering properly. All surfaces of the bisque ware should be wiped with a damp sponge or momentarily placed under a water tap to remove dust and loose particles of clay. The moisture added to the bisque ware by this procedure will prevent an excessive amount of glaze from soaking in and thus allow a little more time for glazing. The extra moisture also helps to reduce the number of air pockets and pinholes that form when the glaze dries too quickly on a very porous bisque. The amount of moisture required depends upon the absorbency of the bisque, the thickness of the piece, and the consistency of the glaze. Should the bisque fire accidentally rise much higher than cone 010, the ware should not be dampened at all. The glaze must be completely cleaned off the bottom of the pot and $\frac{1}{4}$ inch up the side as soon as it is dry enough to handle. An excess of glaze will always run. Never allow a heavy layer of glaze to remain near the foot rim. The cleaning operation may be simplified by dipping the bottom of bisque pots in a shallow pan of hot paraffin prior to glazing.

BRUSHED GLAZES are generally limited to a band or decorative panel of glaze. Small pieces may be glazed satisfactorily by brush; in glazing large pieces, it is difficult to obtain an even coating. In some cases, an elephant-ear sponge may be used in place of the brush. With practice, a large area can be evenly covered. Brush glazes are usually used in children's classes since the pieces are generally small and the youngsters will waste less glaze with this method than by pouring or dipping. Low-temperature and runny glazes are best suited to the brushing method.

DIP GLAZING is perhaps the simplest glazing method. Its chief drawback is that a rather large amount of glaze is required. After the vessel has been cleaned and moistened with a damp sponge, it is plunged into a large pan of glaze. It should be withdrawn almost immediately and shaken to remove the excess glaze. The object is then placed upon a rack to dry and the finger marks are touched up with a brush. Small-sized pots may be quickly dip glazed with metal tongs, which come in several shapes. The slight blemishes caused in the glaze by the pointed tips usually heal over when fired. A more uniform surface generally develops if the glaze is thin enough to allow dipping two or three times within a few seconds.

POURED GLAZES require less initial glaze than dip glazes and can be applied to a greater variety of shapes. For example, the insides of bottles and deep vaselike vessels can be glazed only in this manner. In the case of a bottle, the glaze is poured through a funnel and then the vessel is rotated until all its surfaces are covered. Then the excess is poured out and the bottle is given a final shake to even out the glaze and remove the excess. Glazes that are poured or dipped have to be a little thinner in consistency than those that are brushed on. The interior of bowls may be glazed by pouring in a portion of the glaze, spreading the glaze by rotating the bowl, and then pouring out the excess. Generally this must be done rather quickly or an excessive or uneven amount of glaze will accumulate. To glaze the exterior of bottles, grasp them by either the neck or the foot rim and pour the glaze over the bottle from a pitcher, allowing the excess to run off into a pan beneath. Finger marks are then touched up with a brush and the foot cleaned when it is dry. The exterior of bowls may be glazed in the same manner provided the foot is large enough to grasp, otherwise the bowl may be placed upside down on wooden dowel rods extending across a pan. It is the best practice to glaze the interior of vessels first and the outside later.

SPRAYED GLAZES permit subtle variations in color and more definite control over glaze thickness and coverage. Actually these advantages are more theoretical than real and apply more to the beginner than the experienced potter. The finest Chinese glazes of the past, which we have difficulty in equaling today, were all dipped or poured. Gradations of color were achieved by blowing the color on separately through a lung-powered, bamboo tube atomizer.

The spray method has two major disadvantages: large amounts of glaze are often wasted; and the glaze coating, because of its fragile nature, is easily damaged by handling during the process of loading the kiln. With practice, even glazes can be poured, eliminating these disadvantages and saving time. For the most part, sprayed glazes are most satisfactory on flat shallow bowls or for use in reglazing. Various effects can be easily achieved by grading one glaze into another or by toning down an underglaze with a second that may be more neutral or with a mat. When a viscous glaze covers one that tends to be a little runny, the underglaze may break through and run causing a spotty decorative effect.

As many glaze materials are toxic, glazes should be sprayed only in a booth with an adequate exhaust fan. In order to obtain an even layer of glaze, one should spray the glaze on slowly, building up a coating with a soft "woolly" surface. If the sprayed piece gets too moist, a wet shine may develop, blisters may form, and the glaze may run. If the glaze runs, it will be uneven, regardless of how much more glaze is used. It may be advisable, then, under some conditions, to scrape off the glaze and start again.

DECORATION AND GLAZING

GLAZE DEFECTS

Usually there are several reasons, all logical, why a particular glaze fault may occur. Trying to deduce the cause from one piece may prove quite difficult. When there are a number of pots having the same glaze from a single kiln load available or when there are several glazes on a single body, the problem of deduction is much easier. The following section outlines several factors that can cause glaze defects. Glaze faults may result not only from the composition of the glaze but from the improper selection or preparation of the clay body, faulty kiln operation, or, as most frequently is the case, lack of skill and care in application.

Defects Due to the Body

1. A body that is too porous because of improper wedging, kneading, blunging, or pugging may cause small bubbles, beads, and pinholes to form in the glaze as the body contracts and the gases attempt to escape.

2. Excessive water in the forming of the body may result in conditions somewhat similar to those just listed.

3. An excessive amount of manganese dioxide used as a colorant in a body or slip will cause blisters to form in both the body and the glaze.

4. Soluble sulfates are contained in some clays and come to the surface in drying, forming a whitish scum. Pinholes and bubbles are formed as these sulfates react with the glaze to form gases. This condition may be eliminated by adding 2 percent barium carbonate to the body. A slight reduction fire at the point at which the glaze begins to melt will reduce the sulfates and allow the gas to pass off before the glaze develops a glassy retaining film.

5. If the body is underfired in the bisque and therefore very porous, it may absorb an excessive amount of the glaze. Soluble fluxes in the glaze, because of their higher thermal expansion and contraction rates, may cause the body to crack. In any case, a glaze applied to a very absorptive body may have a coarse if not sandpaper-like surface.

Defects of Application

1. Blisters or pinholes may result if the bisque has not been moistened slightly before glazing. The glaze traps air in the surface pores of the body.

2. Dust or oil on the surface of the bisque may cause pinholes or a scaly surface in the glaze.

3. If the glaze is applied too heavily, it will run excessively and obscure the decoration and perhaps even make the pot stick to the kiln shelves.

4. In addition to flowing excessively, glazes that have been applied too thickly will usually crack upon drying. As a rule, when they are fired, these cracks will not heal up but will pull further apart and bead up at the edges. If the drying contraction is great enough, the adhesion of the glaze to the body will be weak, causing portions to flake off during the initial smoking period of the firing cycle.

5. On the other hand, too thin a glaze application will result in a poor, dry surface. This is especially true of mat glazes, which, as a rule, require a slightly thicker application than gloss glazes.

6. If a second glaze coating is applied over a completely dry first coat, blisters will form. The wetting of the lower glaze layer causes it to expand and pull away from the body.

7. If the bisque ware is considerably cooler than the glaze at the time of application, bubbles and blisters may later develop.

Defects Originating in Firing

1. If freshly glazed ware is placed in the kiln and fired immediately, the hot moisture will loosen the glaze from the body causing blisters and crawling.

2. Too rapid a firing will not allow the normal gases to escape. They will form tiny seeds and bubbles in the glaze. For some especially viscous glazes, a prolonged soaking period is necessary to remove these gas bubbles.

3. Excessive reduction will result in black and gray spots on the body and glaze and will produce a dull surface.

4. Gas-fired kilns with poor muffles using manufactured gas are troublesome to use with lead glazes. The sulphur content in the combustion gases will dull the glaze surfaces and possibly form blisters and wrinkles.

Defects in Glaze Composition

1. Glazes that are not adjusted properly to the body are susceptible to stresses that may cause the glaze and at times even the body to crack. If the glaze contracts at a slower rate than the body does in cooling, it goes into compression. This causes the glaze to crack and, in places, to buckle up and separate from the body. This defect is more commonly known as *shivering*.

2. Slightly similar to shivering and also caused by unequal contraction rates in cooling is *crazing* of the glaze. In this case, the glaze contracts at a greater rate than the body, causing numerous cracks to form. (See also Chapter 4 on clay bodies and quartz inversion and Chapter 6 on ceramic glazes.)

3. Glazes that run excessively during the normal firing temperatures should be adjusted by the addition of kaolin to increase the refractory quality of the glaze or, if possible, by changing the bases. Those that have a lower molecular weight will be less fluid in the glaze melt.

4. A dull surface will result if the proportion of silica to alumina or barium is too low.

5. An excessive amount of tin, rutile, or colored spinels, which are relatively insoluble in the glaze, will also cause a dull or rough-surfaced glaze.

6. Bristol and colemanite glazes not fitted properly to the body will tend to crawl excessively or crack. This may be due in part to an excess of zinc, which has a very high contraction rate at the higher temperatures.

7. Glazes ground too finely, thus releasing soluble salts from the frits, feldspar, and so forth, will develop pinholes and bubbles.

8. Glazes, if allowed to stand too long, may be affected by the decomposition of carbonates, organic matter in ball clay, or gum siccatives. Gases thus formed may result in pinholes and bubbles in the final glaze. In some cases, preservatives like formaldehyde will help. If washed, dried, and reground, the same glaze may be used without difficulty.

GLAZE CALCULATIONS AND CHEMICALS

CHAPTER 8

CALCULATIONS

In Chapter 6, Ceramic Glazes, a trial-and-error method was suggested by which the novice potter might develop a satisfactory glaze and gain a rudimentary understanding of the properties of the common glaze chemicals. Compared to the long history of ceramics, the scientific formulation of glazes is rather recent. The glazes and techniques illustrated in Chapter 1 are the final results of centuries of such trial and error methods. But since we no longer learn ceramics in a father-and-son tradition, it is necessary that we find a quicker and more scientific method of glaze formulation.

All matter composing the earth is made up of approximately one hundred chemical elements that we call atoms. Each has distinctive characteristics. These elements do not occur in nature in a pure form but in compounds, which are groups of atoms held together by an electrical attraction or bond. The atom is much too small to be weighed, but it was possible to determine the relative weight of one type atom to that of another. Oxygen, symbolized by the letter O, was given an arbitrary atomic weight of 16; other atoms were given a weight corresponding to their proportionate weight relationship to oxygen.

Silica, mentioned frequently in the chapters on clay and glazes, is a major ceramic compound and is found in every clay and glaze. The *molecular formula* for silica (more correctly silicon dioxide) is SiO_2. This indicates that the compound consists of one atom of silicon and two atoms of oxygen. From the atomic weight table in the appendix, we find that the weight of silicon is 28. The two oxygen atoms weigh 32, thus giving us 60 as the molecular weight of the compound, silicon dioxide (silica).

Large stoneware vase with wax-resist and stain decoration on a mat glaze fired to cone 10, reduced, 16 in. Louis Raynor, U.S.A.

Silica may be added to a clay body or glaze in the silicon dioxide form but is most commonly found as a part of a more complex compound such as kaolin ($Al_2O_3 \cdot 2SiO_2 \cdot 2H_2O$), or potash feldspar ($K_2O \cdot Al_2O_3 \cdot 6SiO_2$).

The RO, R₂O₃, RO₂ System

As mentioned in Chapter 6, there are three principal parts to a glaze. One of these is silica (SiO_2), which gives the glaze its glassy transparent quality. A second is alumina (Al_2O_3), a refractory element, which contributes toughness and abrasion resistance to the glaze. Since neither of these oxides will melt at temperatures below 3100°F, it is necessary to use a third ingredient, a flux, such as lead oxide or sodium that will lower the melting point and combine with both the silica and alumina to form, after firing, a hard glassy coating on the ceramic body.

With rare exceptions, the glaze components are not single refined oxides but complex compounds that are commercially available at reasonable costs. In order to compare glazes or to understand the effects of these varied chemicals, it is necessary to separate the component oxides into the three major parts comprising the glaze formula. The symbol RO refers to the fluxing agents, which are chiefly metallic or alkaline elements that form their oxides by combining with one atom of oxygen such as CaO or PbO. In a similar manner, alumina (Al_2O_3) may be symbolized by R_2O_3 and silica (SiO_2) by RO_2. A table will perhaps better illustrate this division of the component parts of a glaze.

In the first column are the RO

RO	R₂O₃	RO₂
Bases	Neutrals	Acids
Li_2O*	(Amphoteric oxides)	SiO_2
Na_2O*	Al_2O_3	TiO_2
K_2O*	B_2O_3	ZrO_2
CaO	Fe_2O_3	
MgO	Sb_2O_3	Glass formers
BaO	Cr_2O_3	
ZnO		
FeO		
MnO	Refractory elements	
PbO		
CdO		
Fluxing agents		

* One of the few exceptions; 2 atoms of sodium or potassium unite with 1 of oxygen to form the oxide.

oxides that have the effect of fluxes in either a glaze or a body. They are also called the *base oxides*. The elements in the second column are not as easy to classify. Some of the *neutrals* or amphoteric oxides may on occasion function as either a base or an acid oxide. However, the major oxide in this group, alumina (Al_2O_3), always has a refractory effect in a glaze. On the other hand, red iron oxide (Fe_2O_3) is an active flux as well as a colorant. Boric oxide (B_2O_3) can react either as a base or an acid. Silica is the major oxide in the acid column. The value of both TiO_2 and ZrO_2 in a glaze is for their opacity rather than for their glass-forming effect. The exceptions to these general divisions are rather minor. In practice, the RO, R_2O_3, and RO_2 method of categorizing the main components of a glaze works very well.

The Empirical Glaze Formula

Largely for simplifying calculations, glaze batches are usually reduced to an empirical formula. The *empirical formula* is a glaze formula in which the various active ingredients are expressed in molecular proportions. By contrast, the *batch recipe* is a proportion expressed by the actual weights of the raw chemical compounds making up the glaze.

Since the materials used in the average glaze batch are rather complex compounds, it is a distinct advantage to be able to define the glaze in terms of single oxides that bear the same proportional relationship to each other as when in their more complex form in the glaze batch. These oxides are grouped into RO, R_2O_3, and RO_2 units.

Before a batch recipe is converted to an empirical formula, it is first necessary to know the chemical formulas of the individual raw materials as well as their equivalent weights. The molecular formulas and equivalent weights of the molecular components for all commonly used ceramic materials are listed in the Appendix. The table lists the common commercial name of the raw material in the first column and its molecular formula in the second column. Many compounds are designated by more than one name, names that are often dissimilar as, for example, are whiting and calcium carbonate.

The *molecular weight of a compound* is the sum of the atomic weights of its constituent elements. The equivalent weight will often be the same as the molecular weight of the compound, but in many cases it will be smaller. Take, for example, potash feldspar:

Raw material	Formula	Molecular weight	Equivalent weights		
			RO	R_2O_3	RO_2
Feldspar (potash)	$K_2O\cdot Al_2O_3\cdot 6SiO_2$	556.8	556.8	556.8	92.9

BATCH TO EMPIRICAL FORMULA

Raw material and formula	Batch weights		Equivalent weights		PbO	CaO	Na$_2$O	B$_2$O$_3$	K$_2$O	Al$_2$O$_3$	SiO$_2$
White lead (2PbCO$_3$·Pb(OH)$_2$)	128	÷	(RO)	258.5 =	0.495						
Whiting (CaCO$_3$)	15	÷	(RO)	100 =		0.15					
Borax (Na$_2$O·2B$_2$O$_3$·10H$_2$O)	103	÷	(RO) (R$_2$O$_3$)	381.04 190.7 =			0.270	0.540			
Feldspar (potash) (K$_2$O·Al$_2$O$_3$·6SiO$_2$)	83	÷	(RO) (R$_2$O$_3$) (RO$_2$)	556.8 556.8 92.9 =					0.149	0.149	0.89
Kaolin (Al$_2$O$_3$·2SiO$_2$·2H$_2$O)	38	÷	(R$_2$O$_3$) (RO$_2$)	258.1 129. =						0.146	0.294
Flint (SiO$_2$)	85	÷	(RO$_2$)	60.06 =							1.415
Totals	452				0.495	0.15	0.270	0.540	0.149	0.295	2.599

According to the given formula, when one molecular unit of potash feldspar is added, the glaze will have one unit of potassium oxide, one unit of alumina, and six units of silica. Since one unit each of potassium oxide and alumina form the compound, their individual equivalent weights are 556.8. Since six units of silica are necessary to form the compound, the equivalent weight of silica is $\frac{1}{6}$ of the compound weight, or 92.9. The *equivalent weights* of the oxides of a compound are the same as its molecular weight if the oxide in question appears only once. If more than one unit of an oxide occurs, then its equivalent weight will be found by dividing the compound molecular weight by the number of times the oxide in question appears.

These definitions will become clearer in the actual procedure of converting the following glaze batch recipe to an empirical formula.

Glaze recipe	Raw materials	Parts by weight
A lead-borax	White lead	128
glaze matur-	Whiting	15
ing at cone	Borax	103
04	Feldspar	
	(potash)	83
	Kaolin	38
	Flint	85

Before we can go into the actual calculations, we must first find the molecular formula of each of the compounds making up the glaze, plus the equivalent weights of the oxides contained in these compounds. It is convenient to put this information in the form of a table like the one illustrated. By checking over the raw-material formulas, we can determine which of the oxides need to be indicated in the spaces to the right of the table.

The batch weights of the raw materials are divided by the equivalent molecular weights of the particular oxides concerned, giving the molecular proportions in the form of single oxides. By arranging these oxides with the amounts calculated into RO, R_2O_3, and RO_2 groups, we find that the glaze batch has the following empirical formula:

RO	R_2O_3	RO_2
.495 PbO	.295 Al_2O_3	2.599 SiO_2
.150 CaO	.540 B_2O_3	
.149 K_2O		
.270 Na_2O		

The total of the RO oxides comes to 1.064 instead of the desired unit of one because round numbers have been used in the batch recipe. By dividing each of the above figures by 1.064 we will have the following empirical formula. The RO is now .998, a figure that is accurate enough for comparative purposes.

RO	R_2O_3	RO_2
.465 PbO	.277 Al_2O_3	2.442 SiO_2
.140 CaO	.507 B_2O_3	
.140 K_2O		
.253 Na_2O		

Considerable research has been done on the properties of ceramic materials, and reasonable predictions may be made about the probable change that a particular chemical will cause in a known type of glaze. There are, however, many variable factors such as the length of the glaze grinding time, the thickness of its application, the reactions between glaze and body, the kiln atmosphere, and the rate of temperature rise or fall. Since each or all of these conditions may markedly affect a particular glaze, glaze experimentation is something less than a true science. Successful work largely depends upon the over-all experience and care of the operator in controlling these variables.

The Batch Recipe

To convert an empirical formula to a batch recipe we have to reverse the procedure explained in the previous section. Again, we must lay out a chart form on which to compile our information. This type of conversion will require slightly more familiarity with raw chemical compounds, because we have to select those compounds containing the proper oxides without adding any unwanted elements. The parts of compounds that pass off in the kiln as gases or water vapor are ignored. To make the process clearer, let us take the following *empirical glaze formula* and convert it into a batch recipe.

0.40 Na_2O	0.03 Al_2O_3	2.1 SiO_2
0.46 PbO	0.32 B_2O_3	
0.14 FeO		

The general procedure is as follows: First, if any alkaline fluxes are present (Na_2O or K_2O), try to include as much as possible in a soda or potash feldspar. It is a cheaper source of the flux and, equally important, it is nonsoluble and not as likely to lump up in a glaze like borax. Then fill out the other single oxides. Try to save the alumina for next to the last and take out the silica at the end. Alumina and silica are often included in other compounds, and the balance can easily be taken care of last as either kaolin or silica. Since the silica is always in a larger amount than the alumina and is available in a cheap pure form, save it for the last item.

Several of the calculations on page 201 may seem incorrect at first, so perhaps we should point out a few of these seeming inconsistencies. In the first addition, when we take 0.03 equivalents of soda feldspar, we get six times as much SiO_2 as either Na_2 or Al_2O_3 because the formula for soda feldspar is $Na_2O_3 \cdot Al_2O_3 \cdot 6SiO_2$. Similarly, borax has twice as much B_2O_3 as Na_2O.

Now that we have the needed molecular equivalents of the chemical compounds, we can find the gram batch weights (or pounds) by multiplying each equivalent by the molecular weights of the chemical compound. Thus we get the following:

Raw material	Equivalents		Molecular weights		Batch weights
Soda feldspar	0.03	×	524	=	15.72
Borax	0.16	×	382	=	61.12
Soda ash	0.21	×	106	=	22.26
White lead	0.153	×	775	=	118.58
Red iron oxide	0.07	×	160	=	11.20
Flint	1.91	×	60	=	114.60

GLAZE CALCULATIONS AND CHEMICALS

Oxides in formula	Na_2O	PbO	FeO	Al_2O_3	B_2O_3	SiO_2
Raw material Equivalents needed	0.40	0.46	0.14	0.03	0.32	2.1
Soda feldspar $(Na_2O \cdot Al_2O_3 \cdot 6SiO_2)$ 0.03 equivalents	0.03			0.03		0.18
remainder	0.37	0.46	0.14		0.32	1.92
Borax $(Na_2O \cdot 2B_2O_3 \cdot 10H_2O)$ 0.16 equivalents	0.16				0.32	
remainder	0.21	0.46	0.14			1.92
Soda ash (Na_2CO_3) 0.21 equivalents	0.21					
remainder		0.46	0.14			1.92
White lead $(2PbCO_3 \cdot Pb(OH)_2)$ 0.153 equivalents		0.46				
remainder			0.14			1.92
Red iron oxide (Fe_2O_3) 0.07 equivalents			0.14			
remainder						1.92
Flint (SiO_2) 1.92 equivalents						1.92

Limit Formulas

In our initial experiments with glazes conducted in Chapter 6, no definite limits were mentioned regarding the ratio between the RO, R_2O_3 and RO_2 parts in a glaze. This is because the major purpose of these glaze tests were to gain familiarity with the qualities of the various glaze chemicals. The analysis of many glazes have shown that there are general limits to the amounts of alumina and silica that can be satisfactorily used relative to a single unit of flux. The firing temperature and the type of flux are also important factors.

In the several limit formulas that follow, a number of possible fluxes are indicated; however, the total amount used must add up to a unit of one. In general, the higher proportion of alumina will result in a mat surface, provided the kiln is cooled slowly. Barium will also tend to promote mat surfaces. A study of these formulas indicates how the ratio of alumina and silica rises as the temperature increases. While not intended to serve as glaze formulas, the listing should be a helpful guide to those seeking to change the temperature range of a favorite glaze. Some glaze chemicals are quite complex, and on occasions such additions to a glaze may not have the desired effect. By changing the batch recipes to the empirical formulas and comparing them with the suggested limits, one ought to be able to detect the direction of the error.

Cone 08-04		Lead glazes	
PbO	0.2–0.60	Al$_2$O$_3$	0.15–0.20
KNaO	0.1–0.25	B$_2$O$_3$	0.15–0.60
ZnO	0.1–0.25		
CaO	0.3–0.60	SiO$_2$	1.5 –2.50
BaO	0 –0.15		

Cone 08-04		Alkaline glazes	
PbO	0–0.5	Al$_2$O$_3$	0.05–0.25
KNaO	.4–0.8		
CaO	0–0.3	SiO$_2$	1.5–2.5
ZnO	0–0.2		

Cone 2-5		Lead glaze	
PbO	0.4–0.60	Al$_2$O$_3$	0.2–0.28
CaO	0.1–0.40		
ZnO	0 –0.25	SiO$_2$	2.0–3.0
KNaO	0.1–0.25		

Cone 2-5		Lead-borax glaze	
PbO	0.2 –0.3	Al$_2$O$_3$	0.25– 0.35
KNaO	0.2 –0.3	B$_2$O$_3$	0.20– 0.60
CaO	0.35–0.5		
KnO	0 –0.1	SiO$_2$	2.5 – 3.5

Cone 2-5		Colemanite glaze	
CaO	0.2–0.50	Al$_2$O$_3$	0.2–0.28
ZnO	0.1–0.25	B$_2$O$_3$	0.3–0.6
BaO	0.1–0.25		
KNaO	0.1–0.25	SiO$_2$	2.0–3.0

Cone 8-12		Stoneware glaze	
KNaO	0.2–0.40	Al$_2$O$_3$	0.3–0.5
CaO	0.4–0.70	B$_2$O$_3$	0.1–0.3
MgO	0 –0.35	SiO$_2$	3.0–5.0
ZnO	0 –0.30		
BaO	0 –0.30		

CERAMIC CHEMICALS

The chemicals used by the potter are generally not pure single oxides but usually more complex compounds that are available for industrial uses in a moderately refined form at a low cost. Due to differences in either the original mineral or in refining methods, the ceramic chemicals available from different dealers may vary slightly. Even items from the same dealer may change minutely from year to year. Commercial potteries constantly check new shipments of chemicals. This is seldom done in the small studio; should a favorite glaze react strangely, one ought to consider this factor provided, of course, no change occurred in the normal glazing and firing procedure. The feldspars, in particular, vary in their fluxing power. It is for this reason that we have not stressed the importance of a glaze formula but rather the acquiring of an experimental knowledge of the properties of the glaze ingredients. The batch glazes listed in the Appendix are more for purposes of illustration as they may have to be adjusted slightly to fit the materials available.

For the convenience of students converting an empirical glaze formula into a batch recipe, a listing follows that gives the major sources of the various oxides in the RO, R$_2$O$_3$ and RO$_2$ groups. A more complete chemical description may be found in the alphabetized section at the end of this chapter.

GLAZE CALCULATIONS AND CHEMICALS

Sources of Base (RO) Oxides

Barium oxide (BaO) is a very active flux under some conditions. Its glass formation has a brilliancy second only to the lead silicates. Barium's effect on the thermal expansion of the glaze is less than that of the alkalies and calcia. The best source for Barium is:

Barium carbonate ($BaCO_3$)

Calcium oxide (CaO) in comparison with the alkaline oxides produces a glaze more resistant to abrasion, mild acids, and weathering. It likewise lowers the coefficient of thermal expansion, therefore increasing the tensile strength. Although it is often used in small amounts with other fluxes in low-fire glazes, calcium should not be used as the sole flux at temperatures under cone 3. It is the most common flux used at porcelain temperatures. As with alumina, an excess of calcia tends to produce mat textures. Sources of calcium are:

Calcium carbonate ($CaCO_3$)
Calcium borate ($2CaO \cdot 3B_2O_3 \cdot 5H_2O$), more commonly known as colemanite
Dolomite [$CaMg(CO_3)_2$]
Calcium fluoride (CaF_2), better known as the mineral fluorspar

Lead oxide (PbO) has been mentioned frequently before as one of the major low-fire fluxes. There are several reasons for its popularity. It combines readily with all other fluxes and has a lower coefficient of expansion than the alkaline fluxes. Lead gives a greater brilliancy to the glaze, although at times this may be a disadvantage. The lead glazes melt and flow well and thus tend to reduce pinholes and other defects of the more viscous type of glaze. The chief defects are the poisonous nature of lead compounds, unless they are fritted, and their weakness to attack by strong fruit acids. Lead tends to blacken or film over if slightly reduced. The surface of lead glazes tends to scratch easily unless used in conjunction with an alkaline flux. There are many forms of lead such as:

Galena (PbS)
Litharge (PbO)
Red lead (Pb_3O_4)
White lead [$2PbCO_3 \cdot Pb(OH_2)$].
Lead monosilicate, the fritted lead silicate composed of approximately 16 percent SiO_2 and 84 percent PbO.
Lead bisilicate, another commercial lead silicate having the approximate composition of 65 percent PbO, 33 percent SiO_2, and 2 percent Al_2O_3.

Lithium oxide (Li_2O) is more commonly used by glass manufacturers, but it has several important qualities that make its occasional use in glazes valuable. Lithium (the oxide or carbonate) is expensive because of the small amounts of Li_2O (3 to 8 percent) found in the producing ores. It has a much lower atomic weight than either sodium or potassium (ratio of 1:3 and 1:5), and therefore a smaller amount of material can be used without lessening the fluxing action. This has the effect of decreasing tensions evolving from thermal expansions and contractions, and therefore promoting a more durable glaze. Sources of lithium are:

Lepidolite ($LiF \cdot KF \cdot Al_2O_3 \cdot 3SiO_2$)

Spodumene ($Li_2O \cdot Al_2O_3 \cdot 4SiO_2$)
Lithium carbonate ($LiCO_3$)
Petatile ($Li_2O \cdot Al_2O_3 \cdot 8SiO_2$)

Magnesium oxide (MgO) is frequently found combined with the feldspars and limestones. It lowers the thermal expansion more than other bases, and it is as satisfactory as the alkaline fluxes in developing a durable glaze. In some combinations it will develop a slight opacity. Used with low-fired glazes, magnesium has a refractory effect; it fluxes easily at higher temperatures and becomes quite fluid. Sources of magnesium are:

Magnesium carbonate ($MgCO_3$)
Dolomite [$CaMg\,(CO_3)_2$]
Talc (varies from $3MgO \cdot 4SiO_2 \cdot H_2O$ to $4MgO \cdot 5SiO_2 \cdot H_2O$). In the solid and more impure form, it is also known as steatite and soapstone.

Potassium oxide (K_2O) is similar in fluxing action to sodium. It has a lower coefficient of thermal expansion, increasing the hardness and brilliance of a piece and lowering the fluidity of the glaze. Sources of potassium are:

Potassium carbonate (K_2CO_3), more commonly known as pearl ash
Potash feldspar ($K_2O \cdot Al_2O_3 \cdot 6SiO_2$)
Cornwall stone, a complex compound of variable composition roughly similar to a feldspar and having fluxes of calcium, sodium, and potassium (IRO $\cdot$ 1.08 $\cdot Al_2O_3 \cdot 7.79\ SiO_2$)
Carolina stone, a domestic product similar to Cornwall stone
Volcanic ash, with a ceramic formula of:

0.660 K_2O 0.899 Al_2O_3 9.59 SiO_2
0.230 Na_2O 0.060 Fe_2O_3 0.05 TiO_2
0.096 CaO
0.014 MgO

Sodium oxide (Na_2O) is one of the more common low-fire fluxes. It has the highest coefficient of expansion of all the bases and generally gives a lower tensile strength and elasticity to the silicates formed than most other fluxes. The usual ceramic sources of sodium are as follows:

Sodium chloride (NaC)
Sodium carbonate (Na_2CO_3), more frequently called soda ash
Borax ($Na_2O \cdot 2B_2O_3 \cdot 10H_2O$)
Soda feldspar ($Na_2O \cdot Al_2O_3 \cdot 6SiO_2$)
Cryolite (Na_3AlF_6)

Zinc oxide (ZnO) can contribute several different factors to a glaze. It can be used to replace some of the more soluble alkaline fluxes. Zinc is second only to magnesium in reducing the thermal expansion and to calcium in increasing the strength and resistance of a glaze. It contributes some opacity to the glaze and is helpful in reducing crazing defects.

Zinc oxide (ZnO), the major zinc compound used in ceramics.

Sources of Neutral (R_2O_3) Oxides

Unlike the RO group, which has numerous somewhat similar compounds, the R_2O_3 group is almost limited to alumina (Al_2O_3) or a few oxides that have the same oxygen ratio. The greatest difference between a glass and a glaze is the presence of alumina in the glaze. The alumina content is a most important factor in a successful glaze. It controls the fluidity of the melting glaze and enables it to withstand the temperatures needed to mature the body. Greater amounts of alumina increase the hardness of the glaze and its resistance to abrasions and acids.

Alumina (Al_2O_3) in a glaze may vary from 0.1 to 0.9 molecular equivalents, depending upon firing temperatures. The equivalent ratios between the alumina and the silica groups may be from 1 : 4 to 1 : 20. For glossy glazes the ratio is about 1 : 10. As mentioned before, an increase of alumina will tend to bring about mat textures. A glossy porcelain glaze firing from cones 10 to 12 will have an alumina-silica ratio of between 1 : 7 and 1 : 8, whereas the mats will be 1 : 3.2 to 1 : 3.8. Alumina also has an effect on the colors developed. The normal blue of cobalt oxide will become a rose pink in the absence of alumina. Chromium oxide, which usually gives various green tones, will tend to become reddish in the presence of excess alumina. Sources of alumina are:
  Alumina hydrate [$Al(OH)_3$]
  Feldspar and Cornwall stone (see sections under RO oxides)
  Kaolin (china clay) $Al_2O_3 \cdot 2SiO_2 \cdot 2H_2O$ (see sections under Clay)

Antimony oxide (Sb_2O_3) is primarily used as an opacifier and a coloring agent and is found in:
  Antimonious oxide (Sb_2O_3)
  Basic antimonate of lead, [$Pb_3(SbO_4)_2$], also known as Naples yellow.

Boric oxide (B_2O_3) is one of the neutral oxides (R_2O_3), which, by our previous definition, can react either as bases or acids. The refractory properties of alumina are more like those of the acid silica than any of the bases. Boric oxide has a number of characteristics similar to alumina: the alumina of mat glazes can be satisfactorily replaced by boric oxide; color effects do not change by this substitution; both alumina and boric oxide harm underglaze red and green colors, and both can form mixed crystals. On the whole, however, boric oxide functions as a base since in comparison with silica it increases the elasticity, lowers the tensile strength, and, in limited quantities, lowers the thermal coefficient of expansion. Like lead, it increases the gloss or refractive index of the glaze. Major compounds containing boron are:
  Boric acid ($B_2O_3 \cdot 2H_2O$)
  Borax ($Na_2 \cdot 2B_2O_3 \cdot 10H_2O$)
  Colemanite ($2CaO \cdot 3B_2O_3 \cdot 5H_2O$), technically called calcium borate

Chromic oxide (Cr_2O_3) is derived from the mineral chromite ($FeCr_2O_4$). It is used as a colorant in glazes. The fact that the mineral form is a natural spinel would indicate its use as a stain.

Red or *Ferric Iron* oxide (Fe_2O_3) is commonly used as a coloring agent to form brownish red hues and also to modify copper and cobalt. It would have use as a flux were it not for its strong coloring action. Its presence in many compounds is regarded as an impurity and considerable effort goes into removing iron flecks from whiteware bodies. It conforms to the R_2O_3 oxide ratio but has none of the refractory qualities that alumina has.

Sources of Acid (RO₂) Oxides

The important oxide in this group, silica, has a refractory effect on the glaze while the others function largely as opacifiers or coloring agents.

Silica (SiO_2) combines readily with the bases to form glassy silicates. It is the most common element in the glaze, comprising about 50 percent of it by weight. In a glaze it has the effect of raising the melting point, decreasing its fluidity, increasing resistance of the glaze to water and chemicals, increasing hardness and tensile strength, and reducing the coefficients of thermal expansion of the glaze. The amounts of silica used depend upon the flux and the maturing point of the glaze, but it is generally between 1 and 6 molecular equivalents.

Silica (SiO_2) is commonly obtained from sandstone, quartz sands, or flint pebbles. Silica is found combined with many ceramic materials that have been mentioned before. Below are listed a few of the more frequently used silica compounds.

Ball clay ($Al_2O_3 \cdot 2SiO_2 \cdot 2H_2O$)
Kaolin ($Al_2O_3 \cdot 2SiO_2 \cdot 2H_2O$)
Soda feldspar
    ($Na_2O \cdot Al_2O_3 \cdot 6SiO_2$)
Potash feldspar
    ($K_2O \cdot Al_2O_3 \cdot 6SiO_2$)
Cornwall stone
    ($IRO \cdot 1.16Al_2O_3 \cdot 8.95\ SiO_2$)
Lepidolite ($LiF \cdot KF \cdot Al_2O_3 \cdot 3SiO_2$)
Spodumene ($Li_2O \cdot Al_2O_3 \cdot 4SiO_2$)

Tin oxide (SnO_2) is used primarily as an opacifier in glazes. Although rather expensive, it has a continued wide use because it has greater covering power than any other opacifier.

Tin oxide (SnO_2), also called *stannic oxide*, is the chief form of tin used.

Titanium oxide (TiO_2) is probably the only other oxide in the RO₂ group that has some of the refractory qualities of silicon. Its use in glazes, however, is entirely due to its effect upon other colors and its action as an opacifier.

Titanium dioxide (TiO_2)
Rutile (TiO_2), an impure form containing iron oxide.

Characteristics of Ceramic Chemicals

Albany slip is a slip clay, which is a natural clay containing silica, alumina, and fluxes in the correct proportions to function as a glaze. It is mined in the vicinity of Albany, New York, hence its name. Since it occurs in small pits, its composition and color will vary. Usually it fires a glossy brown-black at temperatures between cones 8 to 12. One shipment that I used, however, fired out a pale, nearly transparent tan. Slip clays are usually very easy to apply and fire with little, if any, defects. A typical composition and formula is as follows:

Composition			
	Percent		*Percent*
Silica	56.75	Magnesia	3.23
Alumina	15.47	Titania	1.00
Ferric oxide	5.73	Alkalies	3.25
Lime	5.78		

GLAZE CALCULATIONS AND CHEMICALS

	Formula	
0.195 K$_2$O	0.608 Al$_2$O$_3$	3.965 SiO$_2$
0.459 CaO	0.081 Fe$_2$O$_3$	
0.345 MgO		

Alumina hydrate [Al(OH)$_3$] is preferred to the calcined form (Al$_2$O$_3$) for some uses since it has better adhesive qualities and stays suspended in the glaze longer. Introduction of alumina for mat effects is considered to be more effective in the hydrate form than in such compounds as clay or feldspar.

Antimonious oxide (Sb$_2$O$_3$) is poisonous and slightly soluble in water. For satisfactory effect as an opacifier, it must be used in glazes firing under cone 1. Antimony is also used to produce yellow and orange colors for glazes. The most common mixture is known as *yellow base* and has the following composition:

Red lead	15
Antimony oxide	10
Tin oxide	4

The mixture is calcined to cone 09, then ground and washed.

Basic antimonate of lead [Pb$_3$-(SbO$_4$)$_2$], also known as *Naples yellow*, is primarily used as a paint pigment. It is a source of low-fire yellows. The presence of lead in Naples yellow is an advantage since antimony will not produce a yellow unless combined with lead or iron.

Barium carbonate (Ba$_2$CO$_3$) is usually used in combination with other fluxes since at lower temperatures it combines very slowly and reacts as a refractory to form mat textures. At higher temperatures it reacts strongly as a flux.

Barium chromate (BaCrO$_4$) is used to produce colors in the pale yellow to light green range. It is generally used in overglaze decoration, as it is fugitive at temperatures over cone 04.

Bentonite (Al$_2$O$_3$·4SiO$_2$·9H$_2$O) is derived from volcanic ash. This formula is not quite correct as bentonite contains other impurities. South Dakota bentonite has the following analysis:

	Percent		*Percent*
Silica	64.23	Lime	0.46
Alumina	20.74	Magnesia	2.26
Iron oxide	3.49		

It generally fires to a light cream color and fuses at about 2400°F. Its chief value is in its use as a plasticizer for short clays. As such it is about five times as effective as ball clay. Purified bentonite will also make a stronger glaze covering and will help prevent settling in the glaze. An addition of about 3 percent is sufficient.

Bicarbonate of soda (NaHCO$_3$) has some use in casting slips and in forming stains with cobalt sulfate. Soda ash (Na$_2$CO$_3$) is the sodium form more commonly used as a flux.

Bismuth subnitrate (BiONO$_3$·H$_2$O) generally contains impurities such as arsenic, lead, and silver carbonates. It melts at a low temperature and is used primarily to produce pearly metallic lusters under reducing conditions. (See Luster Glazes.)

Bone ash in the unrefined state has a formula of $4Ca_3(PO_4)_2 \cdot CaCO_3$ with a molecular weight of 1340. The material generally used today is the refined calcium phosphate $Ca_3(PO_4)_2$ with a molecular weight of 310. It is sometimes used as a glaze flux but more commonly as a body ingredient in bone china, chiefly in the kind produced in England. It lowers the firing temperatures required and increases the translucency.

Borax ($Na_2O \cdot 2B_2O_3 \cdot 10H_2O$) is, next to lead, the major low-fired flux. It has a strong action on all ceramic compounds and may be even used in small amounts in the high-fired glazes that tend to be overly viscous in nature. Borax has a different effect upon coloring oxides than lead, and for this reason it is often used either alone or in combination with lead. Borax absorbs moisture and should therefore be kept dry, or weight calculations will be inaccurate. As mentioned earlier, borax is very soluble in water and should not be used on raw ware.

Boric acid ($B_2O_3 \cdot 2H_2O$) is a flaky material soluble in water. It is available in a fairly pure state at a low price. Although boron is one of the neutral oxides (R_2O_3), it functions more as a base since it increases the gloss as does lead. Unlike silica, an acid, boron lowers the expansion coefficient and increases the elasticity.

Cadmium sulfide (CdS) is a low-fire yellow colorant. It is usually combined in a stain made of cadmium, selenium, and sulphur frits. Unfortunately it is fugitive above cone 010 and can only be used for overglaze decorations.

Calcium borate (see Colemanite).

Calcium carbonate (see Whiting).

Calcium fluoride (see Fluorspar).

Calcium phosphate (see Bone Ash).

Calcium zirconium silicate is a commercially produced opacifier with the composition of ZrO_2, 51.12 percent; SiO_2, 25.41 percent; CaO, 22.23 percent. It does not have the strength of tin but is considerably cheaper. It will lower slightly the maturing temperatures of the lower-fired glazes.

Carolina stone is similar to Cornwall stone.

China clay (see Kaolin).

Chromic oxide (Cr_2O_3) and other chromium compounds are commonly used in glazes to produce green colors. Dichromates are preferred because of the greater amounts of chromium per weight. Care must be taken in the glaze composition for, when combined with tin, a pink will result. Zinc will form a brown, and high-lead glazes may develop a yellow-lead chromate. Reducing conditions in the kiln will blacken the color. In fact even adjacent tin-glazed and chrome-glazed pieces may affect each other in the kiln. Bright low-temperature reds (under cone 010) may be produced by chrome oxide in a high-lead and low-alumina glaze.

Clay (see Chapter 4, Clay and Clay Bodies) is a decomposed feldspathic-type rock consisting chiefly of silicates of aluminum but often containing numerous other ingredients such as quartz, micas, feldspars, iron oxides, carbonates of calcium and magnesium, and organic matter.

Cobalt carbonate ($CoCO_3$) is used to introduce a blue glaze color; in combinations with manganese, iron chromate, or ochre it produces black colorants.

Cobalt oxide (Co_2O_3) is the major blue colorant. It is extremely strong and therefore often fritted with alumina and lime or with lead for lower-fired underglaze colors. The frit allows a lighter and more even color dispersion. Color stains made of cobalt, alumina, and zinc are uniform at all temperature ranges. Small amounts of cobalt in combination with MgO, SiO_2, and B_2O_3 will produce a variety of hues in the pink and lavender range.

Cobalt sulfate ($CoSo_4 \cdot 7H_2O$), unlike the other cobalt compounds mentioned, is very soluble in water. It melts at a low temperature and is primarily used in decorative work or lusterware.

Colemanite ($2CaO \cdot 3B_2O_3 \cdot 5H_2O$) is a natural hydrated calcium borate, which has the advantage of being only slightly soluble in water and therefore does not develop the granular lumps in the glaze so characteristic of borax. Colemanite has wide use as a low-fire flux since the boron present melts at a fairly low temperature. It tends to prevent crazing and also functions slightly as an opacifier. Colemanite may be substituted for calcium in some glazes where its presence would harm the pink or red colors desired. Colemanite may vary slightly in composition depending upon its source, and this factor may cause trouble unless tests are made.

Copper carbonate ($CuCO_3$) is a major green colorant used in glazes. The carbonate form is preferred to the oxide form in the production of blue greens or copper reds under reducing conditions.

Copper oxide is (1) cupric or black copper oxide (CuO) or (2) cuprous or red copper oxide (Cu_2O). Copper is one of the few colorants that does not change greatly under normal oxidizing conditions. Lead fluxes tend to produce a blackish green. When copper and tin are used with an alkaline flux, a turquoise will result. Potash will induce a yellowish green while zinc and copper with fluxes of sodium, potassium, and barium will tend to develop a blue tinge.

Cornwall stone is a complex mixture derived from an English deposit of partially decomposed granite rock. It is composed of quartz (flint), feldspar, lepidolite, tourmaline, fluorspar, and small quantities of other minerals. Cornwall stone has characteristics which lie between those of kaolin and feldspar. It is a major ingredient of many English glazes and bodies and is subject to less firing strains than kaolin and feldspar. Due to the more intimate mixture of naturally occurring minerals, a smaller amount of alkali flux is necessary than would otherwise be needed. Since less bulk is required, there is less shrinkage of both the unfired and fired glaze, thus minimizing glaze defects. Cornwall stone is roughly similar to *petuntze*, the feldspathic powered rock used for centuries by the Chinese as a major ingredient in their porcelain bodies and glazes. Like feldspars, Cornwall stone has variable composition; samples differ in the percentages of silica, potassium, sodium, and so on. If not available, a substitution of 67 parts feldspar, 22 flint, and 11 kaolin may be made for 100 units of Cornwall stone. However, as previously noted, the new glaze will not have identical characteristics.

A material similar to Cornwall stone, called Carolina stone, is mined in the United States but is not commonly available. An analysis of two samples, listed below, show almost identical proportions.

	Cornwall stone *Percentage*	Carolina stone *Percentage*
SiO_2	72.6	72.30
Al_2O_3	16.1	16.23
Fe_2O_3	0.23	0.07
CaO	1.4	0.62
MgO	0.1	trace
K_2O	4.56	4.42
Na_2O	3.67	4.14
CaF_2		
TiO_2	0.06	
Ignition loss	2.54	1.06

Formula for Cornwall stone sample

0.185	CaO	1.162	Al_2O_3	8.95	SiO_2
0.359	K_2O	0.0106	Fe_2O_3	0.0055	TiO_2
0.437	Na_2O		*Molecular weight* 732.57		
0.0185	MgO				

Cryolite (Na_3AlF_6) is used primarily as a flux and an opacifier for enamels and glasses. It has a limited use in glazes and bodies as a source of fluxes and alumina. In some glazes, an addition of cryolite will promote crazing.

Dolomite [$CaMg(CO_3)_2$] is a double carbonate of calcia and magnesia. It has a greater use in glassmaking than in glazes. It is a cheap method of introducing calcia and magnesia into a glaze. Dolomite will promote a longer and lower firing range in clay bodies. Below cone 4, the addition of a small amount of a lower-firing alkaline flux to the dolomite will greatly increase this effect.

Epsom salts (see Magnesium Sulfate).

Feldspar is a crystalline rock composed of the aluminum silicates of potassium, sodium, and calcium. These silicates are never found in a pure state but in a mixture with one or the other predominating. For convenience in ceramic calculations,

GLAZE CALCULATIONS AND CHEMICALS

their formulas are usually given as follows:

Potash feldspar (microcline)
$K_2O \cdot Al_2O_3 \cdot 6SiO_2$
Soda feldspar (albite)
$Na_2O \cdot Al_2O_3 \cdot 6SiO_2$
Lime feldspar (anorthite)
$CaO \cdot Al_2O_3 \cdot 6SiO_2$

The feldspars are a major ingredient of porcelain and whiteware bodies and are often the only source of body flux. If the feldspar content of the body is high, the substitution of soda spar for a potash feldspar will reduce the vitrification point by as much as 100°F. The feldspars are a cheap source of glaze flux and have the additional advantage of being non-soluble. Due to the presence of Al_2O_3 and SiO_2, the feldspar cannot be considered a flux at low temperature ranges even though some flux is contributed to the glaze. The fluxing action is increased by the fineness of the particle size. Potash forms a harder glaze than soda and decreases the thermal expansion. Thus, unless soda is desired for color purposes, potash feldspar should be preferred in the glaze composition.

Ferric chloride ($FeCl_3 \cdot 6H_2O$) is more commonly called *chloride of iron*. It is very soluble in water and must be stored in airtight containers. Its chief use is as a luster decoration on glass or glazes. It produces an iridescent gold-colored film under proper conditions. (See Luster Glazes.)

Ferric oxide (see Iron Oxide).

Ferrous oxide (see Iron Oxide).

Flint (SiO_2) is also called silica or, in foreign publications, quartz. It is commonly obtained from sandstone, quartz sands, or flint pebbles. True flint is obtained from England, France, and Denmark and is prepared by calcining and grinding flint beach pebbles. This cryptocrystalline has a different specific gravity (2.33) from that prepared from quartz sand or sandstone (2.65). In the United States, all silica is called *flint*. The difference between the two is slight. The "pebble" flint reacts a trifle faster in the glaze. The specific gravity is of importance only if it is used in casting slips.

When used alone, silica melts at the extremely high temperature of 3119°F. It forms an extremely hard and stable crystal. It combines under heat, however, with a variety of fluxes at much lower temperatures to form a glass and with the alumina compounds to form the more refractory body structure. An increase in the silica content of a glaze has the effect of raising the maturing temperatures as well as increasing its hardness and resistance to wear. In a glaze, the addition of flint decreases its thermal expansions; in a body it increases such expansions.

Fluorspar (CaF_2), also called *calcium fluoride*, has a limited use as a source of flux in glaze and body compositions. The particle size must be under 100 mesh when used in the body or pinholes are likely to form in the glaze. Fluorspar fluxes at a lower temperature than other calcia compounds. With copper oxides, some unusual blue-green hues can be developed.

Ilmenite ($TiO_2 \cdot FeO$) is the mineral source of titanium and its compounds. Used as a coarse powder-like sand, it produces dark specks in the glaze.

Iron chromate ($FeCrO_4$) is used in combination with manganese and zinc oxide to produce underglaze brown colors or with cobalt to form a black stain. Used alone, it is fugitive above cone 04.

Iron oxides have three forms: (FeO) *ferrous oxide*, (Fe_2O_3) *ferric oxide* or hematite, and (Fe_3O_4) *ferrous-ferric oxide* or magnetite. Iron is the oxide most frequently used to produce tan or brown bodies and glazes. Were it not for its pronounced color, it would have a wide use as a flux. It is responsible for most of the low-firing characteristics and the red color of many earthenware clays. A pink stain can be made with a smaller amount of iron plus alumina, calcium, and flint. When reduced in a suitable glaze, iron will form grey-greens. (See Celadon.)

Kaolin ($Al_2O_3 \cdot 2SiO_2 \cdot 2H_2O$) is also called *china clay* or *pure clay*. Due to its composition and relative purity, kaolin is the highest firing clay. It is an important ingredient of all whiteware and china bodies since it fires out pure white. For glazes, kaolin constitutes a major source of Al_2O_3 and SiO_2. The chief residual deposits are in North Carolina, and sedimentary deposits are found in South Carolina and Georgia. For bodies, the more plastic sedimentary types are preferred. The sedimentary kaolin deposits of Florida are even more plastic and are often termed ball kaolin. (See Chapter 4, Clay and Clay Bodies.)

Lead antimonate (see Basic Antimonate of Lead).

Lead, bisilicate (see Lead Silicate).

Lead, white (see Lead Carbonate).

Lead carbonate [$2PbCO_3 \cdot Pb(OH)_2$] is the white powder more commonly called white lead. It is the major low-fired flux and produces a glossy glaze with relatively few faults. Its major drawback is its poisonous effects if breathed in while carelessly sprayed. A lead-glazed vessel should not be used for storing concentrated citric acid fruit juices. By fritting the lead and silica, this dust hazard and most of the solubility danger can be removed. However, due to its ease of application and free flowing and brilliant surface, lead carbonate continues to be the major low-fired flux. The evolution of CO_2 from the glazes is said to promote a better mixture of the glaze ingredients than that of other lead compounds. The use of lead as a flux will have a different effect on the colorants used than the alkaline compounds. The addition of calcia, silica, or alumina to a lead glaze will increase its hardness and resistance to wear.

Lead oxide as used in ceramics is of two types: (PbO) *litharge* or lead monoxide, and (Pb_3O_4) *red lead* or minium. Litharge is a yellow powder that has a greater use in Europe than in the United States. As litharge occasionally contains impurities and has larger particles than the carbonate form, the latter is the preferred lead compound to use. Due to the greater amount of oxygen, the red form is often used in place of litharge. Ceramic grades of red lead are seldom pure but usually contain 75 percent red lead and about 25 percent litharge. Pound for pound, red lead contains more PbO than the carbonate form.

Lead silicate is a frit made of lead and silica to eliminate the toxic effects of the lead compounds. The two most common types are: *lead monosilicate,* with a composition of 15 percent SiO_2 and 85 percent PbO; *lead bisilicate,* with a formula of 65 percent PbO, 34 percent SiO_2, and 1 percent Al_2O_3.

Lead silicate, hydrous [$2PbSiO_2 \cdot Pb(OH)_2$] has a molecular weight of 807. This material is the basic silicate of white lead. It is used as a substitute for lead carbonate, when the CO_2 released by the carbonate forms pinholes or is otherwise objectionable in the glaze.

Lead sulfide (PbS), also called *galena,* is the black powder that is the raw source of all lead compounds. It has a very limited use in glazes.

Lepidolite ($LiF \cdot KF \cdot Al_2O_3 \cdot 3SiO_2$), also called lithium mica, contains from 3 to 6 percent of lithia. It has some use as a body ingredient in chinaware bodies as well as being a source of flux, Al_2O_3, and SiO_2 in the

higher temperature glazes. It will tend to brighten most glazes, lower thermal expansions, and reduce brittleness. (See Lithium Carbonate.)

Lime (CaO), calcium oxide (see Whiting).

Litharge (PbO) (see Lead Oxide).

Lithium carbonate (Li_2CO_3) is a common source of lithia that is a strong flux in the higher temperature ranges. With lithia, greater amounts of Al_2O_3, SiO_2, and CaO may be used in alkaline glazes, thus producing a more durable glaze while retaining the unusual copper blues characteristic of the alkaline-type glazes. It may be used in place of lead in the medium temperature ranges when volitization is a problem.

Magnesium carbonate ($MgCO_3$), magnesite acts as a refractory at lower temperatures, changing to a flux at higher temperatures. It is valuable to slow down the fluid qualities of crystalline and other runny glazes. It also improves glaze adherence.

Magnesium sulfate ($MgSO_4 \cdot 7H_2$) is better known as *epsom salts.* Its primary use in glazes is as an aid to retard the settling of frits and glazes. Usually 1 percent, dissolved in hot water, will be sufficient and will have no apparent effect on the glaze.

Magnetite (see the Iron Oxides).

Manganese Dioxide (see Manganese Oxide).

Manganese oxide (MnO_2) is used in ceramics as a colorant. It should not be used in concentrations over 5 percent to either body or glaze because blisters may develop. The usual colors produced are in the brown range. With cobalt, a black results; with the proper alkaline fluxes purple and dark reddish hues may develop. When fritted with alumina, a pink colorant will be formed.

Nepheline syenite ($K_2O \cdot 3Na_2O \cdot 4Al_2O_3 \cdot 9SiO_2$) is a material roughly similar to a feldspar and has the following composition.

	Percent
SiO_2	60.4
Al_2O_3	˙23.6
Fe_2O_3	0.08
CaO	0.7
MgO	.1
Na_2O	9.8
K_2O	4.7
Ignition loss	0.7

Molecular formula

Na_2O	0.713	Al_2O_3	1.04
K_2O	0.220		
CaO	0.056	SiO_2	4.53
MgO	0.011		

Molecular weight 447

A major use for nepheline syenite is as a substitute for potash feldspar where it lowers the firing temperatures required. It also produces a greater firing range and increased thermal expansion, which in turn will reduce crazing tendencies in the glaze. Its use in a glaze is roughly similar to potash feldspar with the exception of lowering the maturing point.

Nickel oxide is used in two forms, (NiO) *green nickel oxide* or nickelous and (Ni_2O_3) *black nickel oxide* or nickelic. The function of nickel in a glaze is almost solely as a colorant. Depending upon the flux used and the ratio of alumina, a variety of colors may be produced: with zinc, a blue is obtained; with lime, a tan; with barium, a brown; and with magnesia, a green. None of these hues are particularly brilliant. In general, nickel is used to soften and alter other coloring oxides. In addition, the use of 5 to 10 percent nickel in a proper glaze results in the formation of a crystalline structure.

Ochre is a term given to clays containing varying amounts of red iron or manganese oxides. Their chief use is in paint manufacturing. However, they may be used as glaze or slip colorants to impart tan, brown, or brick-red hues.

Opax is a standard commercially produced opacifier with the following composition:

	Percent		*Percent*
ZrO_2	91.88	NaKO	.92
TiO_2	.40	Al_2O_3, P_2O_5	.39
LiO_2	5.76	Total H_2O	.09
Fe_2O_3	.06		

Opax does not have the power of tin oxide, but it is considerably cheaper and is often used to replace part of the tin oxide that would otherwise be required.

Pearl ash (see Potassium Carbonate).

Petatile ($Li_2O \cdot Al_2O_3 \cdot 8SiO_2$), lithium-aluminum silicate, is chiefly used as an auxiliary body flux to reduce thermal expansions and increase shock resistance. At about cone 06, it converts into beta spodumene that has almost no volume change when heated or cooled. It is a source of lithia and silica for medium- and high-temperature glazes.

Plastic vitrox $(IRO \cdot 1.69Al_2O_3 \cdot 14.64SiO_2)$ is a complex mineral mined in California that has a use in both glaze and body formulas as a source of silica, alumina, and potash. It has similarities to both potash feldspar and Cornwall stone. (See Appendix for comparative analysis.)

Potash feldspar (See Feldspar).

Potassium Carbonate (K_2CO_3) is more commonly called *pearl ash*. It is used primarily to modify color effects. When pearl ash is substituted for the lead, sodium, or calcium content, the colors resulting from copper oxide may be changed from the usual green to either a yellow green or a bright blue.

Potassium dichromate $(K_2Cr_2O_7)$ is used in glazes as a green colorant. When it is calcined with tin, low-fire stains developing pink and red hues are formed. (See Chromic Oxide.)

Praseodymium oxide (Pr_6O_{11}) is a black oxide that is a rare earth compound used in ceramics as a yellow colorant. It is commonly combined with zirconium oxide and silica to form a glaze stain that is stable at all normal firing temperatures.

Pyrophyllite $(Al_2O_3 \cdot 4SiO_2 \cdot H_2O)$ is used primarily in wall-tile bodies where it decreases thermal expansions, crazing, and moisture expansions to which tile is subjected. Since it is nonplastic, it has a limited use in pottery bodies.

Red lead (see Lead Oxide).

Rutile (TiO_2) is an impure oxide of titanium containing small amounts of iron and vanadium. Used as a tan colorant.

Selenium (Se) has its greatest use as a glass colorant. It has a limited use in ceramic glazes and overglaze colors, primarily as cadmium-selenium red frits. These, unfortunately, are fugitive at higher temperatures.

Silica (see Flint).

Silicon carbide (SiC) has many industrial uses. Its value in ceramics is as sole or major ingredient in high-temperature kiln furniture and muffles. When added to an alkaline glaze in small amounts ($\frac{1}{2}$ of 1 percent), the carbon will reduce locally the copper oxides to form artificial copper reds.

Sillimanite $(Al_2O_3 \cdot SiO_2)$ is similar in many respects to Kyanite. Major uses are in high temperature refractory bodies.

Silver chloride (AgCl) is the major silver compound used in luster overglaze preparations (see Lusters). When silver chloride is combined with bismuth and with a resin or fat oil as a binder, an overglaze metallic luster with greenish or yellow tints will form.

Soda ash (see Sodium Carbonate).

Sodium aluminate ($Na_2O \cdot Al_2O_3$) is used to prevent casting slips from setting and to increase the strength of dry ware.

Sodium bicarbonate (see Bicarbonate of Soda).

Sodium carbonate (Na_2CO_3) is commonly called *soda ash*. It is a very active flux, but because of its solubility it is more commonly used in glazes as a frit ingredient. Small quantities of soda ash will reduce the water of plasticity required in a clay body. This increases workability and strength of the body and reduces the shrinkage when it goes from the wet to the dry state.

Sodium silicate ($Na_2 \cdot XSiO_2$) is a compound that may vary from $1Na_2O \cdot 1.6SiO_2$ to $1Na_2O \cdot 3.75SiO_2$. It usually comes in a liquid form and is the major deflocculant used in casting slips. Like soda ash, it greatly reduces the water required to make the clay into a slip form. In doing so, it greatly lessens the rate of shrinkage, the strains of drying, and breakage in the green and dry states.

Sodium uranate ($Na_2O \cdot UO_3$), more commonly called *uranium yellow*, has unfortunately not been available since World War II because of restrictions placed on uranium by the Atomic Energy Commission. Uranium yellows are still available, however, in Europe. Uranium compounds were formerly the best source of yellow colorants. When uranium compounds are combined with various fluxes or with tin and zirconium oxide, a variety of hues from bright yellow to orange to vermillion red can be developed. (See also, Uranium oxide.)

Spodumene ($Li_2O \cdot Al_2O_3 \cdot 4SiO_2$) is an important source of lithia. The use of lithia, which is an active flux, helps to develop unusual copper-blue hues. Spodumene is also used in whiteware and porcelain bodies. When used to replace feldspar, it will reduce the vitrification temperature as well as the shrinkage rate. Strange as it may seem, the crystalline form of spodumene expands at about 1700°F (927°C) instead of shrinking. When a mixture of 60 percent of spodumene and 40 percent of lead bisilicate is used, a nonplastic, press-formed body can be made that at 1970°F (1077°C), will have zero absorption and zero shrinkage.

Steatite, a hydrous magnesium silicate is a massive variety of talc. Most steatite is used in a powdered form for electrical insulators. It has very little shrinkage, and occasionally the rocklike nuggets are turned down in a lathe for special projects. Steatite was used by the Egyptians some 5000 years ago for beads and small figurines. These were generally covered by a turquoise alkaline copper glaze. (See Talc.)

Talc varies from $3MgO \cdot 4SiO_2 \cdot H_2O$ to $4MgO \cdot 5SiO_2 \cdot H_2O$. In the solid and more impure form, it is also known as *steatite* and *soapstone*. Talc is occasionally used in glazes but is more frequently employed as a major ingredient in whiteware bodies firing at moderate temperatures (cones 04-6). Like dolomite, it is used to lower the firing temperatures of the kaolin, ball clays, and feldspars, which are often the other body ingredients. Talc will promote a slight opacity in glazes.

Tin oxide (SnO_2), also called *stannic oxide*, is the most effective of all opacifiers. From 5 to 7 percent will produce a completely opaque white glaze. An excess will produce a dull surface. Tin also has a wide use in stains as it has a considerable effect on the color qualities of most color-forming oxides. Due to its relatively high price, tin substitutes are frequently used. (See Opacifiers.)

Titanium oxide (TiO_2), or more correctly *titanium dioxide*, is a major opacifier when used either alone or in a frit. Like rutile, which is an impure form containing iron, titanium will, if used in any quantity, encourage a semimat surface texture.

Uranium oxide, U_3O_8 (black), is a depleted nuclear fuel used as a yellow colorant in low-fire lead glazes. More efficient as colorants are other forms of uranium, such as sodium uranate, $Na_2O \cdot UO_2$, (orange) and sodium diuranate (yellow). A 5-percent addition of tin oxide aids the color formation while a reduction fire is detrimental. The tin-vanadium, zirconium-vanadium, and praseodymium yellow stains have a greater flexibility and are preferred by most potters.

Vanadium pentoxide (V_2O_5) is a rather weak yellow colorant when used alone. When fritted in the proper composition with tin, it produces a strong yellow color. This stain, known commercially as tin-vanadium stain, has largely replaced the uranium yellows, which are no longer available. It has a wide firing range (cones 06-14), is transparent, and is not affected by a reduction firing.

Volcanic ash occurs in many regions of the American West. It was formed from the dust of volcanic glass erupted in prehistoric volcanic actions. Since the material often floated through the air many miles before being deposited, it is extremely fine and can be used with little preparation. Its composition is roughly similar to that of a granite-type rock (see the formula under RO oxides). An average analysis of Kansas ash is as follows:

	Percent		Percent
SiO_2	72.51	MgO	0.07
Al_2O_3	11.55	K_2O	7.87
Fe_2O_3	1.21	Na_2O	1.79
TiO_2	0.54	Ignition loss	3.81
CaO	0.68		

In most glazes, volcanic ash can be substituted for roughly 70 parts of feldspar and 30 parts of flint. A low-fired 04 glaze may be compounded of 60 percent of ash and 40 percent borax and lead or just lead.

Whiting ($CaCO_3$) is a *calcium carbonate*, produced domestically by processing marble or limestone. European whiting is generally obtained from chalk deposits such as the famous cliffs of Dover. Whiting is the major high-fire flux, although it has a minor use in bodies where a small amount will lower vitrification temperatures and reduce porosity. As a flux, it produces much harder and tougher silicates than will either the lead or alkaline compounds. For this reason small amounts are often added to the lower fired glazes. As with other fluxes, calcium has an effect upon the coloring oxides, particularly chrome greens.

Wollastonite ($CaSiO_3$) is a natural calcium silicate. As a replacement for flint and whiting, it reduces firing shrinkage and improves heat shock. It is used both in bodies and glazes.

Zinc oxide (ZnO) is a strange compound to classify. At high temperatures it is an active flux. When used to excess in a glaze high in alumina and cooled slowly, zinc will produce crystalline structures. Opacity will develop if zinc is used in a high-alumina low-calcium glaze with no borosilicate fluxes at cone 1 or above in amounts of 0.15 equivalents. In general, zinc increases the maturing range and promotes a higher gloss, brighter colors, a reduction of expansions, and, under some conditions, an opacity.

Zirconium oxide (ZrO_2) is seldom used alone as an opacifier in ceramics but is generally combined with other oxides and fritted into a more stable silicate form. Below are listed a few commercial zirconium silicates. None have the strength of tin oxide, but they are considerably cheaper.

Calcium zirconium silicate: 51.12 percent ZrO_2, 25.41 percent SiO_2, and 22.23 percent CaO.

Magnesium zirconium silicate: 53.75 percent ZrO_2, 29.92 percent SiO_2, and 18.54 percent MgO.

Zinc zirconium silicate: 45.78 percent ZrO_2, 23.08 percent SiO_2, and 30.52 percent ZnO.

Zirconium spinel: 39.94 percent ZrO_2, 25.25 percent SiO_2, 19.47 percent ZrO, and 19.41 percent Al_2O_3.

Most of the above compounds are used in combinations with other opacifiers such as tin or the titanium compounds. (See also Opax and Zircopax.)

Zircopax is a standard commercially produced opacifier with the composition of 64.88 percent ZrO_2, 0.22 percent TiO_2, 34.28 percent SiO_2.

Colorants for Glazes and Decoration

Coloring oxides In general, most studio potters obtain their glaze colors from the oxides or carbonates of the more common metals such as iron, copper, nickel, tin, zinc, and manganese. Other oxides, such as vanadium and cobalt, although rarer and more expensive, are extensively used because of a lack of cheaper substitutes. Most of these compounds have been discussed in previous sections. The following list of major colorants indicates the oxide necessary and the amounts generally used to produce a particular color. But just because an oxide is listed as producing a green does not mean that it will

GUIDE TO USE OF COLORANTS

Color	Oxide	Percentage	Temperature	Atmosphere
Black				
{ cobalt		1–2	any	either
{ manganese		2–4		
{ cobalt		1		
{ iron		8	any	either
{ manganese		3		
Blue				
cobalt		½–1	any	either
turquoise copper (alkaline flux)		3–5	low	oxidizing
slate blue nickel (with zinc)		1–3	low	oxidizing
Brown				
rutile		5	any	reducing
chromium (with MgO, ZnO)		2–5	low	either
iron		3–7	any	oxidizing
manganese		5	any	either
nickel (with zinc)		2–4	any	either
Green				
copper oxide		1–5	any	oxidizing
iron		1–4	any	reducing
nickel		3–5	low	oxidizing
Red				
pink chrome-tin (1 to 18)		5	any	oxidizing
coral chromium (with high PbO)		5	low	oxidizing
purple manganese (with KNaO)		4–6	any	oxidizing
copper		1	any	reducing
iron (high SiO_2, KNaO), CaO		2–5	low	oxidizing
Tan				
iron		2	any	either
manganese		2	any	either
rutile		2	any	either
Yellow				
Antimony yellow stain (with high PbO)		3–5	low	either
Praeodymium yellow stain		4–6	any	either
Uranium yellow and orange (with high PbO)		5–8	low	oxidizing
Zirconium vanadium stain		5–10	any	either
Tin vanadium stain		4–6	any	either

produce a green in every case. A study of the section on ceramic materials will reveal that generally the particular color that develops from an oxide depends upon the type of flux used, the proportions of alumina or silica, and the firing temperature. In some cases, even the rate of cooling will have an effect upon the glaze. Therefore, the list of oxides and colors on page 219 is merely for your convenience in determining color possibilities. Before using the oxide, look up its characteristics and the characteristics of the glaze in which you plan to use it.

It is common practice to use two or more colorants in order to modify harsh colors and to obtain subtle variations or mottled color effects. Copper and nickel are often used to soften powerful cobalt hues. Opacifiers are used to brighten colors. Rutile is a frequent addition since it contributes a runny and slightly specked quality in addition to slightly matting a glaze.

Opacifiers are, for the most part, a group of chemicals that are relatively insoluble in the glaze melt. Tin oxide and zirconium oxide are the chief examples of this type. As such, they remain suspended in the glaze and if dense enough prevent the light from penetrating through to the body. Most opacifiers, and of course those of the greatest value, are white. However, some give a slight yellow, pink, or bluish cast to the glaze.

Another type of opacifier is titanium (or zinc under some conditions) that tends to form minute crystalline structures within the glaze. Having a different index of refraction from the major portion of the glaze, it thus breaks up and prevents much of the light penetration. This is the type of crystal formation associated with mat glazes and is the reason why all mats must be, necessarily, either wholly or partially opaque.

Spinel stains Under certain circumstances, the use of the raw coloring oxide may be objectionable. For example, most metallic oxides are very soluble in the melting glaze. In the previous section, we noted that the fluxes and other elements of the glaze had a considerable effect upon

OPACIFIERS

Color	Oxide	Percentage	Temperature	Atmosphere
Pure white	tin	5	any	either
Weak blue white	titanium	8–12	any	either
White	zirconium	8–12	any	either
Weak yellow white	antimony	10–12	low	oxidizing
White	opax (a frit)	10	any	either
White	zircopax (a frit)	10	any	either

GLAZE CALCULATIONS AND CHEMICALS

the color quality. Overglaze and underglaze decoration with any degree of precision or control is impossible with colorants that diffuse into or flow with the glaze. In these cases, a special type of colorant known as a spinel is used.

A *spinel stain* is a colored crystal that is extremely resistant to the attacks of fluxes in the glaze and the effects of high temperatures. In strict chemical terms, *spinel* refers to the mineral magnesium aluminate ($MgAl_2O_3$). However, manganese, iron, and chromium may be present by replacement. The crystal is an octahedron variety of extreme hardness. The ruby gem is a red spinel. By calcining certain oxides together, some very stable colored spinels can be formed. In general, these follow the formula $RO \cdot R_2O_3$. The RO member may be either MgO, ZnO, NiO, CaO, CdO, MnO, or FeO, and the R_2O_3 can be Cr_2O_3, Al_2O_3, or Fe_2O_3.

Preparation of a spinel stain is a lengthy procedure, and it is not recommended unless it is necessary for advanced experimental work. There is a wide range of commercial stains, expertly prepared, available at a reasonable cost. The general idea, however, of the preparation should be understood. More detailed information can be found in the reference texts listed in the Appendix.

It is extremely necessary that the chemicals involved are mixed completely and intimately. To this end the raw chemicals should first be passed through an 80-mesh sieve. It is preferable that they be in the form of soluble salts, that is, the nitrates or sulfates of the oxides just listed. These are thoroughly mixed in a liquid solution. After the water has been evaporated, the dry mixture is placed in a crucible or a kiln and calcined. The temperature will vary with the mixture. If the mixture melts into a solid mass, the mixture should be calcined in a pot furnace so that the crucible can be removed with tongs and the contents poured into water, thus preventing the spinel from hardening into a solid crystalline block. Afterwards, the material is broken up with an iron mortar and pestle into a coarse powder, which is then ball milled. For a uniform color without specks, the particle size of the spinel must be extremely small. This may necessitate grinding in the ball mill for well over a hundred hours. When it is ground fine enough, the stain should be washed several times with hot water to remove any remaining soluble salts. Filters may be necessary at this point to prevent the loss of fine particles.

Other colored stains. Besides the spinels, a number of other chemical compounds are calcined to produce stable colorants at certain temperatures. A discussion of a few of the better-known examples will serve to illustrate some of the numerous possibilities in the preparation of colorants.

AN ULTRAMARINE BLUE can be formed by a silicate of cobalt. It is made by calcining cobalt oxide and flint plus a flux such as feldspar.

GREEN STAINS can be developed by calcining fluorspar and chromium oxide.

YELLOW STAINS such as Naples yellow and yellow base are made from antimony, lead, and tin. Calcium and sodium uranate can also be used, when available, to form various yellow and orange colorants.

PINK AND RED STAINS are made by several methods. One of the most unusual is the precipitation of colloidal gold upon kaolin, which is then calcined and ground to form the stain. Other red stains are formed from a mixture of tin, calcium, flint, and chromium. For further information and specific details, consult the reference texts by Parmelee and Norton and the *Literature Abstracts of Ceramic Glazes* listed in the Appendix.

Underglaze colors were briefly mentioned before in the section on decoration. As the term indicates, they are colors used under the glaze. Since they will eventually be fired at the same temperature as the glaze, the range of colors available is less than for overglaze colors. For example, at the hard porcelain range of cone 14, most, if not all, of the delicate hues available in overglaze colors will burn out completely. This leaves only the blues, browns, grays, gold pinks, reduction reds, and celadon hues available for use at these higher temperatures. It is advisable to run a series of firing tests before attempting any amount of decorative work at such temperatures. The basic reason for the use of underglaze rather than overglaze colors is one of dura-

bility. Its greatest use is in the field of dinnerware, especially restaurant china.

Underglaze colors are made up of a colorant, either a raw oxide or a spinel, a flux such as feldspar to allow the color to adhere to the body, and a diluent like silica, calcined kaolin, or ground bisqueware. The purpose of these last materials is either to lighten the color or to equalize shrinkage. It is rather important that the mixture be adjusted properly to the bisqueware and the final glaze. The glazed surface should show no change in gloss over the decoration. A preliminary firing to red heat is necessary prior to glazing to burn out the vehicle used to adhere the mixture, which may be either a solution of gum tragacanth or oil of lavender thinned with turpentine. Failure to burn off the carbon formed by the adherent will make the glaze bubble and blister over the decoration.

Overglaze colors The major differences between overglaze colors and underglaze colors are the use of a lower melting flux and a wider range of colors. Since the decoration is to be applied to a previously fired glaze, the final firing need only be high enough to allow the flux to melt into the glaze, and seal the color. This is usually at a temperature of cone 016, approximately 1470°F (799°C). The flux is made of varying proportions of lead, borax, and flint, depending upon the color to be used with it. The mixture is calcined lightly, ground, and washed. The colorant, and if necessary, an opacifier, is then added and the whole mixture ball milled to an adequate fineness. A vehicle such as gum or oil is used to help the mixture to adhere to the glazed surface. In commercial production where decoration is standardized and, a little sterile in design, printing methods are used. The colors of both types of decoration are applied by decals or silk screen.

Lusters Since lusters are employed more as a decoration than as a glaze, they are included in this section on decorative coloring materials. As was noted earlier in the discussion of glaze types, a luster is nothing more than a thin layer of metal that is deposited and fused upon the surface of the glaze. There are various methods by which this may be accomplished, some of which will be outlined below. Lusters may give a variety of effects depending upon the transparency or color of the composition and the type of glaze upon which it is applied. In the Persian and Hispano-Moresque pieces, it is usually very effectively combined with underglaze decoration. In fact, luster really comes into its own when it is used to enrich other types of decoration. If used alone in an over-all glaze effect, it tends to look like a rather cheap imitation of either glass or metal. The colors available in lusters are a transparent iridescent, a nacreous silver white, and metallic hues in a variety of yellows, greens, browns, and reds.

Preparation of lusters will vary according to the method of firing employed. In general they are of three types.

1. A mixture composed of a resin, oil of lavender, and a metallic salt is brushed on the glazed ware. The ware is then fired in an oxidizing kiln to a low temperature of between 1100° and 1300°F (593° and 704°C), at which point the carbon in the resin reduces the metallic salt to its metal form. Most lusters contain bismuth nitrate, an active flux, as well as the other metal salts. It is used in combination with zinc acetate, lead acetate, and alumina to produce a clear, iridescent luster. The various metal colorants are always used in the form of a salt that decomposes at the lower temperatures needed to form the luster coating. Yellows may be made with chrome alum and bismuth nitrate. Nickel nitrate, cobalt sulphate, manganese sulphate, and iron chloride will produce a variety of browns, shading from yellowish to reddish hues. Uranium nitrate, if ever again available, develops a greenish yellow. Gold is commonly used to produce red hues and platinum, silvery lusters. Many combinations of these colorants are used and results will be varied, depending in part upon the basic glaze used and the firing schedule. In general the luster mixture will consist of 1 part of the metallic salt, 3 to 5 parts resin, and 7 to 10 parts of oil of lavender. The resin, usually gum dammar, is heated; when it becomes liquid, the nitrate or chloride is added. When the nitrate dissolves, the oil is slowly poured in. The solution is then filtered, or cooled and decanted. Before creating your own formulas, read over the experiments listed in the *Literature Abstracts of Ceramic Glazes.*

2. The method previously discussed is one that is commonly used today to produce lusters. Another type is similar to one used many centuries ago by the Egyptian and Islamic potters, although seldom used today. They first developed lusters and incidentally carried this decorative glaze to its highest level of artistic merit. The chief difference between the two methods is the use of a reduction fire to reduce the metal rather than the reducing agent contained in the resin. The mixture, which is brushed upon the glazed ware, consists of 3 parts metal, usually in a carbonate form, 7 parts red ochre, and an adhesive such as gum tragacanth. Old recipes call for vinegar or wine, but the gum is doubtless more efficient. In the firing cycle, the atmosphere is oxidizing until a low red heat is reached, whereupon reduction is started and continued to the temperature necessary to reduce the metal, usually from 1200° to 1300°F (649° to 704°C).

3. The third method of developing a luster is also seldom used, but in rare cases it occurs by accident. The color is incorporated into the glaze, preferably in the form of a metallic salt. Various combinations may be used in proportions ranging from 0.5 to 8.0 percent of the total glaze. As in the resinate type of luster glaze, the use of bismuth in addition to the other metallic salts will aid luster development. The kiln is fired oxidizing to the maturity point of the glaze, then cooled to 1200° to 1300°F (649° to 704°C). At this point the kiln is relit and fired for about 15 minutes at a reducing atmosphere. Accurate records should be kept on reduction firings as variations of temperature and reduction periods will produce quite different results.

Binders

Various materials may be added to either the clay body or glaze to increase the green or dry strength of the ceramic form or to aid glaze adhesion and to lessen injury to the fragile glaze coating during the kiln loading. The several binders and waxes used in industrial production to increase the body strength are little needed by the studio potter since his plastic clay body is usually adequate in this regard.

Clay   If the glaze contains an excess of 10 percent of kaolin, additional binders may not be needed. If the clay content is low, the addition of about 3 percent bentonite will increase adhesion. It should be mixed with the dry ingredients.

Gums   Traditionally gum arabic or tragacanth have been used as glaze binders. The granular gum crystals are soaked overnight in water and stirred vigorously the following day. About one-quarter ounce will make a quart of creamlike mucilage binder. A couple of drops of carbolic acid are needed to prevent decomposition. One or two teaspoons of this solution per quart of glaze is usually adequate.

Methocel   This synthetic methylcellulose compound not only has advantages over the gums by not deteriorating but it also serves as an agent to prevent setting. This is a problem to which colemanite in particular is susceptible. Normally 1 to 2 percent by dry weight is sufficient. However, do not attempt to add the dry powder to a liquid glaze.

Temporary binders In an emergency, sugar, syrup or wheat flour may be used. Of course, all will ferment and none have the deflocculating action of methocel.

CHAPTER 9

KILNS, OPERATION AND CONSTRUCTION _____

INTRODUCTION

The kiln is the most necessary piece of equipment in the potter's studio. We can make a variety of ceramic pieces by using only our fingers. But a kiln, of one type or another, is necessary if the ware we make is to serve a useful function and have permanence.

Crude figurines and fetishes were made of plastic clay and sun-dried for countless centuries before the discovery that firing would make them hard and durable. This event was certainly an accident and likely occurred independently in several areas of the world. Crude pottery fragments are found at the lowest level of all excavated neolithic villages that date 7000 years and older (circa 5000 B.C.). Pottery making developed shortly after man left the

nomadic life of the hunter to settle in temperate valleys, where wild grains, berries, and fruit supplemented the fish and game diet.

The first kiln was little more than a bonfire in which the sun-dried ware was placed and fired. The finished pieces were quite soft and porous and needed a coating of animal fat to render them waterproof. It seems logical that the next step was to build a chamber of flat stones with a fire box beneath and eventually to make clay bricks for improved construction. As early as 4500 B.C., both in Mesopotamia and Egypt, pottery was decorated with colored slips indicating the use of a kiln with a controlled oxidation. After 3000 B.C., the black smoked ware was only found in the more primitive areas.

Stoneware lantern with scratched and slip decoration. The involved finial contrasts effectively with slab form. Paul Bogatay, U.S.A.

KILN TYPES

Fuel-Burning Kilns

The first kiln was a boxlike affair similar to Figure 1. In time, a fired clay lining that held the heat better replaced the flat stones; the entire exterior was covered with clay or perhaps even dug into a hillside. With a short chimney and dried split wood for fuel, a stoneware temperature could be reached by a skilled potter. The basic problem was to construct a heat retaining chamber for the pots through which the flames from the fire box were drawn by the rising heat in the short stack. The relationship of the fire box size to the kiln chamber is of critical importance as well as is the size and the height of chimney. In more recent designs, the gas or oil burner takes the place of the fire box of the wood-burning kiln. Too high a chimney will increase the draft and cause uneven firings. Insufficient draft will result in a slow and perhaps inadequate heat rise.

As pottery making changed from a home industry into more of a commercial enterprise, larger kilns were needed. These had the shape of a pointed cone, called a bottle-neck kiln, or a large half sphere, commonly called a beehive. Although they were small at first with only a single fire pit, they in time became quite large with multiple fire pits and several loading doors. Until recently, all building brick, sewer tile, and so on were fired in beehive kilns often 30 foot or more across. Salt-glazed tiles are still fired in such kilns since to my knowledge salt glazing has never been practical in the tunnel kilns now used so extensively in the industry.

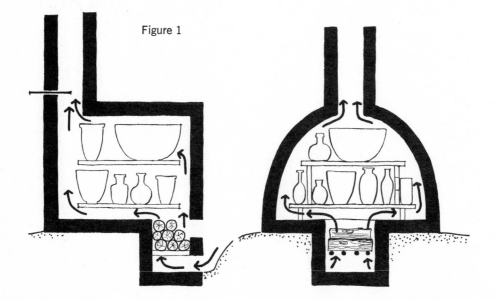

Figure 1

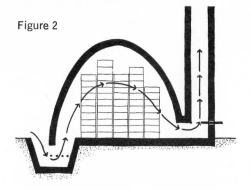

Figure 2

A disadvantage of the large bee-hive and bottle-neck kilns is the difficulty of obtaining a uniform heat throughout. This is more critical in glazed ware than for bricks or unglazed container jars. One solution was to use smaller multiple chamber kilns such as the Japanese climbing kiln. Such a kiln, built on a natural or artificial slope, might have as many as twenty chambers. In addition to providing a more uniform heat, it was quite economical on fuel

since upper chambers serving as a chimney were heated by the rising draft. The major fire pit is at the base. Auxiliary stoking ports are on either side of each chamber. As the lower chamber reaches glaze temperature, its fire pit is sealed and stoking continues up the line until each chamber reaches glaze temperature. The fuel used is wood, generally dried pine, which burns with a long . flame. For a more detailed account of wood-fired kilns, see Bernard Leach's *A Potters Book*. This book, incidentally is a necessity for every potter's library, containing as it does not only a wealth of age-old potter's lore but also the priceless addition of a philosophy of life and art so desperately needed today.

The bottle-neck and beehive kilns used first wood and later coal as fuel. The ash and cinders flowing through the kiln inevitably deposited a film

Figure 3

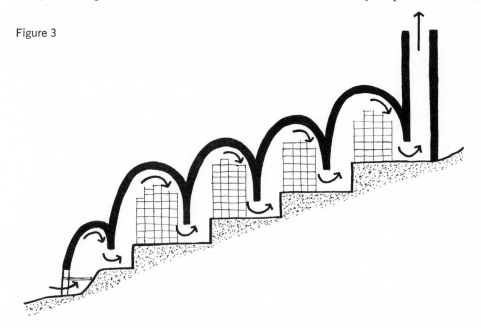

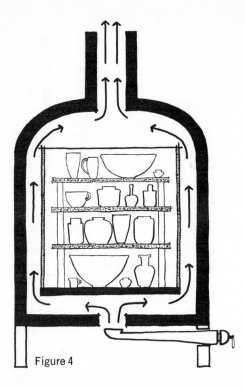

Figure 4

hotter toward the floor. Careful adjustment of draft, air, and fuel can eliminate most of this problem. Reduction is generally accomplished in the modern gas-muffle kiln by inserting moth balls in the peep hole or by removing part of the muffle.

The muffleless downdraft kiln has become increasingly popular in recent years as natural gas and propane, which is a very clean fuel, have become available everywhere. It has several advantages over the muffle-updraft type in that it provides more uniform heat, saves on fuel consumption, has a larger capacity, and makes it much easier to obtain an even reduction. Whereas the updraft and beehive kiln have only a few variations on a basic design, the modern downdraft kiln exhibits a bewildering array of possibilities. However, it is really impossible to say categorically that one type is superior in all aspects to the others. This advance has been largely due to the ease of introducing multiple gas jets into the kiln versus the limited flexibility of older fuels.

The traditional downdraft kiln, and one that has numerous virtues, has burners on both sides of the chamber. The burner flames impinge upon a bag wall, which deflects them upward. The rising heat is then pulled downwards through the loaded ware by the action of the chimney draft. This draft exhausts into the chimney at the rear of the kiln through one or more channels in the kiln floor. Provided the burners, air intake, and chimney are adequate, a uniform heat can be obtained by adjustments in the height of the bag

on the glaze injurious to its surface. To prevent these blemishes, most glazed ware was eventually fired in saggers. A sagger is a topless box made of fireclay and usually round in shape. It is stacked in the kiln one on top of the other, each containing a glazed pot. This method was not only wasteful of kiln space but required much more fuel as the sagger as well as the ware had to be heated to the full temperature. The kiln sketched in Figure 4 was developed to eliminate this problem. It has a central chamber formed by thin muffle walls that protect the ware from the direct flames flowing up from the fire box below. The first muffle kilns were wood and later oil fired. Because of their construction, they usually were not too large and not very efficient on fuel. There is a tendency for the muffle-updraft kiln to be a little

KILNS, OPERATION AND CONSTRUCTION

Figure 5

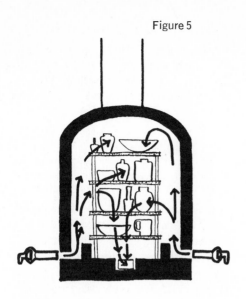

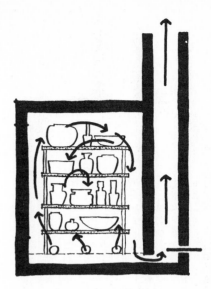

wall, the opening into the chimney, and the regulation of the damper. Numerous modifications of this basic design have been made with varying degrees of success. Occasionally, potters with a space problem have placed all burners on one wall and the chimney outlet opposite as in Figure 6. This has the added advantage of eliminating the space taken up by one bag wall and one combustion area. Properly proportioned, it ought to work quite successfully.

A slight modification of the basic downdraft design consists in placing the burners in such a way that the flames travel the length of the fire chamber as they rise. In this case, the opposing burner heights are staggered. This design (Figure 7) results in a less impeded heat flow than that which the bag wall imposes in the basic design. Continuing further in this direction, we can eliminate the bag walls entirely and place the burners so they develop a circular heat motion in the kiln. Depending upon kiln size, either two or four opposing burners (one in each corner) can be used. If the burners are placed near the ware, a small defecting baffle is used. In one unusual design (Figure 8) two large opposing burners are placed at the top of the kiln chamber and numerous channels in the floor draw off the descending heat into small stacks placed in each corner of the kiln.

Other burner placements fire into channels crossing under the floor

Figure 6

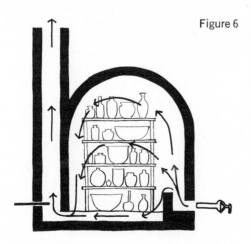

Figure 7

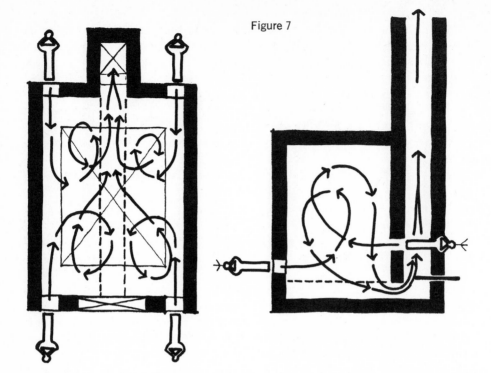

Figure 8

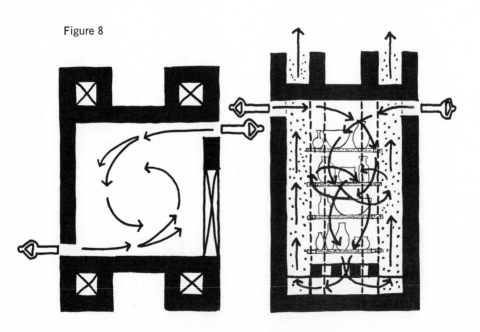

KILNS, OPERATION AND CONSTRUCTION

(Figure 9). Leaving the channels, the gas rises rapidly, its major path being the space left free from shelves and stacked ware. After circling the top, the gases are pulled down by the chimney draft through channels between the burner ports, and then they cross back under the floor before connecting to the chimney at its base. A less complicated variation is seen in the next drawing (Figure 10). Here the burners fire through channels under each side of the floor and join on the opposite wall. The heat travels up and over the ware to be sucked down by the chimney draft through an opening at the floor bottom.

The kiln sketched in Figure 11 is merely a variation of our basic downdraft kiln shown in Figure 5. The double chamber allows for firing a glaze and bisque simultaneously, with little if any extra fuel expenditure. Since the bisque chamber is really only an enlargement of the lower chimney, it can be adapted to many designs. For example, the kiln, in Figure 9 might easily be converted into a double-chamber construction.

The kilns thus far discussed are all loaded from a single door. In a small kiln, this is no problem since the depth is not great and the shelves not too large. Nor is it any inconvenience in a large walk-in kiln. However, these two extremes are seldom found in the average school or studio. The small kilns do not hold enough to be really worth the time it takes to watch or regulate them. The walk-in type is usually beyond most budgets, and unless a tremendous amount of work is produced they are not fired often enough to allow for the educational trial and error sequence to take place as rapidly as is desirable.

In the 20- to 30-cubic foot size, which is most desirable for handling class work or for an active studio potter, the loading presents occasional problems. In such kilns, it is difficult to load the shelves and especially the ware on the top, far side. The car kiln is the answer to those

Figure 9

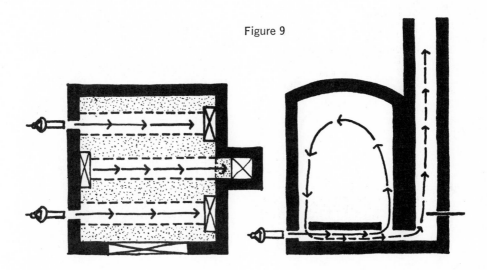

Figure 10

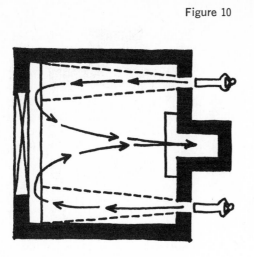
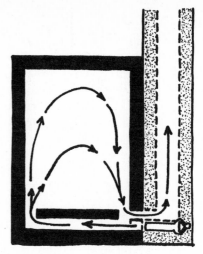

who want a 30-cubic foot kiln with the convenience of a 100-foot walk-in. The kiln in Figure 12 is our basic downdraft design fashioned in such a way that the floor rolls out on rails for loading. The door is often built as an integral part of the car floor assembly. The draft passes out by a channel in the floor, which is quite thick and is dovetailed into the side walls with a minimum clearance. A metal rail on the cars lower side slides in a trough of sand on the kiln side wall to prevent a direct heat flow. The convenience in loading a car kiln is well worth the extra cost, provided it is used frequently. Small potteries that do not need the excep-

Figure 11

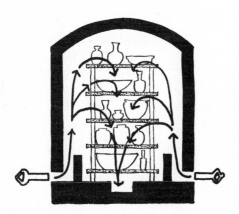
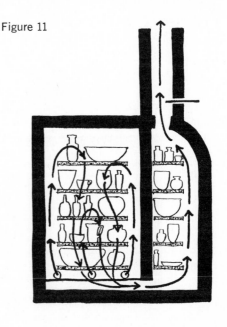

KILNS, OPERATION AND CONSTRUCTION

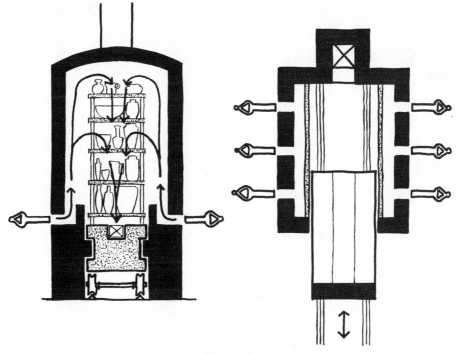

Figure 12

tional capacity of a tunnel kiln often use several car kilns. One additional advantage is that the ware can be taken out and a new load pushed in while the kiln walls retain more heat than would the walls of a standard design during the same operation. (See Chapter 10, Mass Production Methods, for additional information on the large type of kilns used in commercial plants.)

Electric Kilns

No mention has been made thus far of electric kilns. In Scandinavia, where electric power is readily available but natural gas nonexistent, this type of kiln is used by most studio potters. The gas kilns are preferred by American potters due to the re-

duction fire possible and the greater economy.

There are, however, several advantages enjoyed by the small electric kiln that have led to its widespread use in the public schools. By small I mean a kiln about eighteen inches square. Anything below this in size is only a toy and should not be seriously considered for a pottery kiln for either school or studio. Even as test kilns they are questionable as the heat rise and fall is apt to be so rapid that the glazes will not perform in a similar way in the larger kiln. Portability is the great virtue of the electric kiln. Even though it may weigh 300 to 500 pounds; it can be moved into any room with no worry about a chimney, gas lines, or ventilation. Although the operation of a gas kiln is essentially a safe one, it does take a more skilled operator than the electric kiln.

Electric kilns are made in two types: a top loader that has a flat insulated hinged cover, and an upright kiln with a swinging door (see Chapter 11). Up to about eighteen inches in depth, I prefer a top loader for reasons of convenience and economy. The electric elements are placed in grooves in the insulating bricks of the four sides. The top tends to heat up more than the bottom and a cool spot develops in the center of both top and bottom. The front loader is more convenient in the larger kiln size and also more expensive because of construction. The weight of the swinging door calls for a heavier metal frame than the top loader. In order to have an even heat, elements must be recessed into the door and be provided with a flexible power connection.

The elements used in the electric kiln are of three basic types. The most common is the coiled nickel-nichrome wire that is suitable for temperatures not exceeding 2000°F (1090°C). Kanthal elements normally operate up to 2300°F (1260°C) and some types to 2350°F (1288°C). The fairly new Kanthal Super element reaches temperatures in the 3000°F (1650°C) range but at a corresponding higher price. The Kanthal alloy is made in several wire sizes and in strip form for larger kilns. There is a limit to how much volume can be heated to a high temperature by these elements. For the larger and higher firing electric kilns, silicon carbide rods varying in diameter from a $1/4$ of an inch to over 2 inches are used. One such trade-marked element, Globar, has an operating temperature up to 2800°F (1538°C). All kilns of this type that I have seen have needed transformers to alter the 220 volts from A.C. to D.C. These transformers generally cost as much if not more than the kiln. In industry, where a perfect oxidation is necessary at high temperature, there are many Globar installations from small laboratory kilns to large tunnel-car kilns. But for the school or small pottery, the rod type of electric kiln is at an economic disadvantage compared with a gas kiln of similar size.

KILN LOADING AND FIRING

The loading and firing of the kiln is a most important operation, because a little carelessness can spoil all previous efforts. Furthermore, slipshod methods will result in permanent damage to shelves, elements, and the basic kiln structure.

Although pieces can be glazed raw and single-fired, this is not the standard procedure. Usually the ware is first fired at a low temperature called a *bisque fire*. This may be from cone 010 to cone 04 depending upon the clay body and the personal preference of the potter. It must be fired hard enough to be safely handled in the glazing operation but not so dense that the glaze will not adhere readily. These pieces, called bisqueware, may then be glazed. The exception to this procedure is the very thin high-fired porcelain, which is usually bisque fired to a higher temperature than its glaze. (See Chapter 10.)

The raw ware must never be loaded until completely dry. While pieces may be stacked inside one another, their foot rims ought to coincide. Never place a heavy piece on a thin delicate one as it may crack or deform. Large bowls ought to be fired upside down on their rims to prevent possible warping. Thin cups are fired either upside down or a pair are loaded lip to lip to prevent deforming. For a similar reason, casseroles and covered vessels are all fired with covers in place. The covers of jars with tall knobs can often be reversed to save space.

The kiln will have a better chance to fire evenly if loaded completely with a uniform density. Care should be taken to have at least 1 inch clearance from electric elements and 2 to 3 inches in gas kilns from the walls to allow for heat flow and to prevent hot spots from developing.

Even though completely dry, the raw ware always contains a considerable amount of atmospheric moisture. If the temperature of the kiln is raised too rapidly, the trapped moisture converts into steam. The resulting inevitable expansion explodes the piece. With thin ware, this is not so great a problem; the average beginner's pots must be carefully dried during the initial stage of firing. It is advisable to leave the door of the kiln ajar or to keep peep holes open for the escaping moisture during the first hour or two of firing.

Chemical changes in the body during firing are slight at first. By 350° to 400°F (175° to 200°C), all atmospheric moisture should have left the ware causing little or no shrinkage. Depending upon the body composition, the chemical water will leave the ware at temperatures between 950° and 1300°F (510° and 705°C). At this point, considerable shrinkage occurs and the firing should not be too rapid as the body is very weak. As the temperature approaches 1750°F (955°C) and continues to 1850°F (1010°C), needle-like crystals of alumina-silica ($3Al_2O_3 \cdot 2SiO_2$), called mullite, are formed. These give toughness to the body; as the temperature increases, additional free silica forms a glass around these crystals. Due to impurities and varying compositions, clay bodies develop maximum hardness at different temperatures. Earthenware clay matures at about 2000°F (1090°C), stoneware at about 2350°F (1290°C) and pure clay (kaolin) at about 3000°F (1650°C). (See also Clay and Clay Bodies, Chapter 4.)

The larger kilns must be heated up slowly because of the very bulk of the brick, regardless of the character of the load. Whereas a small electric kiln might be bisque fired in 5 to 6 hours, it is good practice to fire a large gas kiln, loaded in the afternoon, all night at a very low burner opening and then fire off more rapidly the next morning. Heavy pieces such as ceramic sculpture might conceivably take twice as long as a normal pottery load.

When the bisque temperature is reached, the elements or burners are turned off. The draft of a fuel-burning kiln must be immediately closed at this point to prevent a cold draft of air from being sucked into the burner ports and through the kiln. After cooling overnight, the draft may be opened to allow for a more rapid cooling. The door should not be opened until the ware has cooled to about 200°F (93°C). Failure to exercise care in this regard leads to cracked pots and shelves and damage to kiln wall and arch. Even though the overheated pot does not immediately crack, strains are often set up in the glaze leading to an eventual crackle.

The *glaze fire*, also called gloss fire, is normally a higher temperature than the bisque. Since the glaze will adhere to anything it contacts, the loading procedure is quite different than for the bisque fire. First, the kiln surfaces, especially the arch, should be cleaned of any exfoliated brick particles that would cause a rough spot in the glaze. A vacuum cleaner is most convenient for this job. Then, glaze particles must be chipped from all shelves, after which the surfaces are brushed with a kiln wash made from equal parts of flint and kaolin. Shelf bottoms should also be carefully brushed off as they tend to pick up particles of brick and kiln wash. A new shelf will take about three coatings. Coating a new silicon carbide shelf with aluminum paint will make the surface pores less apt to soak up a runny glaze. The ends of fireclay stilts may be dipped into aluminum paint to eliminate their tendency to stick to the bottoms of the shelves.

All ware must be dry footed, that is, the bottom as well as about a quarter of an inch of the foot rim must be free of glaze. If the foot is dipped in melted paraffin prior to glazing, the glaze is easily wiped off. As an added precaution, sift a thin layer of flint or flint sand over the kiln-washed surface, it may then be scraped off and reused. If a glaze is known to be runny or if a pot has been reglazed, it is advisable to dust an extra layer of flint or to place the pot on a thin sheet of insulating firebrick.

The lower kiln shelf or floor must be well supported so it will not warp or twist. If this floor is level, there should be little if any trouble when shelves are placed above it. Shelves of any size should have a center support when at all possible. This extra precaution will eliminate the warped shelves that occur so frequently in studios. The effort involved is usually less than that entailed in shimming up twisted shelves so they will not wobble. Rectangular shelves are less apt to crack from expansion and cooling contractions than the square shape.

It is important in the glaze fire that the ware is not too close to the elements or side walls. A hot spot will cause a glaze to run unevenly or a mat glaze to develop a shiny area. Glazed ware ought to be stacked as uniformly as possible with at least a $\frac{1}{4}$ of an inch between pieces.

Shelves ought to be staggered in order to provide a heat flow through the center section of the load.

Freshly glazed pieces should not be immediately loaded although they often are. If the damp bisque is heated too rapidly, steam will form. Even though the piece does not burst, the glaze adhesive may be affected and crawling and flaking may occur. Unless very heavy, the dry glazed ware may be fired more rapidly in the initial stages than is the case for the raw ware, since the major shrinkage has already taken place.

Reduction firing is not feasible as a continuous practice in an electric kiln, where the required free carbon in the air would tend to combine with the normal oxidization on the elements and, in effect, rust them away. The term *reduction firing* should not be confused with *reduction glazes*, which are feldspatic glazes using either iron or copper as a colorant to produce celadon or ox-blood red glazes in a reduced firing cycle.

Most potters reduce their kilns to allow the reduced iron and other impurities in the stoneware body to modify the color of the glaze and give it a slightly mottled effect. The same glaze in an electric kiln, an oxidized gas kiln, or a reduced gas kiln will often appear as quite different glazes. A limited *artificial reduction* affecting the glaze is possible in an electric kiln. It is common only to the copper red and consists of mixing about one-half of one percent of fine silicon carbide into a suitable alkaline copper glaze. The resulting glaze tends to produce a specked red and purple and is rather unlike the traditional reduced copper red.

There are many variables to be considered when discussing a reduction firing. For example, each kiln will perform differently; clay bodies and glazes will each react according to their nature. It might be mentioned that a porcelain body should be used to obtain the traditional Chinese reds.

The term *reduction* refers to the chemical reaction by which, under extreme heat, free carbon will unite with the oxygen combined in ceramic compounds. First, carbon monoxide and then carbon dioxide form and pass out of the chimney as gases. Compounds commonly affected by this exchange are the metallic oxides such as iron and copper that, when dispersed in the glass structure of the glaze as pure collodial metals, form the soft greens and rich reds of the celadon and copper-red glazes.

If we wish to pull the body color into the glaze, the reduction must begin prior to the sintering of any glaze elements. This will vary with the glaze but will usually be in the range between cone 022 and cone 016. Some potters have a short heavy reduction followed by a slightly reduced atmosphere to a temperature about one hundred degrees Fahrenheit (38°C), below the maturity of the glaze, and then they oxidize. Others reduce for a certain period of time and then oxidize again, continuing in a planned sequence. The steady slight reduction is generally preferred by those who wish the body color to be pulled into the glaze. The off-and-on reduction is more desirable in producing copper reds. These may be an over-all red or a red streaked with greens and blues, depending largely upon the firing procedure. In the open-chamber kiln, carbon is introduced into the kiln atmosphere by the incomplete combustion of the fuel. A heavy reduction is, in most cases, accompanied by a temperature drop, which is the one reason for the off-and-on reduction sequence.

Reduction is accomplished by various methods depending upon the kiln construction. In a tight muffle kiln, moth balls or pine splinters are introduced through the peep hole, or some of the muffles are removed. In the average open downdraft kiln, a slight closing of the damper will cut down on the suction of air into the burners and cause a reduction. In the case of a forced-draft kiln, the air intake is partially closed. Such kilns often have auxiliary air sources besides the blower. Occasionally, plugging these vents will bring about reduction.

Whether a reduction is occurring is very simple to ascertain. The flames in the burner ports will be very sluggish and will partly spill out into the kiln room. A ventilation fan and ceiling outlet is a necessity as the air in the kiln room gets pretty foul. A sealed forced-draft burner will not allow observation of the flame. The most accurate test in either system is to remove the peep-

hole plugs with care, for in a heavy reduction the flames will shoot out for a foot or more. By observing this flame, one can make adjustments to the draft. Often a $\frac{1}{2}$ inch movement of the damper will make the difference between a reducing and an oxidizing fire. To determine whether one has a slight reduction or oxidization, place a pine splinter in the peep hole. If the wood chars with an outward flame, which does not begin until it is well past the opening, the kiln is reducing. This action signifies that there is a lack of oxygen in the kiln atmosphere. If the splinter burns and the flame is within the peep hole, the atmosphere is oxidizing.

Mention might be made now of the tendency, particularly among students, to overreduce when firing a kiln. It is true that the underreduced glazes are shiny and bland in color. But in many ways the overreduced kiln is even worse. Instead of a satin smooth surface with gently mottled colors, the overreduced glaze is rough to the touch, dirty in color, blistery, and encrusted with eruptions from the clay body beneath.

Pyrometric cones are used in all kilns to determine the exact heat reached. Cones are triangular pyramids $1\frac{3}{4}$ inches in height with a base of a $\frac{1}{2}$ inch. The cone is pressed into a pad of clay at a slight angle and placed in the kiln a few inches behind the peep hole in the door. Pyrometric cones are composed of materials similar to a glaze and are calculated to bend at a specific temperature (see table in Appendix).

Pyrometric pyrometers are also used to measure kiln temperature. Such instruments consist of a thermocouple, which is inserted into the kiln chamber, and an indicating gauge. The two dissimilar metals in the thermocouple unit give off minute amounts of electrical current when heated, thus activating the instrument needle. They are satisfactory for small electric kilns that are fired at a prescribed schedule. Adjustments may have to be made as the thermocouple ends become corroded. There is a tiny screw on the dial face to adjust the needle to the proper cone temperature. Care must be taken not to hit the thermocouple tips as they become very brittle after repeated firing.

The pyrometer is a very helpful device in determining the desired temperatures for reduction and in serving as a guide to the progress of the firing. Without this indicator, it is difficult to tell immediately how particular adjustments of air, fuel, and draft are affecting the heat rise. On the other hand, with the many variables involved in firing a large gas kiln, the pyrometric pyrometer is not an accurate guide in determining the final temperature. The reason being that glazes will mature at a lower temperature if the firing cycle is prolonged. This combination of time and temperature is commonly called *work heat*. The cone always records it correctly. But the difference between a fast and slow heat rise may result in a pyrometer being a ½ cone off as far as the actual maturity of the glaze is concerned. The usual practice is to use three cones, say 7, 8, and 9, if the firing is to go to cone 8. When cone 7 goes over, one is alerted and checks the cones in both top and bottom peep holes to see that firing is progressing uniformly. Usually, one area is a little hotter; in a properly designed kiln, one should be able to make minor adjustments to fuel and draft at the end of a firing cycle, ending up with a firing that has, at the most, a ½ cone variation.

The firing cycle is not completed by simply turning off the current or the gas. In an electric kiln, the heat tends to rise. A more even fire will evolve if the top elements are cut back to a medium heat when the cone goes over. This allows the bottom section to pick up a little more heat. Fifteen minutes to a half an hour should be sufficient.

A gas kiln may tend to fire hotter at either the top or the bottom. Adjustments to the bag wall, the opening into the chimney, and the burner ports should enable one to obtain a fairly uniform heat. By cutting down on both draft and fuel at the end of the firing cycle a so-called soaking heat is developed that does not create a rise in temperature but tends to equalize hot and cold spots. This is especially important in a reduction fire that causes a disturbed condition in the glaze. Unless fired in an oxidation atmosphere for the last 100 degrees and then soaked at a slightly lower temperature for at least an hour, such glazes will likely have a rough surface with numerous gas blisters.

KILN MATERIALS

Due to the widespread industrial uses for refractories, one can purchase most materials needed for kiln building in any sizable city. If not available locally, a building-material dealer can order the items without difficulty.

Common red building bricks, the softer the better, can be used as inexpensive back-up material for a large kiln. *Refractory firebricks*, which will safely withstand high temperatures, must be used for the inner lining. These are available for operating temperatures of 1600°, 2000°, 2600°, and 2800°F (870°, 1093°, 1260°, 1427°, and 1538°C) and some as high as 3000° and 3200°F (1649° and 1742°C). As the indicated temperature of operation increases, the bricks become denser and heavier and lose some of their insulating ability. They also become more expensive and the highest-temperature brick will cost at least double those in the lowest range. Nevertheless, for continued service, it is advisable to choose an inner lining brick capable of withstanding temperatures 300°F (150°C) higher than the hottest glaze fire anticipated.

If possible, one should shop around a bit as the material for a large kiln comes to quite a sum. Prices are somewhat standard in the industry, but local mark-up and shipping charges will vary a great deal. Thus far I have used bricks from four companies for kiln construction. None were unsatisfactory for the job, although I found differences between brands in the expansion rates between the inner and outer brick courses. While all are qualified to be termed *firebrick*, there are several rather dissimilar compositions made for special purposes. Some are high in alumina or silica, and others use zirconium, silicon carbide, and so on. The bricks used in our ceramic kilns are the most common type, an alumina-silica combination. Most firebricks come in two very different types. The oldest, and still valuable industrially, is a *hard refractory brick* used as a lining where fumes, corrosion, and abrasion occur such as in a steel or glass furnace. A later development in refractories is the *insulating firebrick*, which is light in weight, porous, and has a much greater insulating value than the hard firebrick. For fireboxes, in a wood or an oil burner, the hard brick is preferred. The smaller type kilns, using a clean fuel and not subjected to a great weight of material, might more economically use the insulating firebrick throughout. It should also be noted that the hard firebrick must be cut with a diamond tipped saw whereas the insulating type may be easily cut with a hack saw blade.

The standard sized bricks, called common straights, are 9 by $4\frac{1}{2}$ by $2\frac{1}{2}$ inches. Industrial furnaces subjected to continuous operation are generally constructed of a hard inner firebrick lining, followed by a course or two of insulating firebrick, and sheathed with a final layer of building brick. Beside the common straight brick, angled brick for arches and special shapes for burner ports are commonly available in the hard firebrick.

Castable refractories of high-temperature tolerance are also available. These come in a dry granular state and are mixed and cast much like concrete. They shrink very slightly after being fired. A convenient use for this material is in fireboxes, burner ports, and for kiln arches that may be cast in one piece. Although the weight is downward, it is most advisable to strap the kiln. Constant heating and cooling is apt to cause cracks and a resulting sideward pressure. The insulating properties of the castable refractory is somewhere between that of the hard and insulating firebrick. It is compounded in both high silica and high alumina mixtures.

Other materials of lower-heat tolerance but of high insulating value have occasional use. Electric kilns constructed within a steel frame frequently have transite (a cement-asbestos rigid panel) as both support and additional insulation. Vermiculite, an expanded granular mineral with good insulating qualities, is often used to cover the kiln arch to a depth of 5 to 6 inches. It also comes in a brick form for use as a low-temperature back-up material. Asbestos is also a valuable insulating material but only for back-up purposes. It is available in either a sheet or block form.

Transite is of especial value to the potter since it is also made in a series of tubular shapes of varying lengths and diameters and comes $\frac{1}{4}$ to $\frac{1}{2}$ inch in thickness. If placed in a free airspace, a transite pipe will function adequately as a kiln chimney. But do not ask a lumber dealer for a chimney pipe of transite, for its major use is for sewer and drainage pipes.

Kiln shelves are commonly made of a silicon-carbide composition if intended for use at stoneware temperatures. This material absorbs heat readily but is very tough and resistant to sagging even when heavily loaded. Sillmanite is recommended for earthenware temperatures, as it tends to deform at higher temperature. The same is true of any shelves of stagger or fireclays.

Stilts are commonly made of fireclay. They are usually extruded with a hollow center, which allows for frequent heating and coating without undue expansion stresses. A very good high alumina triangular hollow stilt is made by Alpine, Inc. Satisfactory stilts can also be made from sections of a 2800°F (1538°C) insulation brick. The tendency of all fireclay stilts to cling to a shelf may be lessened by dipping the ends in aluminum paint.

KILN CONSTRUCTION

The unknown and untried experiences in life are its greatest mysteries. Strangely, for many potters, kiln construction is in this category.

The requirements of a kiln are basically very simple: Either an insulated chamber in which heat develops (an electric kiln), or a chamber through which heat passes, gradually raising the temperature inside (a gas kiln).

The Electric Kiln

Needing no chimney or gas lines, the electric kiln is the more simple to construct. Unless one is very technically minded and able to calculate the resistance and ohms of the wire needed, it is advisable to purchase elements that are already measured, cut, and coiled, and otherwise ready to be inserted into a kiln of a prescribed size.

Although insulating bricks larger than the standard straight (9 by $4\frac{1}{2}$ by $2\frac{1}{2}$ inches) are made, they are not commonly available in the small amounts needed for kiln construction. Insulating straights are packed twenty-five to the box. It is wise to make certain that the carton is not damaged as the bricks are easily broken. A brick laid flat giving $4\frac{1}{2}$ inches of insulation is sufficient for the small electric kiln. Since the element channels get much hotter than the kiln interior, the brick operating temperature must be higher. A brick suitable for temperatures up to 2300°F is used only to 2000°F. For stoneware temperatures to 2300°F, bricks suitable at 2600° or 2800°F are used. For temperatures to 2000°F, any brand of insulating brick can be used. However, for the higher temperatures, care must be used not to get a firebrick that has any flecks of iron impurities as they will melt out in the high heat of the element slot and cause the elements to burn up. It only makes sense to figure on a size

that eliminates cutting and extra joints. A popular size is the 18- by 18-inch square (inside), which uses exactly three bricks on a side.

After determining kiln size, an angle iron frame should be welded to furnish support. The corner angles should elevate the kiln 5 or 6 inches off the floor. Two extra angles should brace the floor to support floor bricks. Floor and side panels of transite (cement-asbestos) should be a trifle small to allow for heat expansion.

Normally elements are made in coiled lengths that go two complete turns around the kiln, starting from the center of one side. An angle slot is cut across the brick at this point so the element wire can pass to the next channel. Occasionally, the elements (nichel-nichrome) will come coiled like a door spring. Rather than a hit-and-miss stretching in the kiln, put five nails in a piece of plywood corresponding to the size of the recesses in the kiln chamber. In this manner, the wire can be evenly stretched and will fit properly into the corners. The coils must not touch each other or hot spots will develop. Nichel-nichrome tends to contract on successive firings but can be carefully stretched and put back in place. The high-fire Kanthal element usually comes already stretched and formed, as it is a hard and very resistant wire. The Kanthal-wired kiln should be fired several times up to 2300°F when new, even though it is normally fired lower. At this heat, the elements will sink into their channels and become quite rigid. If Kanthal wire is not fired over 2000°F, it too will contract and pull away from the channels.

Being hard and brittle, it cannot easily be replaced without breaking.

The simple way to install the elements is to cut a section out of the upper brick that is the size of the diameter of the element and then to groove a hollow with a round rasp in the brick below. A slot should be cut and a matching hole drilled in the transite to connect the element to the control panel as each course of brick goes up. Due to its action on the elements, no cement is used. If the frame is made correctly, the bricks should fit tightly. Long finishing nails can be driven through the outer edge of the bricks to prevent shifting.

Prior to the erection of the side walls, a transite panel must be mounted on the outside wall. This should have brass nuts and bolts to serve as connections for the ends of each element. A ventilated and insulated cover with control switches covers this panel. In an 18- by 18- by 18-inch kiln, one usually has four sets of elements controlled by two switches. The low, medium, and high heats are obtained by hooking up the elements on 110 volts, 220 volts in series, or 220 volts in parallel. Unless one has electrical wiring experience, it is most advisable to obtain the help of an electrician. The electric kiln requires a separate fuse and switch box and a number 10, three wire, 220 volt direct line from the entrance box.

The cover may fit flat on top of the kiln walls or be recessed. A simple cover construction is to stagger the bricks on edge. A heavy strap or angle iron is placed on each side, extending 2 inches past the cover. It is bored to take long $\frac{1}{4}$ inch threaded rods, two of which pass through each brick. An angle welded on the rear corner is bolted to the strap overhang forming the cover hinge. A similar rod in the front overhang, inserted into a pipe, serves as a cover handle.

The Gas Kiln

Due to the uniformity of the insulating brick size, it is possible to build a satisfactory small kiln without using any cement. This is especially desirable if one wishes to try a small experimental design because it can be readily changed. Likewise, a flat roof similar to that of the electric kiln can be used. A small kiln firing to 2000°F would need only a single width of 2300°F brick. A simple design (see Chapter 9, Figure 6) with only a single bag wall and using one or two atmospheric burners might be a suitable design for a small kiln of about four cubic feet.

For larger kilns, a heavier wall is necessary for both its greater insulating value and stability. For kilns up to about sixteen cubic feet, a satisfactory insulation consists of an inner lining of 2600° or 2800°F brick on edge, backed up by a 2000°F brick laid on the flat, giving a total wall of 7 inches. Such a kiln can be consistently fired to cone 8 and 9. If cone 12 temperatures are desired, two bricks on the flat, giving 9 inches of insulation, would be more satisfactory. Since the walls may be 3 or 4 feet in height, a high refractory cement should be used. This can be purchased in a dry or wet form. Basically, it is a mixture of fireclay, a flux such as sodium silicate (a liquid, water glass). The wet type sets up a stronger unfired bond that may make construction easier.

It is essential to have a strong base if the kiln is of a moderate size, as the weight of materials will run 3000 to 5000 pounds. In view of the weight of the clay and the other materials, the studio ought to have a concrete floor with perhaps a separate reinforced section under the kiln. It is most inconvenient to bend or stoop to load a kiln. Unless the kiln is of a walk-in size, it is advisable to have a reinforced concrete slab raised off the floor with concrete blocks to the proper height. This also allows one to move the kiln without dismantling. Many kiln designs call for exhaust channels in the floor. Inexpensive common bricks may be used to fill in those floor sections that exceed the necessary insulation thickness.

The refractory cement used in kiln construction is applied in as thin a coating as possible. As the bricks are very uniform, the cement is not used as a leveling device but only as a binding agent. Since they are so porous, the insulating bricks are first soaked in water, drained, and then the necessary surfaces are dipped into a liquid solution of the refractory kiln cement. As quickly as the bricks are in place they are tapped to remove any extra cement. A wooden block is used under the hammer head to prevent crushing the soft brick.

It is inevitable that as a double-layered wall heats up, an uneven expansion will take place and eventually some cracks will occur. This must be expected. Due to the heat, a greater expansion occurs in the inner layer. To equalize this tendency, it is desirable not to use the extremely soft brick that has less expansion on the outer layer. Insulating bricks vary in their physical characteristics, and if possible they should be tested for shrinkage.

Larger kilns may use a common soft building brick as an additional back-up layer. Its insulating value is much lower than that of an insulating firebrick, but it contributes structural strength to the wall. Before the development of insulating firebrick, all kilns were constructed of the hard, nonporous firebrick. It withstands the heat well but also conducts it readily. Large industrial kilns commonly have a hard fireclay lining, backed up by insulating fireclay brick, and with a facing of common brick. As we have switched from impure fuels such as fuel oil and early types of manufactured gas to natural gas and propane, there is less necessity for the studio potter to have a heavy corrosion-resistant kiln lining, which is a relatively poor insulator and is impossible to cut without special equipment.

For the 12- to 16-cubic foot kiln used by most studio potters, a brick-up door is quite satisfactory and eliminates the heavy steel frame needed for a swing door. As the inner brick surface expands and the pressure develops in the kiln atmosphere, the upper bricks in a tall build-up door are forced outward; one should not be alarmed. Sheet-metal strips curved to spring under the tie rod will hold the upper door bricks in place. A paste of asbestos fiber is the best means of sealing up expansion cracks that always occur around a kiln door, regardless of its construction. For the larger kiln, a weighted door that will slide up in a track is a great convenience. To retard abrasion, the facing bricks on the door edge ought to be of a harder texture than the usual soft outside brick. Perhaps the inner lining brick will be needed. This also holds true for the bricks around the burner ports that get greater wear.

The kiln roof arch need be no problem. Usually three or more wide, 1-inch boards are cut to the curve of the arch. About a one-and-one-half-inch rise to a foot of width is adequate. The curved forms are easily covered with masonite and supported by uprights from the kiln floor. A little slack should be allowed, and wedges should be placed under the uprights to facilitate removal. Hard firebrick may be purchased in a variety of wedge shapes. Insulating firebrick presents no problem as it can easily be rasped to the proper angle. Use a wood block as a cutting guide. Take a small cut at first and put all the bricks in place before starting to cement. Before removing the form, angle irons must be placed upright on each corner with connecting tie rods. Although they do stiffen the structure, their major role is to support the two channel irons inserted under the corner angles to take the thrust of the roof arch. A castable arch is normally self-supporting.

But a strapping is still advisable as expansion cracks usually occur that weaken the structure and may cause it to collapse. It is customary to bring the outer wall brick up to a point higher than the arch crown. Above the arch, inexpansive common brick may be used. The hollow thus formed is filled with 6 inches of loose vermiculite insulation that further insulates the roof area. Certain small irregularities, due to construction, will occur in the under surface of the roof arch. Do not attempt to plaster over the surface with the cement as it will sooner or later pull away from the brick and fall down, possibly damaging a vessel. Use the refractory cement only on the joined surfaces of the firebrick. After a preliminary firing or two, brush off the surface of the kiln interior and spray or brush on a couple of coats of aluminum paint. This will greatly retard the exfoliation of brick particles that often spoil glazed pieces on the top shelf.

Salt Kilns

Salt kilns have become popular in recent years among studio potters. This is a single fire operation; since it does not obscure a sharp textural surface to the same extent as an applied glaze, the salt glaze has an especial value for the sculptural orientated potter. The traditional approach has been to use a kiln with a high silica inner lining. The reaction between the sodium and the silica in the clay body forms the sodium silicate glaze on the surface of the fired piece. It also glazes the entire interior surface of the kiln and renders it unsuitable for normal glaze firings.

It is possible to have a rising oxidization until shortly before the glaze temperature is reached as there are no glaze fluxes to seal off the body. A 2-hour reduction at this point will bring the body color to the surface at which time the salting will begin. Most stoneware bodies contain sufficient silica for salt glazing without additions of other materials. Decorating slips, using kaolin as a base, may need additional silica to form the glaze. The salt used is the common coarse rock salt, such as is used on icy highways. It is soaked in water before using. Salt alone can be used at the higher stoneware temperatures down to about cone 5. Below this cone, borax must be mixed with the salt. The color and surface quality vary greatly with the clay and salting technique and the loading distances used. In general, the salt-glazed pieces are consistently more satisfactory at cone 6 or above.

The salt may be introduced into the kiln through a port in the center of the roof arch, through the burner ports, or through similar openings in the fire chamber. The kiln design must be of a downdraft type for successful salt glazing. The most satisfactory introduction method will depend upon kiln proportions and the type of load. A stoneware cone should be placed under the roof opening to scatter the salt for the top-salting method. Small paper cups (such as are used for relish in restaurants) held in a wire loop are easy to insert through the burner ports. The studio

must be extremely well ventilated at this point, as the very poisonous chlorine gas is formed and some will escape into the room atmosphere.

During the first few firings in a new kiln, an extra amount of salt as well as extra time must be used since the kiln walls absorb the salt as well as does the ware. The glaze results in these early firings are not always successful. Normally, about one half of a pound of salt is needed per cubic foot of interior space. The salt is weighed then soaked in water and divided into eight portions. The damper should be cut back at this time to allow the fumes to stay in the kiln as long as possible. A salting is made every fifteen minutes. A row of clay test rings should be placed behind the peep hole. Before the close of the firing cycle, one of these is hooked out on a wire. From successive draws, we can observe the buildup of glaze and determine whether more or less salt is needed. As with every type of glaze fire, it is desirable to have an oxidizing soaking heat of a half hour at a slightly lower temperature to finish off the firing cycle.

During the salting, silica in the body combines readily with the sodium vapors to form a sodium silicate. It particularly coats the burner port areas where most of this chemical change begins. Due to this strong fluxing action, the brick surfaces contract and in time literally melt away. There is also a problem with kiln furniture. Stilts and shelves may best be coated with aluminum paint but never with regular kiln wash. The glaze will stick on a silicon-carbide shelf coated with kiln wash whereas it may be scraped off an uncoated shelf.

Many potters have been disturbed at watching their kilns disintegrate before them even with the knowledge that the last few firings are reputed to be the best. A potter friend, Richard Leach, and no doubt others, have experimented with various linings that might be more resistant to the salt fumes. On the basis of these experiments, a 14-cubic foot (total interior) kiln was constructed using Kaocast (a high alumina castable refractory) as $2\frac{1}{2}$ inches of inner lining faced by 2000°F insulating brick in a $4\frac{1}{2}$-inch layer. Perhaps because the proportions were rather tall (intended for ceramic scupture), salting through a roof port was not as effective as through the burner ports. After approximately thirty firings, there was no indication of salt accumulation on the Kaocast lining, with the exception of the burner ports and the floor and lower 6 inches of the combustion area. This eroded area was chipped away and recast without difficulty. The low bag wall of Kaocast also needed replacement as did the upper bag wall of insulating bricks plus the insulating bricks for the lower section of the kiln door. However, this is a nominal repair in comparison with the traditional salt kiln. A normal glaze firing at cone 6 was possible due to the small amount of absorbed glaze. This, of course, might not be true at a higher fire, although it would doubtless be possible for the first fifteen to twenty firings.

The construction of this kiln was very easy. The floor of Kaocast was poured in one piece over a layer of insulating brick. As the 2000°F sidewall bricks were erected, a waxed 8-inch form was placed inside and a $2\frac{1}{2}$-inch width casting made each day until the desired height was reached. The 4-inch thick arched roof was cast in one piece. The particular Kaocast used had a maximum temperature tolerance of 3000°F. During drying and repeated firings, the Kaocast lining had a shrinkage of about one-quarter of an inch in 3 feet. It dries and fires to a hard concrete-like material. Although very heat resistant, its insulating value is less than insulating brick. All kilns should have a slow and uniform temperature rise and fall. This is especially true of a kiln with a cast lining as in the kiln just described. Perhaps the greatest damage to kilns generally is not through long and continued use but rather careless firing and abrupt cooling.

CHAPTER 10

MASS PRODUCTION METHODS

INTRODUCTION

Were a contemporary hand potter suddenly to be transported into a Greek or Chinese studio of even two thousand years ago, he would not find the routine much different. Changes such as we find in either equipment or techniques are at the most slight modifications rather than new developments. On the other hand, both the twentieth- and the first-century potter would find the modern commercial pottery a little confusing at first glance.

The development of mechanization in ceramics is roughly two hundred years old. However, as early as the Etruscan period (fifth to sixth century B.C.), bisque molds had been used on a small scale for shaping one surface or sections of ceramic forms. Slip casting, in a limited fashion, was practiced in China as early as the T'ang dynasty (618 to 906 A.D.). By the early eighteenth century, slip casting in bisque molds was becoming a fairly common method in European potteries. The usual technique was to carve the original from a solid block of soft alabaster. From this model, the clay molds were pressed and bisque fired. With such a design development, it is no wonder that the artifacts produced completely lost the characteristics that are unique to clay. More catastrophic was the invention of Plaster of Paris, around 1750, which made available an inexpensive and convenient material superior in several respects to the bisque mold. Duplicate forms in a variety of shapes could now be made accurately and quickly. This period also saw the first developments in steam power that, in time, was to revolutionize the processing of clay and glaze chemicals that until then had been performed tediously by hand.

The major gain of these technical changes was a lowering of prices on a wide range of ceramic products.

Stoneware coffee decanter with pulled handle. Olive green slip glaze at cone 8. Irwin Whitaker, U.S.A.

Unfortunately, the numerous small hand potteries were gradually forced out of business. The pottery workshop now became a factory and its owner not a potter but a businessman. Even before industrialization, many of the larger hand potteries were owned by outside interests. Many potters otherwise capable, failed through lack of business foresight and management skills.

The lamentable fact about the demise of the small hand pottery is that the responsibility for design passed from the potter to one whose primary goal was financial gain. The widespread use of plaster for molds and even original models meant an abrupt change in the age-old traditions of the craft. Instead of evolving from the qualities of the clay, the plaster models more often copied forms originally in metal, glass, and even leather and basket fiber. The introduction of ceramic decals made from copper engravings, although technically quite an achievement, represented the final straw. Now we could have a ceramic teapot, copied from a silver pattern, decorated with a decal whose design was pirated from woven tapestry. The truly sad part is that a good design, in a mass production industry, need cost no more than one in poor taste. The mechanization of the pottery, admittedly crude in the beginning, occurred first in England and then spread throughout the continent. Due to close trade conditions with England, American potters of the colonial era were hardly established before being inundated by a flood of these tasteless imports. As factories were established in the United States, they tended to copy the foreign imports in style since for years these had an uncritical public acceptance and were considered to be superior to the local products.

Our present day factories, with their testing laboratories, have bodies and glazes compounded from local materials that are the technical equal of the import. Manufacturing methods are not too different from one country to another as inventions spread rapidly. With a few exceptions, however, our ceramic industry has continued to copy designs from the foreign import. This situation is not unique to the ceramic industry. The copying of Danish furniture and French and Italian clothing are typical examples in other fields of present-day business tactics.

American dinnerware factories are now experiencing severe competition from abroad, especially from England, Germany, and Japan. These countries have traditionally had strong ceramic industries, many of which were extensively modernized after the war. They produce efficiently a wide variety of ceramic wares. While we have spoken of the mechanization of ceramics, a point must be made to the effect that there are still numerous operations that must be performed by hand. Because of the labor involved and the differences in wages, it is not possible to compete in price—except by excessively high tariffs. However, many of the imports are in the higher price category, which would indicate that, as in Colonial days, our problem is still one of public taste and of the necessity to encourage a quality of ceramic design equal to the technical achievement of American industry in this and in other fields.

It is quite obvious throughout the text that I do not feel that the design of our production ceramics is adequate. But in fairness, I must state that there are other factors involved, beside those mentioned, before a product is available in your local store. If, for example, the factory sales manager, the wholesale buyer, the salesman on the road, or the store buyer does not like the piece, it will never get on the store shelf. Finally, the salesgirl may not like it and will not show it to a customer in other than a depreciating manner.

Were it not that there are many shops abroad, and a few in America with consistently well-designed contemporary merchandise, I would feel that I was dreaming of a shopper's utopia. Public taste may not be very good, but under the present circumstances it often has little chance to a choice. There is a tendency today to shrug off all our problems as being one of formal education. This is a convenient sort of wishful thinking. For most people, taste is formed in the home, factory, or shop environment. In a materialistic society such as ours, business management must take a greater responsibility for our cultural growth; no other segment of our community has the resources or possess such persuasive authority to encourage a public awareness of values that transcend those of price and utility.

SLIP-CASTING TECHNIQUES

Slip casting is a method of making ceramics in which liquid clay is poured into a hollow absorbent mold. After a few short minutes, a film of clay appears on the inner surface of the mold. As water is absorbed, the clay layer becomes denser. When the desired thickness develops, the mold is upended and the center portion, which is still liquid, is poured out. This clay coating continues to harden and eventually shrinks away from the mold. Simple cup forms can be made in a single piece mold. Undercut and more complicated shapes require two, three, or occasionally more pieces in the mold, such as the teapot illustrated.

These multiple sections are keyed together with ball-and-socket projec-

Filling molds with the liquid clay slip. (Courtesy of Syracuse China)

tions and are held together during pouring with heavy rubber bands, such as one might cut from an automobile inner tube. As the water soaks into the plaster mold, the level of slip in the cavity falls and a small amount must be added. In forming the original model, a collar is formed on the top a few inches in depth to serve both as funnel for the slip and as a clay reservoir. The angle of the collar serves as a guide in trimming the top edge of the formed piece. This is done with a fettling knife when the cast piece has become firm. At this stage, the mold sections are carefully removed and the casting seams on the piece are scraped off and sponged to achieve a smooth surface.

Due to technical problems related to uneven shrinkage and air pockets, some pieces may be cast in sections and luted together later with slip. This is particularly true of small handles. Depending upon the character of the clay, this may be done either at a leather-hard or dry stage.

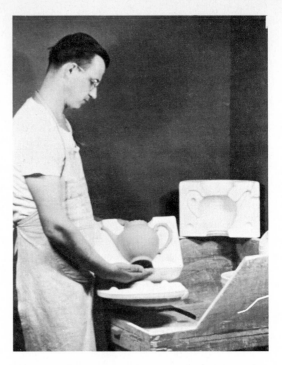

Removing slip-cast creamer from three-piece mold. (Courtesy of Syracuse China)

This is quite different from the more plastic throwing clay bodies, sections of which should be joined as soon as one is able to handle the pieces without distortion.

Cup handles are joined to the cup with slip. (Courtesy of Syracuse China)

Cup handles are cast 12 to a mold and removed and separated when leather hard. (Courtesy of Syracuse China)

MASS PRODUCTION METHODS

CASTING SLIPS

Unlike a clay used in throwing, a clay body for jiggering and casting need not be very plastic. In fact, the plastic clays are often avoided since their greater water absorption means more shrinkage, which is usually accompanied by warping. Various types of binders are used to impart a greater green and dry strength to the ware. This more than compensates for the substitution of less plastic ingredients.

Of critical importance in a casting slip is the use of *deflocculants* such as sodium silicate and soda ash. The use of about one percent of these chemicals to the dry weight of the clay will greatly reduce the amount of water needed to make a fluid slip. It also retards the settling of the heavier slip particles. Georgia kaolin, which has a uniform particle size, is the major kaolin used in casting slips. One negative feature of the slip body is that the bland smoothness is relatively uninteresting when compared to the color and texture of a throwing clay. Some typical casting slips for various temperatures are:

Talc body
(cones 06–05)

Plastic vitrox	165
Ball clay	350
Talc	490

Parian body
(cones 3–4)

Feldspar	600
Kaolin	300
Ball clay	100

Poreclain body
(cones 8–9)

Flint	200
Feldspar	375
Kaolin	300
Ball clay	150

A common name for sodium silicate is water glass. It is a liquid formed by melting soda ash and silica sand. The term is a general one since the proportion of sodium to silica may vary greatly. "N" brand solution is the trade name given to the type commonly used as a deflocculant in ceramics. Soda ash (sodium carbonate), either alone or in combination with sodium silicate, is a more effective deflocculant than sodium silicate in casting slips having organic matter such as found in ball clay. Slip should not be stored for long periods, especially in warm weather, as fermentation occurs that may cause pin holes in the cast ware.

A standard practice is to use about three parts "N" brand sodium silicate by weight to one part soda ash. The proportions will depend upon the body formula. If it includes a large amount of clay, perhaps a one to one mixture of soda ash and "N" silicate solution would be more satisfactory. After weighing, the soda ash should be dissolved in hot water and then both deflocculants added to the water. As a starter, a good idea is to take 100 pounds of slip body and slowly add it to a large crock containing 50 pounds of water (8.3 pounds to a gallon), which is about six gallons. More or less of the slip body might be needed, depending upon the ingredients and the deflocculant action. The resulting slip should have a thick creamy consistency. A blunger is desirable to mix the ingredients, although a large wire whisk may be used for test batches. Slip should always be screened before using, as any lumpy particles will settle and give a poor casting. Care must be taken in screening and filling the mold so as not to trap air bubbles in the slip.

It is desirable not to use over 1 percent deflocculant in relation to the dry ingredients weight. Even less if possible, as an excess will slowly seal up the pores of the plaster mold with an insoluble film of calcium silicate, making it difficult to remove the casting and eventually spoiling the mold completely. Soda ash is more troublesome in this regard than the

A large blunger for thoroughly mixing the body ingredients with water. (Courtesy of Syracuse China)

silicate. Drying out the molds from the outside will help to prevent this accumulation on the inner mold surface.

JIGGERING METHODS

It is impractical to throw flat shapes of any size on the potter's wheel as every novice potter soon learns. Countless generations of potters have used bisque molds to shape one surface of flat dishes and to support the soft clay while drying. With the use of plaster molds, the forming process is quite rapid and accurate. The plaster surface reproduces a smoother surface than is possible with a bisque mold.

The composition and requirements of the clay used for jiggering is different from the throwing clay used by the hand potter. Since the ware is supported by the mold during the initial drying period, it need not be

as plastic. In fact, as the plastic clay shrinks more in drying with the increased likelihood of warpage, it is used in limited amounts. To make up for this loss in green and dry strength, various binders are used such as lignin extract and methocel.

The body ingredients are weighed and mixed in a blunger as in the preparation of a casting slip. This liquid is screened and pumped into a filter press, which is an accordianlike machine of metal and canvas that squeezes the excess water from the slip leaving the plastic clay. This clay comes from the filter press in slabs about one to one and a half inches in thickness and 16 to 24 inches

MASS PRODUCTION METHODS

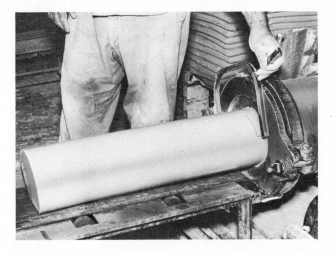

A section of plastic clay is cut off after extrusion from the pug mill. (Courtesy of Syracuse China)

square. These slabs are then placed in the hopper of a pug mill, which is much like a meat grinder in operation. At one end is a vacuum attachment, which, combined with the compressing action of the screw blades, removes even the smallest air pockets from the clay. This feature not only eliminates possible body defects but also renders the clay more plastic. This factor is of importance although not as essential as in throwing clay.

The jigger operation trims off the bottom profile of a dinner plate. (Courtesy of Syracuse China)

The clay may be extruded from the pug mill in a variety of diameters depending upon its use. The size used for the plate shown in the jigger machine would be 6 to 8 inches. A slice about one inch in thickness is cut off the pugged clay with a wire and placed over a square of canvas on the bench. This clay slice is then hit with a mallet-like weight that compresses it into a slab of about one-half inch in thickness. This clay bat is in turn slapped down over a plaster plate mold resting on the jigger head. The next step is to force out any air remaining between the clay and the plaster mold. This is usually done with the moistened hand as the jigger head slowly revolves. The next operation brings the steel template down toward the mold, further compressing the clay and cutting away the excess to form the bottom contours of the plate and the foot rim. The mold bat and plate are then placed on a conveyor belt that carries them through a dryer. In the final operation, the plate is removed from the mold and the seam where the template and mold meet is trimmed away.

Jiggering Methods

A rough cup shape is thrown on the potters wheel and later expanded in mold by the action of the jigger template. (Courtesy of Syracuse China)

It is difficult to obtain a perfectly uniform thickness in slip casting. Heavy cups with attached handles are often slip cast. But the thinner porcelain cups are jigged since even the slightest variation would be noticeable. The procedure in jiggering cups and bowl shapes is slightly different since the mold is now a hollow form and the template is shaped to the inside surface of the piece. One method of jiggering cups is to throw a wad of clay into the mold and allow the template to force the clay down and outward to form the walls of the cup. Another method consists of throwing a rough cup form on a potter's wheel. This is then placed into the mold and jiggered as in the other procedure. The particular method used would depend largely upon the characteristics of the clay body and to some extent upon the shape desired.

PRESS FORMING

Certain forms can be duplicated very economically by the use of molds in hydraulic presses. Most of our electrical insulators are made in such a fashion, using a nearly dry body with wax as a forming lubricant. The process illustrated is more adaptable to pottery production, provided the shapes are simple and without undercuts. Male and female dies are used that shape the form and, under great pressure, squeeze out the excess clay. An unusual feature is that the hard but porous gypsum plaster die has a tubular grid embedded in the plaster. Compressed air flowing from these

MASS PRODUCTION METHODS

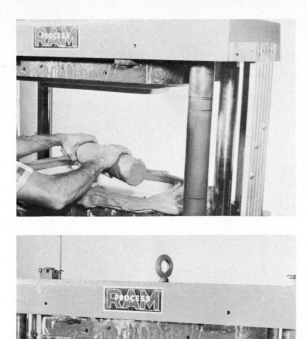

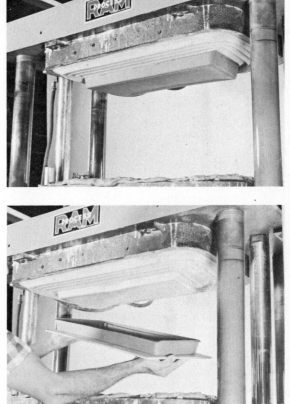

(Pressing photos courtsey of Ram Incorporated)

tubes into the die allow the clay form to be released immediately after forming. The illustrations show a wad of stiff but plastic clay being placed into the die. The pressing operation is very rapid. Compressed air released into the lower die breaks the clay suction and the press rises. The operator removes the newly formed tray on a supporting panel after the compressed air releases it from the upper die.

PRODUCTION KILNS

The term *commercial production* covers a wide range of activities from the manufacture of huge tonnages of building bricks to the forming of minute electrical insulators. Special kilns were developed to fire this ever-increasing volume. The solution was not to build a larger version of the small pottery kiln (see Chapter 9 on kilns) since a larger kiln was difficult to fire uniformly and had a long-time cycle of firing, cooling, and loading. Instead, part of the kiln was made movable, as the car kiln. The car kiln is easy to load and unload and does not lose as much heat in the process. By placing a door at each end of the kiln, the loading cycle was speeded

An envelope kiln about to be rolled over a load of freshly glazed pottery. (Courtesy of the West Coast Kiln Company)

up even further and is called a shuttle kiln.

As lightweight, high-temperature refractories became common, an envelope type of kiln was developed. In this design, two permanent kiln beds are built; the kiln moves back and forth over them. Its advantages are the use of a smaller floor area and use of lighter kiln furniture, since there is not even the vibration of a moving kiln car. These kilns are made in a variety of sizes, but they are primarily intended for small-sized pottery or special-order production. The huge production of our

larger potteries would not be possible without the tunnel kiln, which has continuous operation with no stoppage for cooling or loading.

In the adjacent photo, we see a loaded car kiln entering the tunnel. The chamber is approximately five by nine feet and two hundred feet in length. The cars, fitted tightly together, move through the kiln at a slow but constant speed, taking 70 to 90 hours to warm up, fire, and cool. The entering temperature is 300°F, which gradually increases to 2300°F in the center section and then tapers off as the cars move away from the burners. As you can see, the kiln cars have a heavily insulated floor. A channel iron on the car side usually projects into a sand seal on the kiln wall, which protects the under carriage from a direct flow of heat. Hot air escaping toward the end sections are piped back to preheat the burner-port air. This factor, plus the continuous operation for months on end, makes for a most economical system.

As would be imagined, loading of this kiln is quite different from that of a small studio kiln. Due to a long firing cycle and a great number of duplicate shapes, a very tight load is

Car entering kiln with a load of cups stacked lip to lip. (Courtesy of Syracuse China)

possible. However, thin dinnerware pieces must be supported to prevent warpage. Cups are loaded in pairs, lip to lip, with a weak cement to prevent accidental slippage. Dry refractory clay is shot into openings between the stacked dinner plates for support. A coaster of high alumina content is placed under each piece to prevent their sticking to the shelves. It is common practice, in dinnerware manufacture, to fire the bisque to the maturity of the body while it is well supported.

Removing biscuit plates from kiln car. (Courtesy of Syracuse China)

After glazing, the ware is fired at a lower temperature with no shrinkage and less chance of warping. A potter can keep a small kiln relatively clean and need not worry about dust and brick particles in an open glaze fire. This is not true of large kilns firing continuously for long periods. To protect the ware in the glaze fire, it is loaded into box-like forms of fireclay called saggers. Illustrated is a sagger of cups after the glaze fire. A layer of bitstone (coarse silica sand), which does not adhere easily to the thin glaze on the foot rim, covers the sagger bottom. The high-fire porcelains are always fired on the foot rim in the individual sagger. The foot rims will be unglazed but smoothly polished. Chinaware, previously high fired, such as the sagger load of saucers illustrated, are completely glazed. They rest on dowels of porcelain that are inserted in the sagger wall as the pieces are loaded. This porcelain spur will cause a tiny blemish in the glaze but it does provide a great economy in loading and firing. The kiln car illustrated shows the loading of saggers containing glazed cups and dinner plates.

(Courtesy of Syracuse China)

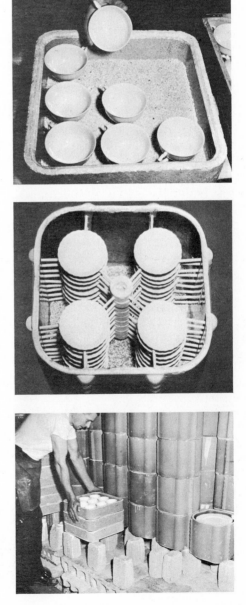

DESIGNING FOR PRODUCTION

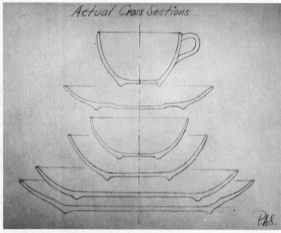

Actual Cross Sections

P.A.S.

(Design models courtesy of Peter A. Slusaishi)

It is evident from the processes of casting, jiggering, and pressing illustrated earlier in this chapter that there are limitations as to the form of the production item. Undercuts of even the slightest degree must be avoided in jiggered or pressed ware. Although reverse shapes can be slip cast, the process calls for multiple piece molds at considerable extra expense.

The designer usually works up a variety of designs and then gradually eliminates those that are obviously nonfunctional, too commonplace, or too difficult to reproduce. Since the cup is the most used item in a dinner set, it is often the starting point. When its shape has been roughly determined, other pieces are designed relating to it. It is essential that the designer have a feeling for a clay form and knowledge of how it may deform in firing. Heavy dinnerware is not very popular. Therefore, the foot rim and wall thickness must be only of a dimension necessary to support the form. Due to the firing shrinkage, all sketches are oversized.

After the cross sections are determined, a plaster model is made. A metal template made from the profile drawing is placed on the turning rig. Plaster is poured around the pin in small amounts until the form is completed. A circular movement of the template trims off the excess and develops a solid plaster model.

Additional refinements to the model may be made with cutting tools while it is still on the wheel head, as illustrated. After the plaster cup model is complete, it is coated with a plaster separator. A retaining collar is put in place and fresh plaster is poured over the cup model to form the original jigger mold. The illustration shows the trimming of the mold to fit the wheel head of the jigger machine. It is necessary to have a mold for each cup to be made in the day's production, which may run in the thousands. The adjoining photo shows the top and bottom sections of the case mold used to make the jigger block mold. The ball and socket projections allow for an accurate positioning of the sections prior to pouring the block mold. The case molds are made of a harder and denser plaster mix than that used for the jigger cup mold, which must readily absorb water from the clay after it is jiggered.

In the case of jiggered ware, only one surface is shaped by the plaster form. The inner cup surface is formed by the jigger template. The first photo shows the steel template being checked for clearance. In the next photo we see a half section of the cup handle on a plaster or marble base. After the retaining walls are in place and the surface shaped, a layer of plaster is poured in forming one half of the mold. Keys are carved out of the fresh plaster, and the complete handle section is put in place. English crown soap is commonly used as a mold separator. If the plaster mold is dry, it must be moistened before soaping and casting otherwise the soap would be drawn into the dry cast causing the two sections to stick. After finishing the cast, it is a simple matter to carve pouring openings into the damp plaster. Before pouring a clay handle, however, the mold sections must be dry. For the pilot design project, a single handle mold is adequate; in production, a dozen handles are normally cast at a time.

Designing the plate and saucer is a somewhat different operation from designing the cup. In this case, the plaster mold is shaped to form the inside, or upper contour of the plate. The template is cut to form the bottom surface of the saucer, as illustrated. The process from the initial sketches to the completed place setting as shown is a lengthy one, and several years may elapse before actual marking can begin. The mold for slip casting is slightly different from that for jiggering, as it usually consists of three sections, as illustrated. However, simple tapered tumbler shapes may be cast in a single mold.

above Steel template being checked.

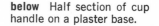

below Half section of cup handle on a plaster base.

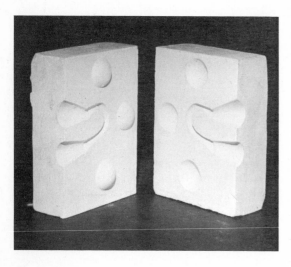

left Two halves of a plaster mold.

MASS PRODUCTION METHODS

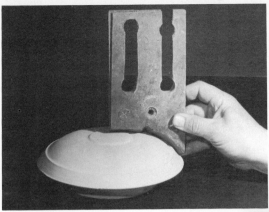

Template cut to form bottom surface of saucer.

The three sections of a plaster mold used in slip casting.

Completed place settings.

MIXING PLASTER

There is marketed a variety of plasters of varying hardnesses and setting rates, depending upon uses for model making, block molds, or case molds. Theoretically, 18.6 pounds of water will set up 100 pounds of plaster. In practice, at least 60 pounds of water will be needed to get the proper flow. The less water used, the stronger the cured plaster will be. Plaster normally sets in about twenty minutes but must be poured sooner. This time will depend upon the amount of mixing. The plaster must be sieved into the water to avoid large lumps until the water will absorb no more. The plaster is allowed to set three–four minutes to become thoroughly wetted. Small batches may be then mixed by hand and larger ones with a power mixer. After a few minutes of mixing, The plaster will begin to thicken. It must be poured now. Once it starts to set it is useless and must be discarded; not down the sink, for it will clog the drains.

Jerry Rothman decorating experimental tiles in Interpace Studio.

THE POTTER IN INDUSTRY

As indicated previously, industrialization has had drastic effects in several areas of pottery making. Research has developed more durable bodies, and mechanical methods have kept prices moderate. Against these positive factors there is the mediocre level of design that is evident throughout the industry. In time, competition and an improved public taste may effect a change. But the customer can only buy what is on the market.

Indicative of a possible new trend is the rather recent formation by two potteries, Bennington in Vermont and Interpace in California, of design staffs drawn from the ranks of creative, producing potters. This seems a most logical development and one that has proven successful in Scandinavia for many years. Shown in the illustrations are several potters at work at the Interpace Studios. Also included are examples of production ware as well as individual, one-of-a-kind pieces.

Flowing organic clay forms titled *Not in Central Park #3*. Unglazed, golden ocher color, 24 in. Jerry Rothman, U.S.A.

above Interpace designer, Harrison McIntosh, with one of the many decorative tiles developed in the studio.
left Stoneware bottles, carved and inlay decoration with grey-blue and beige mat glaze. Height 11½ and 7 in. Harrison McIntosh, U.S.A.

Franciscan dinnerware pattern. Ruppert Deese, Interpace Studios, U.S.A.

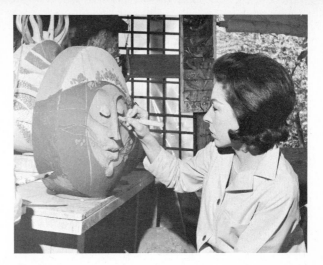

above Interpace designer, Francis Chun, with experimental dinnerware border pattern. **above, right** Interpace designer, Helen Watson at work at a one-of-a-kind decorative sculpture piece.

Ruppert Deese applying decoration to plaster form. Design will be transferred to the clay when bowl is jiggered, Interpace Studios, U.S.A.

right *Seated woman,* constructed largely from thrown forms. Pressed decorative details, cone 10, Dora De Larios, Interpace Studios, U.S.A. **below** Glazed, decorative building tile by Interpace, U.S.A.

11 # STUDIO EQUIPMENT_____

The purpose of this chapter is to illustrate a cross section of the equipment available on the market and with their current prices. The addresses of these manufacturers and many others are listed in the Appendix. In some cases, the items may have to be purchased through a local dealer. Inquire about discounts, as they are often available to schools.

CERAMIC KILNS

A thorough study of Chapter 9, which deals with kilns, is advisable to better acquaint the prospective buyer with the advantages as well as drawbacks of the various designs. The 3- to 5-cubic foot electric kiln, which generally suffices for the limited ceramic program of the secondary school, will be most inadequate for the college situation. And even the optimum college kiln capacity will depend largely upon the percentage of advanced and graduate students. It would be wise to plan for extra capacity, as there has been a steady increase in enrollment in ceramics courses. In the author's pres-

Candelabra of an involved, open, sculptural design tending toward a functional goal. Kenneth Green, U.S.A.

ent teaching situation, two 3-cubic foot electric kilns, an 8-cubic foot gas up-draft, a 10-cubic foot gas downdraft (salt), and a 12-cubic foot gas downdraft kiln are used for three classes of fifteen students each. All fire to cone 8, although the two electrics are usually used for bisque and cone .04 glazes. During the last month of each session, all of the kilns are in constant use.

The techniques of loading and firing are equally important for the student to learn as are those of forming and glazing. If there are a number of relatively small kilns, as in the author's case, these techniques can be taught. But the individual studio potter will find that firing a small kiln load is a time-consuming

left Paragon top-loading electric kiln for temperatures to cone 8; chamber 17 by 17 by 18 in. deep. Price FOB, Dallas, Texas, $287.50. center Unique front-loading electric kiln for temperatures for cone 8–10; chamber 17 by 17 by 17 in., weight 600 pounds. Price FOB Trenton, New Jersey, $415.00; stand $32.00 extra. right Mendell updraft gas kiln, capacity 8 cubic foot; chamber 23 by 23 by 26 in. high. Price FOB El Monte, California, with cone 6 lining, $975.00; cone 12, $1,175.00; crating extra.

above West Coast updraft open fire gas kiln, capacity 12 cubic foot; chamber 24 by 24 by 36 in., cone 10–12. Price FOB La Puente, California, $1,200.00; crating extra. above, right Alpine updraft gas kiln with forced air and automatic shut-off controls, capacity 16 cubic foot, cone 8–10. Price FOB Culver City, California, complete, $1,885.00; crating extra. right Denver Fire Clay updraft gas kiln with muffle, capacity 12 cubic foot, chamber 29 by 24 by 30 in. Price FOB Denver, Colorado, with cone 6 lining, $1,550.00; cone 12, $1,650.00; crating $30.00.

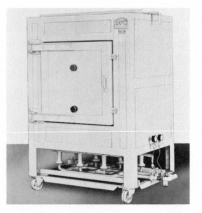

left Unique heavy-duty downdraft kiln, capacity 30 cubic foot, temperatures cone 8–12. Forced draft with automatic shut-off controls. Price approximately $4,800.00, depending upon location of construction. **right** Unique heavy-duty downdraft car kiln, capacity 30 cubic foot, temperatures cone 8–12. Forced draft with automatic shut-off controls. Price approximately $5,400.00 depending upon location of construction.

proposition. The author's personal studio kiln has an 18-cubic foot capacity. However, if I were to be potting on a full-time basis, a kiln with a 30- to 50-cubic foot capacity would be more practical. The sizes referred to are for the loading capacity and do not include the necessary combustion or muffle areas. In comparing kilns for purchase, this factor must be determined. Normally about two inches is left between the load and the kiln or bag wall for the flow of heat and combustion gases. A large ceramic department or a small workshop pottery might consider a car kiln. Although more expensive, they offer economy in loading and firing costs.

All gas kilns should be provided with a heat-sensing regulator on the burners and an automatic shut-off device for safety reasons. The more elaborate installations have auto-matic shut-off controls. With a forced draft, this is sufficient; if the kiln uses atmospheric burners, one must also be on hand to close the draft damper when the gas is turned off. In any case, I prefer to use cones and a final soaking period. Therefore, I

Denver Fire Clay shuttle-car kiln, capacity 20 cubic foot. Over-all length 24 feet, shipping weight 7,000 lbs. Updraft design, car area 24 by 60 by 25 in. Double door design makes possible the use of an additional car for faster operation. Price FOB Denver, Colorado, $3,400.00; crating $225.00.

Unique pyrometer with insulated leads and thermocouple. Price $32.50.

do not consider the automatic shut-off necessary. Several devices have been made that use a cone and a sliding spring mechanism to turn off the power in electric kilns. Due to the eventual corrosion of the metal parts, there is apt to be a problem of sticking and failure. While the thermocouple does not measure the work heat of the kiln and is therefore slightly inaccurate, it is most convenient in determining reduction temperatures as well as indicating the progress of the heat rise. Thermocouples may be inserted, if need be, through the peep hole. There is a great difference in the serviceability of the various market brands.

POTTER'S WHEELS

Although numerous wheels are illustrated here, there are many others on the market made equally as well and that operate as efficiently. None are made in large quantities, and, therefore, the price of a good wheel is relatively high. While an expert can get a passable result on any wheel, the beginner needs a good wheel in order to gain experience and skill. The bargain wheels one sees advertised so often in craft magazines are all but worthless.

Potters are usually conditioned by the wheel on which they first learn to throw and soon develop strong preferences. Personally, I prefer the simple kick wheel for beginning students. When in difficulty, they usually forget to kick and the wheel slows down at the proper time. Most kick wheels are easy to maintain and have the convenience of an integral seat and attached splash pan. The advanced students who are throwing large pieces and studio potters will prefer the variable-speed electric wheel. Many kick wheels are available with motor attachments, which represent a compromise solution.

Oak Hill traditional wheel, waterproof plywood. Flywheel 31 in. diameter, iron weights of 80 lbs. Aluminum wheel head 14 in. in diameter. Shipping weight 170 lbs. Price FOB Davenport, Iowa, $130.00.

Randall kick wheel, welded steel frame, 9-in. recessed aluminum wheel head, 19-in. aluminum splash pan and adjustable bucket seat. Flywheel 28 in. in diameter, standard weight 115 lbs., adjustable if desired. Shipping weight 200 lbs. Price FOB Alfred, New York, $235.00.

Soldner kick wheel, welded pipe frame and 80-lb. reinforced concrete fly wheel. Flat 14-in. aluminum wheel head, 15-in. snap-on splash pan available. Work table 20 by 38 in. Price FOB Aspen, Colorado, $150.00 unpainted; $175.00 painted.

Skutt variable speed bench type wheel, ⅓ H.P. motor with adjustable belts at 50–165 or 35–125 rpm. Wheel head 12 in. in diameter, also cast aluminum housing; weight 75 lbs. Price FOB Portland, Oregon, $230.00.

above Alpine heavy-duty wheel, ½ H.P. variable speed motor with foot control, 0–150 rpm. Price FOB Culver City, California, $325.00. **below** Denver Fire Clay bench type electric wheel, ¼ H.P. variable speed motor, 0–200 rpm. Aluminum wheel head 12 in. in diameter. Price FOB Denver, Colorado, $317.00; shipping weight 120 lbs.

They ought to be tested first in order that the single speed usually available is the one at which the purchaser generally works. In addition to the kick and power wheels shown, there is the treadle type of wheel. The treadle, activated by one foot, turns the wheel head and a light flywheel. A copy of the Leach wheel, which is of this type, is made by Denton Vars of St. Paul, Minnesota.

Randall heavy-duty power attachment for Randall kick wheel previously shown, ½ H.P. Price FOB Alfred, New York, $110.00.

CLAY MIXERS

The process of preparing a plastic clay suitable for throwing can be very laborious and time consuming. The standard public school practice of purchasing bagged moist clay at high prices is not economically feasible when one uses upwards of three tons of dry clay during the school year. Furthermore, some provision must be made to reclaim the many pounds of dry clay trimmings, discarded pots, and so on. The blunger and filter-press process seems unnecessarily involved for the small studio. Many schools have had considerable success using commercial bread-dough mixers. They are very expensive but are occasionally available second hand. Some models are huge, and the problem is to find a moderately sized unit.

Unfortunately, none of the commercial types of the pug mill are small enough for school or studio use. The small laboratory models, on the other hand, are too small to be of any value to the potter. The only exception is the Walker pug mill illustrated, which has been designed for the school and individual studio potter. It takes up relatively little studio space and in a few hours time can mix up a week's supply of plastic clay. Any mixture of moistened clay scraps, dry powdered clay, or water can be run through the mill. As ceramic programs have grown, the pug mill has become almost as necessary as the kiln and the potter's wheel.

Walker Jamar studio-sized stainless steel pug mill. Over-all length 5 ft. 10 in., operating width with tamper 3 ft. 3 in. Totally enclosed motor, ¾ H.P. with 150–1 reduction unit. Hopper size 16 by 20 in., height 36 in., discharge 20 in. off floor level, minimum capacity 300 lbs. plastic clay per hour. Shipping weight 475 lbs. Price FOB Duluth, Minnesota, $850.00; crating included.

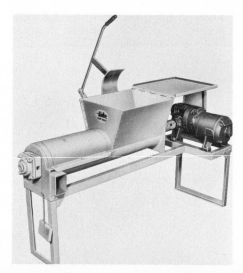

Craftools porcelain ball-mill jars; gallon, ½ gallon, and quart sizes at $34.00, $19.50, and $16.50 each.

GLAZE-ROOM EQUIPMENT

In recent years, the commercial ceramic chemicals have greatly improved in quality and fineness. This has relieved the potter of most of the glaze grinding formerly necessary. Often glazes may be mixed satisfactorily using only a wire whisp. Certain coarse materials, however, may still need to be ground by hand with a mortar and pestle or in a ball mill. A variety of brass screen sieves in mesh sizes of 80, 60, 30, 15, and 8 are desirable. The finer mesh is for glazes and the larger for grog.

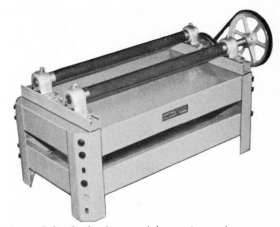

above, left Craftools porcelain mortar and pestle, 16 oz. and 32 oz. sizes at $5.25 and $7.70 each. **left** Craftools brass glaze sieves, 30–100 mesh from $9.80 to $10.90 each. **above** Craftools 20-in. ball mill complete with motor, size for two, one gallon jars, $58.50.

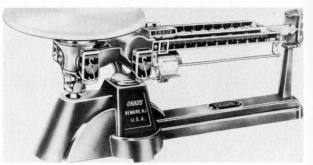

Craftools portable paint sprayer, also suitable for glazes. Complete with ¼ H.P. motor, gun, hose, and nozzles. Price $62.50.

Ohaus triple-beam gram scale; several models available from local dealers. Price for model illustrated $19.50.

right Craftools portable spray booth, opening 30 by 24 in. with exhaust fan and fibre-glass filters. Price $64.50. **far right** Craftools cast-iron banding wheel, ball bearing. Head 8 in. in diameter. Price $13.25.

There are certain glaze and decorative effects that can be obtained more effectively by spraying. Both a portable and a large permanent spray booth are illustrated. The spray gun and compressor used is roughly similar to a standard paint sprayer. Personally, I prefer to dip or pour glazes as the process is quicker and the glazed surfaces are less likely to be injured in loading. Gram scales and decorating wheels are a necessity in every glaze room. Dipping tongs are convenient for glazing small pieces.

Craftools ceramic spray booth, complete with exhaust fan, filters, compressor, spray gun, and hose; shipping weight 450 lbs. Booth opening 36 by 42 in. Price FOB Woodridge, N. J., $495.00.

SPECIAL EQUIPMENT

A shop lift, consisting of a 2-foot square, low steel platform on wheels, with a hydraulic or vertical winch lift, is a great labor saver in the studio. Bagged clay, chemicals, wet clay in cans, and so on, if placed on low pallets, can be conveniently moved. The usual capacity of the shop lift for about five hundred pounds makes it possible to easily move small kilns, remove doors for repairs; it even aids in loading large sculptural pieces into the kiln.

Ware racks are invaluable in the glaze room to store pieces and to aid in loading and unloading the kiln. Draped with plastic, these racks can serve as extra damp room storage. In this case, it is better to use 6-inch boards instead of a solid shelf so that the thrown piece can be placed immediately on drying boards after being cut off the wheel head.

Unique welded steel ware rack on casters; 65 by 22 by 28 in.; shelves extra. Price $72.50.

Every studio ought to have a few large bats that can be used to dry out special body mixtures. A 24 by 30 by 10 inch slab with a cast center cavity, which will hold about one hundred pounds of slip, is a useful size. Wedging tables in many studios are entirely too small and flimsy for continual school use. A welded angle frame about 3-feet square is desirable. If about six inches thick, the plaster will not get damp too quickly.

Metal edge reinforcements such as those used by plasterers will prevent chipping when cast into place. Such tables are also desirable for rolling out clay for slab construction, although a sanded table may also be used. Plaster surfaces must be occasionally scraped, as the finer collodial clay particles tend, in time, to seal the surface and prevent absorption.

APPENDIX

APPENDIX

REFERENCE TABLES

ATOMIC WEIGHTS OF COMMON ELEMENTS

Element	Symbol	Atomic number	Atomic weight
Aluminum	Al	13	26.97
Antimony	Sb	51	121.76
Barium	Ba	56	137.36
Bismuth	Bi	83	209.00
Boron	B	5	10.82
Cadmium	Cd	48	112.41
Calcium	Ca	20	40.08
Carbon	C	6	12.01
Chlorine	Cl	17	35.457
Chromium	Cr	24	52.01
Cobalt	Co	27	58.94
Copper	Cu	29	63.54
Fluorine	F	9	19.00
Gold	Au	79	197.20
Hydrogen	H	1	1.008
Iridium	Ir	77	193.10
Iron	Fe	26	55.84
Lead	Pb	82	207.21
Lithium	Li	3	6.94
Magnesium	Mg	12	24.32

ATOMIC WEIGHTS OF COMMON ELEMENTS—Continued

Element	Symbol	Atomic number	Atomic weight
Manganese	Mn	25	54.93
Molybdenum	Mo	42	95.98
Neon	Ne	10	20.183
Nickel	Ni	28	58.69
Nitrogen	N	7	14.008
Oxygen	O	8	16.00
Palladium	Pd	46	106.70
Phosphorus	P	15	30.98
Platinum	Pt	78	195.23
Potassium	K	19	39.096
Silicon	Si	14	28.06
Silver	Ag	47	107.88
Sodium	Na	11	22.997
Sulphur	S	16	32.066
Tin	Sn	50	118.70
Titanium	Ti	22	47.90
Uranium	U	92	238.07
Vanadium	V	23	50.95
Zinc	Zn	30	65.38
Zirconium	Zr	40	91.22

COMMON CERAMIC RAW MATERIALS

Material	Formula	Compound molecular weight	Equivalent weight	Fired formula
Aluminum hydroxide	$Al_2(OH)_6$	156	156	Al_2O_3
Antimony oxide	Sb_2O_3	292	292	Sb_2O_3
Barium carbonate	$BaCO_3$	197	197	BaO
Bone ash (Calcium phosphate)	$Ca_3(PO_4)_2$	310	103	CaO
Boric acid	$B_2O_3 \cdot 3H_2O$	124	124	B_2O_3
Borax	$Na_2O \cdot 2B_2O_3 \cdot 10H_2O$	382	382	$Na_2O \cdot 2B_2O_3$
Calcium borate (colemanite)	$2CaO \cdot 3B_2O_3 \cdot 5H_2O$	412	206	$2CaO \cdot 3B_2O_3$
Calcium carbonate (whiting)	$CaCO_3$	100	100	CaO
Chromic oxide	Cr_2O_3	152	152	Cr_2O_3
Cobalt carbonate	$CoCO_3$	119	119	CoO
Cobalt oxide, black	Co_3O_4	241	80	CoO
Copper carbonate	$CuCO_3$	119	119	CuO
Copper oxide, green (cupric)	CuO	80	80	CuO
Copper oxide, red (cuprous)	Cu_2O	143	72	CuO
Cornwall stone[a]	$(1RO \cdot 1.16Al_2O_3 \cdot 8.95SiO_2)$	732	652	same
Cryolite	$Na_3 \cdot AlF_6$	210	420	$3Na_2O \cdot Al_2O_3$
Dolomite	$CaCO_3 \cdot MgCO_3$	184	184	$CaO \cdot MgO$
Feldspar, potash	$K_2O \cdot Al_2O_3 \cdot 6SiO_2$	557	557	same
Feldspar, soda	$Na_2 \cdot Al_2O_3 \cdot 6SiO_2$	524	524	same
Kaolin (China clay)	$Al_2O_3 \cdot 2SiO_2 \cdot 2H_2O$	258	258	$Al_2O_3 \cdot 2SiO_2$
Kaolin (calcined)	$Al_2O_3 \cdot 2SiO_2$	222	222	$Al_2O_3 \cdot 2SiO_2$
Iron chromate	$FeCrO_4$	172	172	$FeCrO_4$
Iron oxide, red (ferric)	Fe_2O_3	160	160	Fe_2O_3
Iron oxide, black (ferrous)	FeO	72	72	FeO
Flint (quartz, silica)	SiO_2	60	60	SiO_2
Fluorspar (calcium fluoride)	CaF_2	78	78	CaO
Lead carbonate (white lead)	$2PbCo_3 \cdot Pb(OH)_2$	775	258	PbO
Lead monosilicate	$3PbO \cdot 2SiO_2$	789	263	same
Lead oxide (litharge)	PbO	223	223	PbO
Lead oxide, red	Pb_3O_4	685	228	PbO
Lepidolite	$LiF \cdot KF \cdot Al_2O_3 \cdot 3SiO_2$	356	356	same
Lithium carbonate	Li_2CO_3	74	74	Li_2O
Magnesium carbonate	$MgCO_3$	84	84	MgO
Manganese carbonate	$MnCO_3$	115	115	MnO
Manganese dioxide (black)	MnO_2	87	87	MnO

Material	Formula	Compound molecular weight	Equivalent weight	Fired formula
Manganese oxide (greenish)	MnO	71	71	MnO
Nepheline syenite[b]	$1RO \cdot 1.04Al_2O_3 \cdot 4.53SiO_2$	447	447	same
Nickel oxide, green	NiO	75	75	NiO
Nickel oxide, black	Ni_2O_3	166	83	NiO
Petalite	$Li_3O \cdot Al_2O_3 \cdot 8SiO_2$	197	197	same
Plastic vitrox[c]	$1RO \cdot 1.69Al_2O_3 \cdot 14.64SiO_2$	1139	1139	same
Potassium carbonate (pearl ash)	K_2CO_3	138	138	K_2O
Pyrophyllite	$Al_2O_3 \cdot 4SiO_2 \cdot H_2O$	360	360	$Al_2O_3 \cdot 4SiO_2$
Sodium bicarbonate	$NaHCO_3$	84	168	Na_2O
Sodium carbonate (soda ash)	Na_2CO_3	106	106	Na_2O
Spodumene	$Li_2O \cdot Al_2O_3 \cdot 4SiO_2$	372	372	same
Talc (steatite)	$3MgO \cdot 4SiO_2 \cdot H_2O$	379	126	$3MgO \cdot 4SiO_2$
Tin oxide (stannic oxide)	SnO_2	151	151	SnO_2
Titanium dioxide (rutile impure TiO_2)	TiO_2	80	80	TiO_2
Wollastonite	$Ca \cdot SiO_3$	116	116	same
Zinc oxide	ZnO	81	81	ZnO
Zirconium oxide	ZnO_2	123	123	ZrO_2

[a] Formula for Cornwall stone

K_2O	0.4453	Al_2O_3	1.0847	SiO_2	7.796
Na_2O	0.2427	Fe_2O_3	0.0065		
CaO	0.1873				
MgO	0.0821		*Mol. weight* 652		
CaF_2	0.0421				

[b] Formula for Nepheline syenite

Na_2O	0.713	Al_2O_3	1.04	Si_2O_3	4.53
K_2O	0.220				
CaO	0.056		*Mol. weight* 447		
MgO	0.011				

[c] Formula for Plastic vitrox

CaO	0.045	Al_2O_3	1.693	SiO_2	14.634
MgO	0.058	Fe_2O_3	0.005		
Na_2O	0.054				
K_2O	0.842		*Mol. weight* 1139.40		

ANALYSIS OF COMMON CLAYS AND CHEMICALS

Material	SiO_2	Al_2O_3	Fe_2O_3	TiO_2	CaO	MgO	K_2O	Na_2O	Li_2O	Ignition loss
Red Dalton clay	63.2	18.3	6.3	1.3	0.3	0.5	1.6	1.2		6.4
Barnard clay	41.4	6.7	29.9	0.2	0.5	0.6	1.0	0.5		8.4
Monmouth stoneware	56.8	28.5			0.3	0.3	0.3	1.3		12.2
Jordon stoneware	69.4	17.7	1.6	1.3	0.1	0.5	1.5	1.39		6.4
Albany slip	57.6	14.6	5.2	0.4	5.8	2.7	3.2	0.8		9.5
Ball clay	51.9	31.7	0.8	1.5	0.2	0.2	0.9	0.4		12.3
Sagger clay	59.4	27.2	0.7	1.6	0.6	0.2	0.7	0.3		9.4
Fireclay	58.1	23.1	2.4	1.4	0.8	1.1	1.9	0.3		10.5
Georgia kaolin	44.9	38.9	0.4	1.3	0.1	0.1	0.2	0.2		14.21
English kaolin	47.25	37.29	0.84	0.05	0.03	0.28	1.80	0.04		12.21
Kyanite	59.05	36.5	0.16	0.67	0.03	0.01		0.18		0.21
Pyrophyllite	73.5	20.0	0.5		0.1		1.4	1.2		3.3
Bentonite	64.32	20.7	3.47	0.11	0.46	2.26	2.9			5.15
Volcanic ash	72.51	11.55	1.21	0.54	0.68	0.07	7.87	1.79		3.81
Plastic vitrox	75.56	14.87	0.09		0.22	0.20	6.81	0.29		2.04
Feldspar, potash	68.3	17.9	0.08		0.4		10.10	3.10		0.32
Cornwall stone	72.6	16.1	0.23	0.06	1.4	0.1	4.56	3.67		2.54
Nepheline syenite	60.4	23.6	0.08		0.7	0.1	9.8	4.6		0.7
Lepidolite	55.00	25.0	0.08				9.0	1.0	4.0	0.92[a]
Spodumene	62.91	28.42	0.53		0.11	0.13	0.69	0.46	6.78	0.28

[a] plus 5 percent Fluorine.

ANALYSIS OF SEVERAL STANDARD FELDSPARS[a]

Material	SiO_2	Al_2O_3	Fe_2O_3	CaO	MgO	K_2O	Na_2O	Ignition loss
Spruce Pine #4	67.90	19.01	0.05	1.54	trace	4.98	6.22	0.08
Bell	68.30	17.90	0.08	0.40	trace	10.10	3.10	0.32
Eureka	69.8	17.11	0.1	trace		9.4	3.5	0.2
Kingman	66.0	18.7	0.1	0.1		12.0	2.8	0.2
Oxford	69.40	17.04	0.09	0.38		7.92	3.22	0.3
Chesterfield	70.60	16.33	0.08	0.30		8.50	3.75	0.4
Buckingham	65.58	19.54	trace	0.16	0.20	12.44	2.56	0.32

[a] The variable quality of the feldspar fluxes is a major reason why glaze recipes may need to be changed unless materials are identical.

WATER OF PLASTICITY OF VARIOUS CLAYS

Washed kaolin	44.48–47.50
White sedimentary kaolin	28.60–56.25
Ball clays	25.00–53.30
Plastic fire clays	12.90–37.40
Flint fire clays	8.89–19.04
Sagger clays	18.40–28.56
Stoneware clays	19.16–34.80
Brick clays	13.20–40.70

$$\text{Water of plasticity} = \frac{\text{weight of plastic sample} - \text{weight of dry sample}}{\text{weight of dry sample}} \times 100$$

OXIDE EQUIVALENTS OF SELECTED COMMERCIAL FRITS[a]

Company		K_2O	Na_2O	CaO	PbO	Al_2O_3	B_2O_3	SiO_2	Formula weight
Pemco	54		0.32	0.68			0.64	1.47	191
	67	0.12	0.19	0.69		0.37	1.16	2.17	311
	926	0.01	0.31	0.68		0.11	0.61	1.90	225
	83		0.28		0.72	0.20	0.26	2.43	276
	316				1.00	0.25		1.92	364
	349	0.09	0.09	0.58	0.24	0.19	0.36	2.80	313
Ferro	3124	0.02	0.28	0.70		0.27	0.55	2.56	279
	3134		0.32	0.68			0.63	1.47	210
	3211			1.00			1.11		133
	3223		1.00				2.00	5.00	502
	3419		0.28		0.72		0.57	0.89	276
	3386	0.02	0.08		0.90	0.13	1.77	4.42	499
	3396		0.50		0.50		1.00	2.00	332
Hommel	285	0.10	0.90			0.21	0.94	2.72	315
	267	0.13	0.31	0.56		0.29	1.24	2.05	301
	266		0.32	0.68		0.32	1.10	1.31	245
	22			0.47	0.53		0.98	2.88	385
	240		0.28		0.72		0.56	0.90	271
	13		0.30		0.70		0.39	0.41	227

[a] In most cases the above frits will constitute a complete glaze at cone 06.

COLOR SCALE FOR TEMPERATURES

Color	Degrees C	Degrees F
Lowest visible red	475	885
Lowest visible red to dark red	475–650	885–1200
Dark red to cherry red	650–750	1200–1380
Cherry red to bright cherry red	750–815	1380–1500
Bright cherry red to orange	815–900	1500–1650
Orange to yellow	900–1090	1650–2000
Yellow to light yellow	1090–1315	2000–2400
Light yellow to white	1315–1540	2400–2800
White to dazzling white	1540 and higher	2800 and higher

AVERAGE TEMPERATURES TO WHICH VARIOUS CERAMIC PRODUCTS ARE FIRED

Products	Degree F
Heavy clay products	
Common brick—surface clay	1600–1800
Common brick—shale	1800–2000
Face brick—fireclay	2100–2300
Enamel brick	2100–2300
Drain tile	1700–1900
Sewer pipe	2030–2320
Roofing tile	1960–2140
Terra cotta	2070–2320
Pottery	
Flower pots	1580–1850
Stoneware (chemical)	2650–2700
Stoneware (once fired)	2318–2426
Semivitreous ware	2282–2354
Pottery decalcomanias	1400–1500
Refractories	
Firebrick—clay	2300–2500
Firebrick—silica	2650–2750
Silicon carbide	3236–3992
Whitewares	
Electrical porcelain	2390–2500
Hotel china—bisque	2390–2436
Hotel china—glost	2210–2282
Floor tile	2318–2498
Wall tile—bisque	1886–2354
Wall tile—glost	1186–2246

MELTING POINTS OF SELECTED COMPOUNDS AND MINERALS

	Degree C	Degree F
Alumina	2050	3722
Barium carbonate	1360	2480
Barium oxide (O_2)	450	842
Borax	741	1365
Calcium oxide	2570	4658
Cobaltic oxide (O_2)	905	1661
Copper oxide (CuO)	1064	1947
Corundum	2035	3695
Cryolite	998	1830
Dolomite	2570–2800	4658–5072
Ferric oxide	1548	2518
Fire clay	1660–1720	3020–3128
Fluorspar	1300	2372
Kaolin	1740–1785	3164–3245
Lead oxide (litharge)	880	1616
Magnesium carbonate (dissociates)	350	662
Magnesium oxide (approx.)	2800	5072
Mullite	1810	3290
Nepheline syenite	1223	2232
Nickel oxide (O_2)	400	752
Orthoclase feldspar (potash)	1220	2228
Potassium oxide	red heat	
Rutile	1900	3452
Silica	1715	3119
Silicon carbide (decomposed)	2200	3992
Sillimanite	1816	3301
Sodium oxide	red heat	
Tin oxide	1130	2066
Titanium oxide	1900	3452
Whiting (dissociates)	825	1517
Zircon	2550	4622

TEMPERATURE EQUIVALENTS
ORTON STANDARD PYROMETRIC CONES[a]

Cone number	Large cones		Small cones		Seger cones (used in Europe) Degrees C
	150°C[b]	270°F[b]	300°C[b]	540°F[b]	
020	635	1175	666	1231	670
019	683	1261	723	1333	690
018	717	1323	752	1386	710
017	747	1377	784	1443	730
016	792	1458	825	1517	750
015	804	1479	843	1549	790
014	838	1540			815
013	852	1566			835
012	884	1623			855
011	894	1641			880
010	894	1641	919	1686	900
09	923	1693	955	1751	920
08	955	1751	983	1801	940
07	984	1803	1008	1846	960
06	999	1830	1023	1873	980
05	1046	1915	1062	1944	1000
04	1060	1940	1098	2008	1020
03	1101	2014	1131	2068	1040
02	1120	2048	1148	2098	1060
01	1137	2079	1178	2152	1080

[a] From the Edward Orton, Jr., Ceramic Foundation, Columbus 1, Ohio.
[b] Temperature rise per hour.

TEMPERATURE EQUIVALENTS
ORTON STANDARD PYROMETRIC CONES—Continued

Cone number	Large cones		Small cones		Seger cones (used in Europe) Degrees C
	150°C[b]	270°F[b]	300°C[b]	540°F[b]	
1	1154	2109	1179	2154	*1100*
2	1162	2124	1179	2154	*1120*
3	1168	2134	1196	2185	*1140*
4	1186	2167	1209	2208	*1160*
5	1196	2185	1221	2230	*1180*
6	1222	2232	1255	2291	*1200*
7	1240	2264	1264	2307	*1230*
8	1263	2305	1300	2372	*1250*
9	1280	2336	1317	2403	*1280*
10	1305	2381	1330	2426	*1300*
11	1315	2399	1336	2437	*1320*
12	1326	2419	1335	2471	*1350*
13	1346	2455			*1380*
14	1366	2491			*1410*
15	1431	2608			*1430*

CONVERSION FORMULA

Centigrade to Fahrenheit

$$\text{example}: 100°\text{C} \times \frac{9}{5} = 180 \quad 180 + 32 = 212°\text{F}$$

Fahrenheit to Centigrade

$$\text{example}: 212°\text{F} - 32 = 180 \quad 180 \times \frac{5}{9} = 100°\text{C}$$

GLAZE, STAIN, AND BODY RECIPES

Ceramic glaze formulas used to be discussed with a great deal of secrecy. Fortunately, this attitude has passed. What is done with a glaze is much more important than how it is made. The text has stressed the technical side of ceramics in order to make more studio time available for actual potting than might otherwise be possible.

Regardless of the variety of glazes and decorative devices described the student should not be too impressed by technique, however important it may be. Many of the finest potters use only a few standard glazes and stains and a minimum of decoration. Techniques are important and should be studied, but they should not overshadow the search for ideas.

The list of glazes in this section will supplement the earlier discussions of glaze types and the function of the various glaze chemicals. For convenience the glazes are listed as batch recipes. It must be stressed again that before two of these glazes can be compared with any certainty, they must be converted into empirical formula form.

LOW-FIRE LEAD[a] AND ALKALINE GLAZES

Cones 05–03, Lithium blue

26.9	Lithium carbonate
13.6	Kaolin
53.9	Flint
2.8	Bentonite
3.7	Copper carbonate

Cones 08–09, Chromium red

200.6	Red lead
14.4	Potassium bichromate
6.12	Soda ash
25.8	Kaolin
54.0	Flint

Cones 04–02, Barium mat glaze

20	Whiting
129	White lead
64	Potash feldspar
39	Barium carbonate
21	Calcined kaolin
37	Flint

Cones 04–02, Alumina mat

142.0	White lead
35.0	Whiting
63.5	Potash feldspar
40.0	Calcined kaolin
12.0	Kaolin

Cone 04, Lithium semiopaque (from K. Green)

26.9	Lithium carbonate
25.0	White lead
12.0	Bone ash
9.0	Soda feldspar
15.6	Kaolin
53.9	Flint
2.8	Bentonite

Cone 04, Semigloss rutile (from K. Green)

80.0	White lead
6.1	Plastic vitrox
19.0	Kaolin
16.1	Flint
7.0	Rutile

[a] In substituting red for white lead, approximately eleven and one-half percent less material is needed for the same PbO.

Cone 04, Semimat (very fluid)	
301.0	White lead
85.0	Potash feldspar
6.5	Kaolin
23.0	Rutile
7.5	Whiting
57.5	Borax
12.5	Calcined kaolin

Cone 04, Lead-borax turquoise fluid	
47.5	Whiting
103.0	Borax
4.0	Soda ash
77.0	White lead
107.5	Potash feldspar
51.0	Flint
2.0	Kaolin
37.0	Tin oxide
13.7	Copper carbonate

Cone 04, Colemanite crackle glaze	
102	Potash feldspar
123	Colemanite
43	Barium carbonate
33	Flint

Cone 04, Burnt-red glaze	
164.0	White lead
24.5	Whiting
38.5	Kaolin
9.5	Zinc oxide
100.0	Flint
20.2	Tin oxide
13.5	Red iron oxide

Cone 04, Volcanic-ash mat (from A. Garzio)			
40	Colemanite	60	Volcanic ash
10	Whiting	35	Kaolin
5	Barium carbonate	6	Zinc oxide
		12	Tin oxide
12	White lead		
8	Borax		

Cone 04, Volcanic ash	
60	Volcanic ash
20	Colemanite
10	White lead
10	Borax

MEDIUM-FIRE GLAZES, CONES 2–6

Cones 1–2, Clear glaze	
50.0	White lead
14.9	Soda feldspar
3.2	Whiting
2.7	Zinc oxide
9.4	Flint
14.8	Cornwall stone
.2	Gum tragacanth

Cone 2, Glaze	
31.9	Feldspar
8.6	Whiting
26.1	Red lead
5.4	Kaolin
5.7	Ball clay
19.7	Flint

Cone 2, Plastic vitrox	
310	White lead
179	Potash feldspar
474	Plastic vitrox
106	Whiting

Cone 2, Colemanite	
24.0	Calcined zinc oxide
113.0	Potash feldspar
51.5	Colemanite
20.0	Barium carbonate
19.0	Steatite
66.0	Flint

MEDIUM-FIRE GLAZES, CONES 2–6—Continued

Cones 1–4, Mat		Cone 6, Semimat glaze		Cone 4, Glaze	
40.0	Feldspar	9.8	Whiting	15.3	Whiting
6.0	Whiting	2.1	Talc	23.0	White lead
7.5	Barium carbonate	11.0	Barium carbonate	30.0	Feldspar
6.1	Zinc oxide	4.3	Calcined zinc oxide	7.0	Kaolin
2.0	Talc	42.5	Soda feldspar	7.7	Flint
5.0	Kaolin	8.3	Kaolin		
3.8	Ball clay	8.0	Ball clay		
18.2	Flint	14.0	Flint		

PORCELAIN AND STONEWARE GLAZES, CONES 8–14

Cone 8, Lepidolite (crackle glaze)		Cones 8–10, Semimat	
60	Lepidolite	66.4	Feldspar (potash)
138	Potash feldspar	8.0	Whiting
20	Cryolite	25.6	Kaolin
20	Bone ash		
40	Whiting		**Cones 8–10, Semigloss black**
40	Colemanite	100	Albany slip clay
		3	Cobalt oxide, black

Cone 8, Feldspar		Cone 8, Semimat	
44.5	Soda feldspar	36.0	Potash feldspar
12.0	Whiting	25.4	Kaolin
7.3	Kaolin	17.3	Whiting
36.2	Flint	11.9	Flint
		8.1	Rutile

Cone 8, Semimat ash glaze		Cones 7–8, Semimat volcanic-ash glaze (from Angelo Garzio)	
40	Potash feldspar	100	Volcanic ash
40	Mixed hardwood ashes	28	Colemanite
20	Ball clay	72	Nepheline syenite
		60	Whiting
		28	Magnesium carbonate
		64	Kaolin
		20	Flint

PORCELAIN AND STONEWARE GLAZES, CONES 8–14—Continued

Cones 9–10, White mat
(from R. Eckels)

45.3	Feldspar, potash	5.0	Zinc oxide
19.3	Whiting	3.0	Rutile
11.6	Flint	2.0	Tin oxide
24.0	Kaolin		

Cones 8–11, White opaque

35.1	Feldspar (potash)
9.9	Kaolin (Florida)
13.5	Whiting
1.0	Borax
16.2	Flint
1.8	Zinc oxide
23.4	Zircopax

Cones 10–13 (from A. Garzio)

105.0	Feldspar (potash)
37.5	Whiting
37.5	Ball clay
9.0	Kaolin
6.25	Zinc oxide

Cones 10–12, Mat

38.0	Feldspar (potash)
21.0	Whiting
20.0	Kaolin
15.9	Silica
4.1	Titanium oxide

REDUCTION GLAZES

Cone 04, Celadon

154.8	White lead
12.0	Whiting
396.48	Godfrey spar (soda)
192.0	Soda ash
11.7	Red iron oxide
19.0	Tin oxide

(Grind dry, use immediately if wet. Fire: Reduction, cone 012–07; oxidizing, cone 07–04.)

Cone 04, Copper luster

173	White lead
25	Manganese oxide
64	Cornwall stone
24	Flint
3	Copper oxide
5	Cobalt oxide

(Black when thin, copper when thick. Fire: Reduction cone 012–07; oxidizing cone 07–04.)

Cone 2, Artificial Copper-red reduction
(from Harder)

158.0	Soda feldspar
132.0	Borax
3.5	Soda ash
31.0	Fluorspar
58.0	Kaolin
83.0	Flint
8.8	Tin oxide
1.5	Copper carbonate (plus ½ of 1 percent silicon carbide [180 mesh carborundum])

Cone 8, Copper-red reduction

108.0	Cornwall stone
126.0	Flint
15.5	Zinc oxide
36.0	Barium carbonate
16.5	Soda ash
85.0	Borax
8.0	Copper carbonate
8.0	Tin oxide

Cone 6, Copper-red reduction (from Curtis)

40	White lead
40	Red lead
20	Whiting
10	Kaolin
100	Flint
100	Borax
15	Boric acid
15	Soda ash
5	Tin oxide
2	Copper oxide (Fire smoky to cone 012; strong reduction to cone 07; oxidizing fire to cone 6.)

Cones 6–8, Celadon reduction

61.3	Potash feldspar
7.5	Whiting
4.9	Kaolin
24.8	Flint
1.5	Red iron oxide (Fire smoky to cone 012; strong reduction to cone 07; oxidizing fire to cone 6.)

Cone 8, Artificial reduction (from Baggs)

179.0	Soda feldspar
10.6	Soda ash
152.0	Borax
40.0	Whiting
67.0	Kaolin
96.0	Flint
10.0	Tin oxide
1.6	Copper carbonate
3.5	Silicon carbide

Cones 8–10, Celadon

78	Feldspar (potash)
6	Whiting
14	Flint
2	Red iron oxide

Cones 9–10, Copper red

13.0	Ferro frit #3191
44.0	Feldspar (soda)
14.0	Whiting
3.0	Kaolin (Florida)
25.0	Flint
1.0	Tin oxide
0.2	Copper carbonate

(Add .2 silicon carbide for artificial reduction.)

CRYSTALLINE GLAZES

Cones 07–05, Aventurine

172.9	Borax
9.8	Borium carbonate
12.4	Boric acid
6.4	Kaolin
177.0	Flint
67.0	Red iron oxide

(Grind and use immediately or frit [without the clay].)

Cones 3–4, Aventurine

79	Ferro frit #3304
16	Red iron oxide
5	Kaolin (Florida)

Cones 3–4, Zinc crystal		Cone 8, Zinc crystal (pale green)	
13.1	Soda ash	11.06	Sodium carbonate
15.2	Boric acid	6.28	Whiting
21.7	Zinc oxide	20.30	Zinc oxide
41.8	Flint	40.10	Silica
6.6	Rutile	5.01	Titanium (rutile)
6.0	Ball clay	17.25	Kaolin (Florida)
		3.00	Copper carbonate

(Grind and use immediately or frit without the clay.)

(Grind and use immediately or frit [without the clay].)

Cone 11, Zinc crystal		Cone 11, Titanium crystal	
100	Feldspar	50	Soda ash
35	Whiting	100	Flint
35	Flint	50	Zinc oxide
50	Zinc oxide	20	Titanium oxide

Cones 9–10, Zinc crystal (from M. Hansen)

		#1		#2		#3	
74	Pemco frit #283	plus MnO_2	5 percent	$CuCO_3$	3 percent	NiO	1 percent
21.5	Zinc oxide	$CuCO_3$	5 percent	Rutile	5 percent	$CuCO_3$	3 percent
4.5	Flint	Rutile	4 percent				
1.0	Bentonite						

CERAMIC STAINS[a]

(For preparation, see Chapter 8)

#1 Pink stain		#2 Pink stain	
50	Tin oxide	50.5	Tin oxide
25	Whiting	19.0	Whiting
18	Flint	7.5	Fluorspar
4	Borax	20.5	Flint
3	Potassium dichromate	7.5	Potassium dichromate

(Calcine to cone 8; stain is lumpy and must first be broken up in iron mortar, then ground.)

(Calcine to cone 8 and grind.)

[a] These stains must be finely ground to obtain the desired color.

#3 Crimson stain

22.9	Whiting
6.6	Calcium sulfate
4.4	Fluorspar
20.8	Flint
43.7	Tin oxide
1.6	Potassium dichromate

(Calcine to cone 8 and grind.)

#4 Ultramarine stain

50	Chromium oxide
12	Flint
38	Cobalt oxide (CoO, cobaltous)

(Calcine to cone 8 and grind.)

#5 Blue-green stain

41.8	Cobalt oxide (CoO)
19.2	Chromium oxide
39.0	Aluminum oxide

(Calcine to cone 8 and grind.)

#6 Orange stain

29.8	Antimony oxide
12.8	Tin oxide
14.9	Red iron oxide
42.5	Red lead

(Calcine to cone 6 and grind.)

#7 Black stain

43	Chromium oxide
43	Red iron oxide
10	Manganese dioxide
4	Cobalt oxide

(Calcine to cone 8 and grind.)

#8 Turquoise stain

56	Copper phosphate
44	Tin oxide

(Calcine to cone 6 and grind.)

#9 Red-brown stain

22	Chromium oxide
23	Red iron oxide
55	Zinc oxide

(Calcine to cone 8 and grind.)

#10 Brown stain

64.6	Zinc oxide
9.7	Chrome oxide
9.7	Red iron oxide
8.0	Red lead
8.0	Boric acid

(Calcine to cone 8 and grind.)

#11 Yellow stain

33.3	Antimony oxide
50.0	Red lead
16.7	Tin oxide

(Calcine to cone 6 and grind.)

#12 Black stain

65	Chromium oxide
35	Red iron oxide

(Calcine to cone 8 and grind.)

CLAY BODIES

The body preferred by the studio potter is quite different from that used by the commercial pottery. For slip casting or jiggering a uniformity of texture is desired for obvious technical reasons. Likewise any impurities imparting color to the body are frowned upon. Therefore, bodies used in commercial production are carefully selected, ground, and refined. Plasticity is of a minor importance, and since it is associated with high shrinkage rates, it is usually avoided.

Local supplies of earthenware and plastic fire clays are available, at least in the midwest. Since they are widely used in cement, plaster, and mortar mixtures they are competitively priced and generally quite reasonable.

Because the volume of clay used in the school studio will normally run from one ton to five tons per year both the initial cost and shipping charges are important. Thus clay that can be obtained locally has a decided advantage even if it needs a certain amount of sieving or small additions. Occasionally a truckload of raw clay may be purchased very reasonably from a local brick or tile works.

Earthenware bodies present no real problem of supply in the Midwest since there are many brick and tile factories which also sell bagged clay. Many are shale clays with coarse particles which will cause trouble unless they are run through a sieve of from 15 to 20 meshes per inch. Some earthenware clays contain soluble sulfates which will form a whitish scum on the fired ware. Adding 1 or 2 percent barium carbonate will eliminate this fault. Many such clays will not be very plastic unless they are aged. The addition of about five percent of bentonite, which is extremely plastic, will usually render a short clay workable. Often two clays which alone are not suitable can be mixed together to form a good body. Only experimentation will indicate the necessary changes.

Occasionally the body will lack sufficient flint to fuse with the fluxes it contains. Cream-colored clays may be further lightened in color and rendered more plastic by the addition of ball clays. Talc has some plasticity and is often used in low-fire whiteware bodies as a source of both flux and silica. Feldspar, nepheline syenite, plastic vitrox, are also added to various bodies to contribute fluxing qualities.

Stoneware and porcelain bodies are largely compounded bodies. In fact, it is extremely rare for a single clay to satisfy all throwing and firing requirements. There is no clay which by itself will make a porcelain body. Oriental porcelain is made from one or two claylike minerals which are fairly plastic. Since nothing in the Western world compares with petuntze, porcelain bodies must be compounded from clay and various mineral compounds.

Both stoneware and porcelain will form hard vitrified bodies at cone 10. The major difference between the two is that stoneware contains various impurities, chiefly iron, which gives it a gray or tan color. Both types are compounded for varying temperatures and, in the case of porcelain, for different degrees of translucency. Greater translucency is usually obtained by increasing the silica ratio which has the accompanying defect of an increase in firing warpage.

Both fire clay and stoneware clays differ chiefly from pure clay (kaolin) in that they contain various fluxes and impurities which lower the fusion point and impart a gray, tan, or buff color.

The familiar crocks and old-fashioned jugs which we occasionally still see were made of stoneware clays. As manufacturers today desire completely white bodies, not many items are made of stoneware. Therefore, local sources of stoneware clays may not be available, or the transportation costs may be excessive. Fire clays, which have a more universal industrial use can be substituted for stoneware. Some fire clays are very plastic and fine enough for throwing purposes. They often contain some iron impurities which give the body a flecked appearance. Depending upon the temperature and appearance desired, it may be necessary to blend in an earthenware or stoneware clay or ingredients such as feldspar, talc, or silica.

The following section lists several types of clay and porcelain bodies. They are included merely as suggestions since it usually will be necessary to vary these recipes depending upon raw materials available locally.

Cone 2, Light-red clay body

60	Red clay
25	Flint
15	Kaolin

Cone 2, Cream clay body

12	Ball clay
2	Kaolin
7	Soda feldspar
5	Flint
2	Red clay

Cones 2-8, Stoneware body

20	Jordan clay or Monmouth
25	Ball clay
30	Plastic fire clay
10	Nepheline syenite
5	Flint
12	Grog (fine size for wheel work)

Cones 8-10, Stoneware body

100	Jordan or Monmouth
100	Fire clay
60	Grog (fine, 60-mesh)
60	Flint

Cone 8, Stoneware body

40	Ball clay
40	Fire clay
20	Earthenware (for color and texture)

Cones 8-10, Porcelain body

45	Kaolin
25	Feldspar (potash)
16	Ball clay
13	Flint

Cones 8-12, Porcelain body

7	Ball clay
7	Kaolin
7	Feldspar (potash)
5	Flint

Cones 10-15, Porcelain body

25	Ball clay
25	Kaolin
25	Feldspar (potash)
25	Flint

Engobes are essentially clay slips with the significant difference that some engobes are intended to be used on either dry or bisque ware, thus necessitating additions of flint, feldspar, and occasionally a flux to the clay slip in order to adjust the differing shrinkage rates. The general purpose of the engobe is to provide a smoother surface and usually a different colored base for glaze or brushed decoration.

If the engobe is to be used on a damp piece, a sieved slip of the throwing body may be used, providing the color is not objectionable. The usual colorants may be added, avoiding the chrome oxides that react unfavorably with tin. One percent of a strong oxide, like cobalt, is sufficient, although from 5 to 7 percent may be needed of iron or vanadium. Blistering will result if over 7 percent of manganese is used. Five percent of an opacifier is often needed to lighten the color.

Engobes used on leather-hard ware must be adjusted to reduce shrinkage by calcining part of the clay and by additions of flint and feldspar. On dry ware, the clay content of the engobe can rarely be over 40 percent with the balance of flint and feldspar. A 5-percent addition of borax will toughen the surface and aid adhesion.

When used on bisque ware, the engobe must have a clay content of less than 25 percent, lest it shrink excessively and flake off the pot. Furthermore, it must contain sufficient fluxes to fuse with the bisque surface. Its characteristics resemble those of an underfired glaze. In view of the low clay content, a binder may be necessary.

Too thick an application on any surface, whether leather-hard clay or bisque ware, will crack or flake off. On the other hand, a thin coating will allow the body color to show through. In addition to the usual finely ground coloring oxides, one may add coarsely ground ores, ilmenite, rust chips, chopped copper scouring pads, and so on, to the engobe. Such additions melt out into the covering glaze with interesting effects that are limited to the pattern or area of the applied engobe.

SOURCES OF MATERIALS AND EQUIPMENT*

The cost of materials is an important factor in developing a ceramic program, especially if it is to be paid out of the general budget for the course. A rough estimate for the cost per student per semester is about $10 to $15, depending upon shipping costs which may be considerable in certain cases. The cost per student for advanced students, who produce more pottery, is, of course, greater. In addition to the cost of materials, the firing expense, which may also be charged to the department, must be considered. Breakage of kiln shelves are another continuing expense.

* The addresses of all dealers and manufacturers listed here appear on pp. 304–306. Information on regional dealers not listed will be appreciated by the author.

All this indicates the desirability of a businesslike approach to the problem of purchasing. The lower figure of $10 per student reflects the savings possible by purchasing in quantity. Supplies bought from a hobby-shop dealer, will cost a good deal more than $10 per student.

The cost of clay, which seems so cheap per pound, can be very deceiving. The rate at which a few classes can use up a ton of clay is really surprising. For most types of clay the shipping costs will be greater than the cost of the clay itself. Of course, local clays can be dug, but the trouble and labor of processing local clay may make this solution undesirable. Fortunately clay is commonly used in mortar and cement where, in proper amounts, it helps to provide not only a cheaper but a stronger bond. As such it is available from most building supplies dealers in 50-pound bags, usually priced at about $1.00 per bag. These clays are generally shale earthenware which needs sieving. Often bentonite or flint or talc are necessary to make it suitable. But even then these clays represent considerable savings. In a similar manner, many fire clays can be procured from local dealers where they are normally sold for repairing furnaces and industrial ovens. With a little doctoring these fire clays, which are often quite plastic, can be converted into satisfactory stoneware bodies.

Coloring oxides, which are used in small amounts can be purchased in small quantities. Even a small department, however, should purchase the more common chemicals like lead, flint, borax, or the feldspars, in 100-pound lots. These may not be used up during the term but the savings in purchasing the larger quantity are so great that the greater purchase is warranted.

In ordering it is occasionally advisable to buy a few bulky but cheap items so that the shipment will not have to travel at the expensive parcel-post rate but can be sent instead by freight or motor truck.

Supply Dealers

East Coast

CLAYS

Hammill & Gillespie, Inc.
O. W. Ketcham Architectural Tile Co.
Langley Ceramic Studio
Mandl Ceramic Supply Co.
Newton Pottery Supply Co.
Pottery Arts Supply Co.
Roder Ceramic Studio
Rowantree Pottery
Stewart Clay Co.

United Clay Mines
Jack D. Wolfe, Inc.
Local building-supplies dealers

KILNS

W. H. Fairchild (electric)
L. & L. Manufacturing Co. (electric)
Roder Ceramic Studio (electric)
Unique Kilns (gas and electric)

KILN BURNERS

Hauck Mfg. Co.
Johnson Gas Appliance Co.

KILN SHELVES, ETC.

New Castle Refractories, New Castle, Pa.

MISCELLANEOUS EQUIPMENT

Craftools, Inc.
B. F. Drakenfeld, Inc.
Roder Ceramic Studio

CERAMIC CHEMICALS

Ceramic Color & Chemical Mfg. Co.
Gare Ceramic Supply Co.
Langley Ceramic Studio
Newton Pottery Supply Co.
Standard Ceramic Supply Co.
Vitro Manufacturing Co.
Whittaker, Clack and Daniels, Inc.
Jack D. Wolfe, Inc.

POTTER'S WHEELS

Craftools, Inc. (kick and electric)
Randall Wheel (kick)
Standard Ceramic Supply Co.

FRITS

Pemco Corp.
Vitro Manufacturing Co.

PUG MILLS

Walker Jamar Co.

INSULATING MATERIALS

Armstrong Cork Co.
Babcock and Wilcox Co.
Johns-Manville Co.

USED EQUIPMENT

Hermer Kleiner
Perry Equipment Supply Co.

Midwest and South

CLAYS

Cedar Heights Clay Co. (fireclay)
Christy Firebrick Co.
Croxall Chemical and Supply Co.

General Refractories Co.
Hammill & Gillespie, Inc.
V. R. Hood, Jr.
Illinois Clay Products Co.
Kentucky-Tennessee Clay Co. (ball)
La Mo Refractory Supply Co.
Trinity Ceramic Supply Co.
Western Stoneware Co. (Monmouth)
Zanesville Stoneware Co.
Local building-supplies dealers

KILNS

Allied Engineering Corp. (gas)
American Art Clay Co. (electric)
Harrop Ceramic Service Co. (electric)
Paragon Industries, Inc. (electric)

KILN BURNERS

Hauck Mfg. Co.
Johnson Gas Appliance Co.

KILN SHELVES, ETC.

New Castle Refractories, New Castle, Pa.

CERAMIC CHEMICALS

Ceramic Color & Chemical Mfg. Co.
Croxall Chemical and Supply Co.
George Fetzer
Harshaw Chemical Co.
Illini Ceramic Service
Kraft Chemical Co.
Trinity Ceramic Supply Co.

FRITS

Ferro Corp.
Harshaw Chemical Co.

POTTER'S WHEELS

American Art Clay Co. (kick and electric)
H. B. Klopfenstein & Sons (kick)
Nils Lou (electric)
Oak Hill Industries Inc.
Randall Wheel
Denton M. Vars

MISCELLANEOUS EQUIPMENT

American Art Clay Co.
Binks Manufacturing Co. (spray equipment)
De Vilbiss Co. (spray equipment)
Tepping Ceramic Supply Co.
U.S. Stoneware Co. (ball mills)

PUG MILLS

Walker Jamar Co.

INSULATING MATERIALS

A.P. Green Fire Brick Co.
Illinois Clay Products Co.
Johns-Manville Corp.
La Mo Refractory Supply Co.

West and Pacific Coast

CLAYS

L. H. Butcher Co.
Cannon Co.
Denver Fire Clay Co.
Garden City Clay Co.
Hy-Land Mfg. & Supply Co.
Van Howe Co.
S. Paul Ward, Inc.
Western Ceramic Supply Co.
Westwood Ceramic Supply Co.

KILNS

Advanced Kiln Co. (gas)
A. D. Alpine, Inc. (gas)
Denver Fire Clay Co. (gas and oil)
E. W. Mendall (gas)
Skutt & Sons (electric)
West Coast Kiln Co. (gas)

CERAMIC CHEMICALS

L. H. Butcher Co.
Hy-Land Mfg. & Supply Co.
Van Howe Co.
S. Paul Ward, Inc.
Western Ceramic Supply Co.
Westwood Ceramic Supply Co.

POTTER'S WHEELS

A. D. Alpine, Inc. (electric)
Denver Fire Clay Co. (electric)
Skutt & Son (electric)
Paul Soldner (kick)

MISCELLANEOUS EQUIPMENT

L. H. Butcher Co.
Van Howe Co.
S. Paul Ward, Inc.
Westwood Ceramic Supply Co.

Addresses of Listed Dealers

Advanced Kiln Co., 944 East Slauson, Los Angeles, Calif.

Allied Engineering Corp. (division of Ferro Corp.), 4150 East 56th St., Cleveland 5, Ohio

Alpine, A. D., Inc., 11837 Teale St., Culver City, Calif.

American Art Clay Co., 4717 West 16th St., Indianapolis 24, Ind.

Armstrong Cork Co., Lancaster, Pa.

Babcock and Wilcox Co., 161 East 42nd St., New York 17, N.Y.

Binks Manufacturing Co., 3128 Carroll Ave., Chicago 12, Ill.

Butcher, L. H., Co., 15th and Vermont Sts., San Francisco, Calif.

Cannon & Co., Box 802, Sacramento, Calif.

Cedar Heights Clay Co., 50 Portsmouth Rd., Oak Hill, Ohio

Ceramic Color and Chemical Manufacturing Co., P.O. Box 297, New Brighton, Pa. 15066

Christy Firebrick Co., 506 Oliver St., St. Louis 1, Mo.

Craftools, Inc., 1 Industrial Rd., Wood-Ridge, N.J. 07075

Croxhall Chemical and Supply Co., P.O. Box 757, East Liverpool, Ohio 43920

Denver Fire Clay Co., 3033 Black St., Denver, Colo. 80217

De Vilbiss Co., 300 Phillips Ave., Toledo 1, Ohio

Drakenfeld, B. F., Inc., 45 Park Pl., New York 7, N.Y.

Fairchild, W. H., 712 Centre St., Freeland, Pa.

Ferro Corp., 4150 East 56th St., Cleveland 5, Ohio

Fetzer, George, 1205 17th Ave., Columbus 11, Ohio

Garden City Clay Co., Redwood City, Calif.

Gare Ceramic Supply Co., 165 Rosemont St., Haverhill, Mass.

General Refractories Co., 7640 Chicago Ave., Detroit 4, Mich.

Green, A. P., Fire Brick Co., Mexico, Mo.

Hammill & Gillespie, Inc., 225 Broadway, New York, N.Y. 10007

Hauck Mfg. Co., 123 10th St., Brooklyn, N.Y. 11315

Hommel, O., Co., P.O. Box 475, Pittsburgh 30, Pa.

Hood, V. R., Jr., Box 1213, San Antonio 6, Tex.

Hy-Land Mfg. & Supply Co., 4990 East Asbury St., Denver, Colo. 80222

Illini Ceramic Service, 439 N. Wells St., Chicago 10, Ill.

Illinois Clay Products Co., Barber Bldg., Joliet, Ill.

International Clay Machinery Co., 1145 Bolander St., Dayton 1, Ohio

Johns-Manville Co., 22 East 40th St., New York 16, N.Y.

Johnson Gas Appliance Co., Cedar Rapids, Iowa

Kentucky-Tennessee Clay Co., Mayfield, Ohio

Ketcham, O. W., Architectural Tile Co., 125 North 18th St., Philadelphia, Pa.

Kleiner, Herman, Creektown Pottery, Mount Holly, N.J.

Klopfenstein, H. B., & Sons, Route 2, Crestline, Ohio

Kraft Chemical Co., 917 West 18th St., Chicago 8, Ill.

L & L Manufacturing Co., Box 348, Upland, Pa.

La Mo Refractory Supply Co., 323 Iris Ave., New Orleans 21, La.

Langley Ceramic Studio, 413 South 24th St., Philadelphia, Pa.

Lou, Nils, 1501 Asbury Road, St. Paul, Minn.

Mandl Ceramic Supply Co., R.R. #1 Box 369A, Pennington, N.J.

L. W. Mendall, 12330 E. Rush St., El Monte, Calif. 91733

Newton Pottery Supply Co., Newton, Mass.

Oak Hill Industries, R.R. #4, Davenport, Iowa

Paragon Industries, Inc., Box 10133, Dallas, Tex. 75207

Pemco Corp., 5601 Eastern Ave., Baltimore 24, Md.

Perry Equipment Supply Co., 1421 North 6th St., Philadelphia, Pa.

Pottery Arts Supply Co., 2554 Greenmount Ave., Baltimore 18, Md.

Randall Wheel, Box 774, Alfred, N.Y., 14802

Roder Ceramic Studio, 500 Broadway, Clifton Heights, Pa.

Rowantree Pottery, Blue Hill, Me.

Skutt & Sons, 2618 S.E. Steele St., Portland 2, Oregon

Soldner, Paul, Box 917, Aspen, Colo.

Standard Ceramic Supply Co., P.O. Box 4435, Pittsburgh, Pa. 15205

Stewart Clay Co., 133 Mulberry St., New York, N.Y.

Tepping Ceramic Supply Co., 3517 Riverside Dr., Dayton, Ohio

Trinity Ceramic Supply Co., 9016 Diplomacy Row, Dallas 35, Tex.

Unique Kilns, 530 Spruce St., Trenton, N.J. 08638

United Clay Mines Corp., Trenton 6, N.J.

U.S. Stoneware Co., Akron 9, Ohio

Van Howe Co., 1185 South Cherokee Ave., Denver, Colo.

Vars, Denton M., 825 West Minnehaha Ave., St. Paul 4, Minn.

Vitro Manufacturing Co., 60 Greenway Dr., Pittsburgh 4, Pa.

Walker Jamar Co., 365 S. First Ave. E., Duluth, Minn. 55802

Ward, S. Paul, Inc., 60 Mission St., South Pasadena, Calif.

West Coast Kiln Co., 635 Vineland Ave., LaPuente, Calif.

Western Ceramic Supply Co., 1601 Howard St., San Francisco, Calif.

Western Stoneware Co., Monmouth, Ill.

Westwood Ceramic Supply Co., 610 Venice Blvd., Venice, Calif.

Whittaker, Clarke and Daniels, Inc., 260 West Broadway, New York 13, N.Y.

Wolfe, Jack D., Co., Inc., 724 Meeker Ave., Brooklyn 22, N.Y.

Zanesville Stoneware Co., Zanesville, Ohio

Sources of Material and Equipment in Canada

CLAYS

A. P. Green Firebrick Co.
Rosemount Avenue, Weston, Ontario

Baroid of Canada Ltd.
5108 Eighth Avenue, S.W., Calgary, Alberta

Jean Cartier
1029 Bleury Street, Montreal, P.Q.

Clayburn Harbison, Ltd.
1690 West Broadway, Vancouver, B.C.

Magcobac Mining Co.
510 Fifth Street, S.W., Calgary, Alberta

Mercedes Ceramic Supply
8 Wallace Street
Woodbridge, Ontario

Pembena Mountain Clay
945 Logan, Winnipeg, Manitoba

Pottery Supply House
491 Wildwood Road, P.O. Box 192, Oakville, Ontario

Saskatchewan Clay Products
P.O. Box 970, Estevan, Saskatchewan

GLAZE MATERIALS

Barrett Co., Ltd.
1155 Dorchester Blvd., W. Montreal 2, P.Q.

Blyth Colors, Ltd., Toronto, Ontario

Greater Toronto Ceramic Center
167 Lakeshore Road, Toronto 14, Ontario

E. Harris & Co. of Toronto, Ltd.
73 King Street, East Toronto, Ontario

Lewiscraft Supply House
28 King Street, West, Toronto, Ontario

Mercedes Ceramic Supply
8 Wallace Street, Woodbridge, Ontario

Pottery Supply House
491 Wildwood Road, P.O. Box 192, Oakville, Ontario

KILNS

Ferro Enamels
26 Davis Road, P.O. Box 370, Oakville, Ontario

Hurley Bennett
1497 Pierre Avenue, Windsor, Ontario

Mercedes Ceramic Supply
8 Wallace Street, Woodbridge, Ontario

Pottery Supply House
491 Wildwood Road, P.O. Box 192, Oakville, Ontario

POTTERS WHEELS

Hurley Bennett
1497 Pierre Avenue, Windsor, Ontario

Mercedes Ceramic Supply
8 Wallace Street, Woodbridge, Ontario

Pottery Supply House
491 Wildwood Road, P.O. Box 192, Oakville, Ontario

C. W. Ride
North Hatley, P.Q.

W. H. Williams
144 Westwood Avenue, Hamilton, Ontario

Sources of Materials and Equipment in England

CLAYS

English China Clay Ltd.
18 High Cross Street, St. Austell, Cornwall

Fulham Pottery
London, S. W. 6

Pike Bros.
Wareham, Dorset

Potclays, Ltd.
Wharf House, Copeland Street, Hanley, Stoke-on-Trent

Price Bros.
Burslem, Stoke-on-Trent

Watts Blake & Bearn Ltd.
Newton Abbot, Devon

GLAZE MATERIALS

Blythe Color Works, Ltd.
Cresswell, Stoke-on-Trent

E. W. Good & Co., Ltd.
Barker Street, Longton, Stoke-on-Trent

George Goodwin & Son, Ltd.
Westwood Mills, Lichfield Street, Hanley, Stoke-on-Trent

W. Podmore & Sons, Ltd.
Caledonian Mills, Shelton, Stoke-on-Trent

Reeves & Sons, Ltd.
Enfield, Middlesex

Wengers Ltd., Etruria
Stoke-on-Trent

KILNS (electric)

Applied Heat Co., Ltd.
Elecfurn Works, Otterspool Way, Watford-by-Pass, Watford, Herts

British Ceramic Service Co., Ltd.
Park Avenue, Wolstanton, New-
castle, Staffs.

Cromartie Kilns
Dividy Road, Longton, Staffs.

Kilns & Furnaces Ltd.
Keele Street Works, Tunstall, Stoke-
on-Trent

KILNS (gas)
Dowson & Mason Gas Plant Co., Ltd.
Alma Works, Levenshulme, Man-
chester 19

Bernard W. E. Webber Ltd.
Alfred Street, Fenton, Stoke-on-
Trent

POTTER'S WHEELS
Corbic, Gomshall, Surrey

Judson & Hudson, Ltd., Keighley,
Yorks

Potters Equipment Co.,
73/77, Britannia Road, London, S.W.
6

Alec Tiranti Ltd.,
72 Charlotte Street, London, W. I.

Bernard W. E. Webber Ltd.
Alfred Street, Fenton, Stoke-on-
Trent

MISCELLANEOUS EQUIPMENT
Fulham Pottery, London, S.W. 6

W. Podmore & Sons, Ltd.
Shelton, Stoke-on-Trent

Alec Tiranti Ltd.
72 Charlotte Street, London, W. I.

REFERENCES

References for the Student Potter

Kenny, John B., *The Complete Book of Pottery Making*. Philadelphia: Chilton, 1949. A good text for the beginning student, this book is clearly written and has many excellent illustrations of forming techniques.

Leach, Bernard, *A Potter's Book*. Transatlantic Arts, 1951. Mr. Leach, perhaps the best-known independent studio potter today, has written an extremely readable book, and from the creative point of view, it cannot be recommended too highly. Illustrated.

Norton, F. H., *Ceramics for the Artist Potter*. Reading, Mass.: Addison-Wesley, 1956. Mr. Norton covers the entire range of ceramics from the forming processes to the chemistry of glazes, with numerous illustrations.

Rhodes, Daniel, *Clay and Glazes for the Potter*. Philadelphia: Chilton, 1957. An extremely clear treatment of clays, glazes, and calculations. A recommended text.

————, *Stoneware and Porcelain*. Philadelphia: Chilton, 1959. A companion book to *Clay and Glazes for the Potter*. In addition to a discussion of stoneware and porcelain, the book contains a great deal of useful studio information, including a chapter on kilns. A recommended text.

Supplemental Texts

Andrews, A. T., *Ceramic Tests and Calculations*. New York: Wiley, 1928. A standard text for ceramic glaze, clay, and frit calculations.

Billington, Dora M., *The Technique of Pottery*. B. T. Batsford Ltd., London W1, 1962. A very readable and complete ceramic text by an experienced English potter and teacher.

Binns, Charles, *The Potter's Craft*, 3d ed. New York: Van Nostrand, 1947. The text is of a general nature and is intended for the beginning student. Mr. Binns is well known for his research work on glazes.

Eley, Vincent, *A Monk at the Potter's*. Leicester, Eng.: Ward, 1952. This interesting account of a young monk who decided to start a pottery at his monastery also contains some very practical information.

Hetherington, A. L., *Chinese Ceramic Glazes*. Los Angeles: Commonwealth Press, 1948. A small, very readable volume, dealing primarily with Sung iron and copper glazes.

Home, Ruth M., *Ceramics for the Potter*. Peoria, Ill.: Bennett, 1953. This volume contains some very useful information on clays and glazes from both the historical and contemporary viewpoints. There is also a section on native Canadian clays.

Koenig, J. H., and W. H. Earhart, *Literature Abstracts of Ceramic Glazes*. Ellenton, Fla.: College Institute, 1951. Condensations with formulas of all important articles on glazes appearing in American trade magazines, Ceramic Society publications, and British, German, and other foreign publications.

Leach, Bernard, *A Potter in Japan*. Faber and Faber, London, 1960. An account of Mr. Leach's return to Japan, visits with potters, friends of his early years in Japan.

———, *Elements of Ceramics*. Reading, Mass.: Addison-Wesley, 1952. An introductory text for ceramic engineers, containing technical information on minerals, clays, and glazes, and on various commercial refining and production processes.

Parmelee, Cullen W., *Ceramic Glazes*. Chicago: Industrial Publications, 1951. A very complete and comprehensive text on ceramic glaze materials, slips, glazes, chemical reactions, and glaze calculations.

Rosenthal, Ernst, *Pottery and Ceramics*. Harmondsworth, Middlesex, Eng.: Pelican, 1949. A complete survey of the ceramic field, primarily from an industrial viewpoint.

Searle, A. B., *The Glazer's Book*. London: The Technical Press, 1948. A small, clearly written text on ceramic chemicals, glazes, and calculations.

Wildenhain, Marguerite, *Pottery: Form and Expression*. New York: American Craftsmen's Council, 1959. This beautifully illustrated book by one of America's foremost potters has a moving expression of the art of living as well as the art of ceramics.

Historical Background

Consult bibliography at end of Chapter 1.

Magazines and Professional Journals

Ceramic Age, 9 Chester Bldg., Cleveland 14, Ohio. An industrial magazine of little interest to the studio potter.

Ceramic Data Book, Industrial Publications, 5 S. Wabash Ave., Chicago 3, Ill. Published annually, covering supplies and manufacturers of ceramic equipment.

Ceramic Industry, 5 S. Wabash Ave., Chicago 3, Ill. Like *Ceramic Age,* an industrial trade magazine.

Ceramic Monthly, 4175 N. High St., Columbus, Ohio 4321. Oriented toward the hobby potter; many useful articles.

Craft Horizons, 29 West 53rd St., New York 19, N.Y. Covering all craft fields, with numerous articles on contemporary American and foreign ceramics; well illustrated.

Design Quarterly, Walker Art Center, 1710 Lyndale Ave. S., Minneapolis 3, Minn. A well illustrated periodical covering contemporary design, often ceramics.

Journal of the American Ceramic Society, Columbus, Ohio. Technical articles, usually of an industrial nature but occasionally of interest to the studio potter.

Foreign Publications

Dansk Kunstaandvaerk, Palaegade 4, Copenhagen, Den. Covers the entire Danish design field, well illustrated; many sections are in English.

Designed in Finland, Finnish Foreign Trade Assn., E. Esplanaadik 18, Helsinki. Illustrated booklet on Finnish design published each year with English text.

Domus, Via Monte di Pieta 15, Milan, Italy. Covers the decorative arts fields, emphasizing architecture; beautifully illustrated.

Form, Svenska Slöjdföreningen, Nybrogatan 7, Stockholm, Sweden. This journal of the Swedish Design Society covers all design fields; well illustrated. Contains a short English section.

Kontur, Svenska Slöjdföreningen, Nybrogatan 7, Stockholm, Sweden. Beautifully illustrated booklet published once a year on Swedish design and crafts. English text.

La Ceramica, Via F. Corridoni 3, Milan, Italy. Although an industrial publication, many articles concern studio potters and ceramic sculptors. English summary very short.

Vrienden van de Nederlandse Ceramick, Paulus Potterstraat, Amsterdam—Z 1. Illustrated journal of the Dutch ceramic society. English summary.

GLOSSARY
OF CERAMIC
TERMS

See Chapter 8 for a more complete coverage of ceramic chemicals.

absorbency The ability of a material (clay, plaster of Paris, and so forth) to soak up water.

acid One of three types of chemicals which constitute a glaze, the other two being the bases and the intermediates or neutrals. The acid group is symbolized by the radical RO_2. The most important acid is silica (SiO_2).

Albany slip A natural clay containing sufficient fluxes to melt and function as a glaze. It develops a dark brown-black glaze at cone 8-10 without any additions. Since it is mined in several localities in the vicinity of Albany, New York, its composition may vary slightly from time to time. Similar clays, found in various sections of the country, were much used by early American stoneware potteries.

alkali Generally, the base compounds of sodium and potassium but also the alkaline earth compounds, lime and magnesia. They function as fluxes, combining easily with silica at relatively low temperatures.

alumina (Al_2O_3) A major ingredient found in all clays and glazes. It is the chief oxide in the neutral group (R_2O_3) and imparts greater strength and higher firing temperatures to the body and glaze. When added to a glaze, it will assist in the formation of mat textures.

ash Generally, the ashes of trees, straw, leaves, and so forth. It is commonly used in the Far East to provide from 40 to 60 percent of high-temperature glaze ingredients. Depending upon the type, it will contain from 40 to 75 percent silica, from 5 to 15 percent alumina, and smaller amounts of iron, phosphorus, lime, potash, and magnesia.

aventurine A glaze composed of a soda, lead, or boric oxide flux with often an excess of iron oxide (over 6 percent). If it is cooled slowly, iron crystals will form and these crystals will sparkle and glisten beneath the surface of the glaze.

bag wall A baffle wall separating kiln chamber from combustion area.

ball clay An extremely fine-grained, plastic, sedimentary clay. Although ball clay contains considerable organic matter, it fires out white or near white in color. It is usually added to porcelain and whiteware bodies to increase plasticity.

ball mill A porcelain jar filled with flint pebbles and rotated with either a wet or dry charge of chemicals. It is used to blend and to grind glaze and body ingredients.

barium carbonate ($BaCO_3$) Used in combination with other fluxes to form mats in the low-temperature range. A very small percentage (1 to 3) added to a clay body will prevent discoloration caused by soluble sulphates, such as the whitish blotches often seen on red bricks and earthenware bodies in general.

basalt ware A hard, black, unglazed stoneware body developed about 1775 by the Wedgwood potteries in England in an effort to imitate classical wares.

bat A disk or slab of plaster of Paris on which pottery is formed or dried. It is also used to remove excess moisture from plastic clay.

batch Raw chemicals comprising a ceramic glaze which have been weighed out in a specific proportion designed to melt at a predetermined temperature.

bentonite An extremely plastic clay formed by decomposed volcanic ash and glass which is used to render short clays workable and to aid glaze suspension.

binders Various materials; gums, polyvinyl alcohol, methylcellulose used to increase glaze adherence or to impart strength to a cast or pressed clay body.

biscuit or **bisque** Unglazed low-fired ware.

bisque fire Preliminary firing (about cone 010) prior to glazing and subsequent firing at a higher temperature.

bitstone Coarse crushed quartz used in saggers to support thin porcelain in the bisque.

blowing The bursting of pots in a kiln caused by a too-rapid temperature rise. The water content of the clay turns into steam and forces the body to expand and explode.

blunger A mixing machine with revolving paddles used to prepare large quantities of clay slip or glazes.

bone china A hard translucent chinaware produced chiefly in England. The body contains a large amount of bone ash (calcium phosphate) which allows it to mature at cone 6 ($2232°F$). It is not very plastic and therefore difficult to form; it also tends to warp.

calcine To heat a ceramic material or mixture to the temperature necessary to drive off the chemical water, carbon dioxide, and other volatile gases. Some fusion may occur in which case the material must be ground. This is the process used in the production of plaster of Paris, Portland cement, ceramic stains, and so forth.

casting (or Slip Casting) A reproductive process of forming clay objects by pouring a clay slip into a hollow plaster mold and allowing it to remain long enough for a layer of clay to thicken on the mold wall. After hardening, the clay object is removed.

chemical water Water (H_2O) chemically combined in the glaze and body compounds. At approximately 450°C (842°F) during the firing cycle this water will begin to leave the body and glaze as water vapor. Little shrinkage occurs at this point although there is a loss in weight.

china A loosely applied term referring to whiteware bodies fired at low porcelain temperatures. They are generally vitreous, with an absorbency of less than 2 percent, and may be translucent.

china clay *See* **kaolin.**

clay Basically, a decomposed granite-type rock. To be classed as a clay the decomposed rock must have fine particles so that it will be plastic. Clays should be free of vegetable matter but will often contain other impurities which affect their color and firing temperatures. They are classified into various types, such as ball clays, fire clays, and slip clays. Pure clay chemically is $Al_2O_3 \cdot 2SiO_2 \cdot 2H_2O$.

coefficient of expansion The ratio of change between the length of a material mass and the temperature.

coiling A hand method of forming pottery by building up the walls with ropelike rolls of clay and then smoothing over the joints.

combing A method of decoration developed by dragging a coarse comb or tip of a feather over two contrasting layers of wet clay slip or glaze.

Cornwall stone (also Cornish stone) A feldsparlike material found in England and widely used there for porcelain-type bodies and glazes. Compared to American feldspar, it contains more silica and a smaller amount, though a greater variety, of fluxes. It comes closest to approximating the Chinese *petuntze,* which is a major ingredient of Orient porcelain bodies and glazes.

crackle glaze A glaze containing minute cracks in the surface. The cracks are decorative and often accentuated by coloring matter that is rubbed in. They are caused by the different rates at which the body and glaze cool and contract after firing.

crawling Separation of the glaze surface, caused by too heavy application, which cracks upon drying, or from uneven contraction rates between glaze and body.

crazing An undesirable and excessive crackle in the glaze which penetrates through the glaze to the clay body. It should be remedied by adjusting the glaze or body composition to obtain a more uniform cooling and contraction rate.

crocus martis Purple red oxide of iron, used as a red-brown glaze colorant.

crystal glazes Glazes characterized by crystalline clusters of various shapes and colors embedded in a more uniform and opaque glaze. The crystals are larger than in aventurine and may on occasion cover the entire surface. The glaze ingredients generally used are iron, lime, zinc, or rutile with an alkaline flux. A slow cooling cycle is also necessary for the development of the crystals.

cupric and **cuprous oxides** Copper oxides (CuO, Cu_2O), the major green colorants. They will also produce red under reducing conditions.

damp box A lined metal cabinet in which unfinished clay objects are stored to prevent them from drying out.

deflocculant Sodium carbonate or sodium silicate used in a casting slip to reduce the amount of water necessary and to maintain a better suspension.

delft ware A light-colored pottery body covered with a lead-tin glaze with overglaze decorations in cobalt on the unfired glaze. Delft was first made in Holland in imitation of Chinese blue and white porcelain.

della Robbia ware Ceramic sculpture of glazed terra cotta, generally in relief, produced in Florence by Lucca della Robbia or his family during the fifteenth century. The glaze used was the lead-tin majolica type developed in Spain.

dipping Glazing pottery by immersing it in a large pan or vat of glaze.

dryfoot To clean the bottom of a glazed piece before firing.

dunting Crackling of fired ware in a cooling kiln—the result of opening the flues and cooling too rapidly.

earthenware Low-fired pottery (under 2000°F), usually red or tan in color with an absorbency of from 5 to 20 percent.

eggshell porcelain Translucent, thin-walled porcelain ware.

empirical formula Generally a glaze formula expressed in molecular proportions.

engobe A prepared slip which is half way between a glaze and a clay; contains clay, feldspar, flint, a flux, plus colorants.

equivalent weight A weight which will yield one unit of a component (RO or R_2O_3 or RO_2 in a compound). This is usually the same as the molecular weight of the chemical compound in question. In ceramic calculations, equivalent weights are also assigned to the RO, R_2O_3, and the RO_2 oxide groups which make up the compound. If one of these oxide groups contains more than one unit of the oxide, its equivalent weight would be found by dividing the compound molecular weight by this unit number. (See Chapter 8.)

eutectic The lowest melting mixture of the materials composing the eutectic. This is always lower than the melting points of the individual materials.

faience Earthenware covered with a lead-tin glaze. A French term for earthenware derived from the Italian pottery center at Faenza, which during the Renaissance produced this ware partially in imitation of Spanish majolica ware. *See also* **majolica** and **delft ware.**

fat clay A plastic clay such as ball clay.

ferric and **ferrous oxides** (Fe_2O_3 and FeO) Red and black iron oxide. As impurities in clay they lower the firing temperature. They are the chief source of tan and brown ceramic colors and, under reducing conditions, the various celadon greens (*see* **reduction**).

fire box Combustion chamber of a gas, oil, or wood-fired kiln, usually directly below the kiln chamber.

fireclay A clay having a slightly higher percentage of fluxes than pure clay (kaolin). It fires tan or gray in color and is used in the manufacture of refractory materials, such as bricks, muffles, and so forth for industrial glass and steel furnaces. It is often quite plastic and may be used by the studio potter as an ingredient of stoneware-type bodies.

flues Passageways around the kiln chamber through which the heating gases pass from the fire box to the chimney.

flux Lowest-melting compound in a glaze such as lead, borax, soda ash, or lime and including the potash or soda contained in the feldspar. The flux combines easily with silica and thereby helps break the higher-melting alumina-silica compounds eventually to form a glass.

foot The ringlike base of a ceramic piece, usually heavier than the surrounding body.

frit A partial or complete glaze which is melted and then reground for the purpose of eliminating the toxic effects of lead or the solubility of borax, soda ash, and so forth.

frit china A glossy, partly translucent chinaware produced by adding a glass frit to the body.

galena Lead sulphite, used as a flux for earthenware glazes, more common in Europe than in the United States.

glaze A liquid suspension of finely ground minerals which is applied by brushing, pouring, or spraying on the surface of bisque-fired ceramic ware. After drying the ware is fired to the temperature at which the glaze ingredients will melt together to form a glassy surface coating.

glaze fire A firing cycle to the temperature at which the glaze materials will melt to form a glasslike surface coating. This is usually at the point of maximum body maturity and it is considerably higher than the first bisque fire.

globar A patented carborundum-type material used in the form of rods for elements in electric kilns firing at temperatures up to cone 18. Such kilns must be used with a special transformer.

glost fire A glaze firing which is at a lower temperature than the bisque fire, usually employed only with thin chinaware which warps badly at high temperatures. In this case the bisque ware has previously been fired to its maximum body temperature. To prevent warping in the high bisque fire, the ware is placed upside down on its rim or with protective disks on the lips. Some pieces may be embedded in a layer of flint sand.

greenware Pottery which has not been bisque fired.

grog Hard fired clay which has been crushed or ground to various particle sizes. It is used to reduce shrinkage in such ceramic products as sculpture and architectural terra cotta tiles, which, because of their thickness, have drying and shrinkage problems. From 20 to 40 percent grog may be used depending upon the amount of detail desired and whether the pieces are free standing or pressed in molds.

gum arabic or **gum tragacanth** Natural gums used as binders to enable the glaze to adhere better to the body. Binders are necessary for fritted glazes containing little or no raw clay. They are also useful when a bisque fire accidentally goes too high, or in reglazing. The gum, of course, burns completely out during the firing.

hard paste True porcelain which is fired to cone 12 or above (2420°F) ; also called *hard porcelain.*

ilmenite ($TiO_2 \cdot FeO$) An important source of titanium. In the granular form it is used to give dark flecks to the glaze. It is often sprinkled upon the wet glaze without previous mixing.

iron oxide *See* **ferric oxide.**

jiggering, jollying An industrial method of producing pottery. A slab of soft clay is placed upon a revolving plaster bat shaped in the negative of the object to be formed. As the wheel head turns, a metal template on a moving arm trims off the excess clay and forms the bottom, or the reverse side.

kanthal A special metal alloy produced in Sweden for wire or strip elements in electric kilns firing from 2000° to 2400°F.

kaolin ($Al_2O_3 \cdot 2SiO_2 \cdot 2H_2O$) Pure clay, also known as china clay. It is used in glaze and porcelain bodies and fires out to a pure white. Sedimentary kaolins found in Florida are more plastic than the residual types found in the Carolinas and Georgia.

kiln A furnace made of refractory clay materials for firing ceramic products.

kiln furniture Refractory shelves and posts upon which ceramic ware is placed while being fired in the kiln.

kiln wash A protective coating of refractory materials applied to the surface of the shelves and the kiln floor to prevent excess glaze from fusing the ware tight. An inexpensive and effective wash may be made from equal parts of flint and kaolin.

kneading Working clay with the fingers or with the heel of the hand in order to obtain a uniform consistency.

lead White lead (basic lead carbonate, $2PbCo_3 \cdot Pb(OH)_2$), red lead (Pb_3O_4), and galena (lead sulphide, PbS) are among the most common low-fired fluxes.

leather hard The condition of the raw ware when most of the moisture has left the body but when it is still soft enough to be carved or burnished easily.

limestone A major flux in the medium- and high-fire temperature ranges when it is powdered in the form of whiting (calcium carbonate). If a coarse sand is used as a grog, it should not contain limestone particles. Calcined lime will expand in the bisque and cause portions of the body to pop out.

luster A type of metallic decoration thought to have been discovered in Egypt and further developed in Persia during the ninth and fourteenth centuries. A mixture of a metallic salt, resin, and bismuth nitrate is applied over a glazed piece and then refired at a lower temperature. The temperature, however, must be sufficient to melt the metal which leaves a thin layer of metal on the decorated portions.

luting A method of joining together two pieces of dry or leather-hard clay with a slip.

majolica Earthenware covered with a soft tin-bearing glaze, often with a luster decoration. The ware originally came from Spain and derived its name from the island of Majorca which lay on the trade route to Italy. Faenza ware was greatly influenced by these Spanish imports. All Renaissance pottery of this type is now generally called majolica ware.

mat glaze A dull-surfaced glaze with no gloss but pleasant to the touch, not to be confused with an incompletely fired glaze. Mat surfaces may be developed by the addition of barium carbonate, or alumina, and a slow cooling cycle.

maturity The temperature or time at which a clay or clay body develops the desirable characteristics of maximum nonporosity and hardness; or the point at which the glaze ingredients enter into complete fusion, developing a strong bond with the body, a stable structure, maximum resistance to abrasion, and a pleasant surface texture.

molds A form or box, usually made of plaster of Paris, containing a hollow negative shape. The positive form is made by pouring either wet plaster or slip into this hollow. *See* **casting**.

muffle A lining, made of refractory materials, forming the kiln chamber and around which the hot gases pass from the fire box to the chimney. The purpose is to protect the ware from the direct flames of the fire and the resulting combustion impurities. Some of these panels may be removed for a reduction fire.

muffle kiln A kiln with muffle features in contrast to a kiln using saggars. *See* **saggars**.

mullite Interlocking needlelike crystals of aluminum silicate ($3Al_2O_3 \cdot 2SiO_2$) which form in high-temperature bodies between 1850° to 2200°F. This formation is responsible for much of the greater toughness and hardness of stoneware and porcelain, and in particular for the closer union developed between the glaze and the body.

neutral fire A fire which is neither oxidizing nor reducing. Actually this can only be obtained in practice by a slight alternation between oxidation and reduction.

opacifier A chemical whose crystals are relatively insoluble in the glaze, thereby preventing the light from penetrating the glass formation. The color most sought after is white although for some purposes others may be as effective. Tin oxide is by far the best opacifier. Zirconium, titanium, and zinc oxides are also used. Many other oxides are effective in certain combinations and within limited firing ranges. These are commercially available in frit forms under trade names, such as Zircopax and Opax.

overglaze Decoration applied with overglaze colors, either on the raw glaze or on the glazed and fired ware. In the latter case, the firing of the overglazed ware is at a lower temperature than the glaze fire.

overglaze colors Colors containing coloring oxides or ceramic stains, a flux, and some type of binder. The fluxes are necessary to allow the colors to melt into the harder glaze to which they are applied. The lower temperatures at which most underglazes are fired (about cone 016-013) allow the use of colorants which are unstable at higher temperatures.

oxidizing fire A fire during which the kiln chamber retains an ample supply of oxygen. This means that the combustion in the fire box must be perfectly adjusted. An electric kiln always gives an oxidizing fire.

paste The compounded bodies of European-type porcelains.

peach bloom A copper-red reduction glaze with a peachlike pink color (Chinese).

peeling Separation of the glaze or slip from the body. Peeling may be caused when slip is applied to a body which is too dry, or when a glaze is applied too thickly or to a dusty surface.

peep hole A hole placed in either the fire box, kiln chamber, or muffle flues of a kiln through which one can observe the cones or the process of combustion.

petuntze A partially decomposed feldspar-type rock found in China, roughly similar in composition to Cornwall stone. With kaolin it forms the body of Oriental porcelains.

plaster of Paris Hydrate of calcium sulphate, made by calcining gypsum. It hardens after being mixed with water. Because it absorbs moisture and it can be cut and shaped easily, it is used in ceramics for drying and throwing bats, as well as for molds and casting work.

plasticity The quality of clay which allows it to be manipulated and still maintain its shape without cracking or sagging.

porcelain (Chinese) A hard, non-absorbent clay body, white or gray in color, which rings when struck.

porcelain (hard) A hard, nonabsorbent clay body which is white and translucent. In both types of hard porcelain the bisque is low fired and the glaze is very high (generally cone 14-16).

pottery Earthenware; a shop in which ceramic objects are made.

pressing Forming of clay objects by pressing soft clay between two plaster molds, such as in the production of cup handles.

pug mill A machine for mixing plastic clay.

pyrometer An instrument for measuring heat at high temperatures. It consists of a calibrated dial connected to wires made of two different alloys, the welded tips of which protrude into the kiln chamber. When heated, these tips set up a minute electrical current which registers on the indicating dial.

pyrometric cones Small triangular cones ($1\frac{1}{8}$ and $2\frac{5}{8}$ inches in height) made of ceramic materials which are compounded to bend and melt at specific temperatures, thus enabling the potter to determine when the firing is complete.

quartz   Flint or silica (SiO_2).

raku   A soft, lead-glazed, hand-built groggy earthenware made in Japan and associated with the tea ceremony.

reducing agent   Glaze or body material such as silicon carbide, which combines with oxygen to form carbon monoxide during the firing.

reduction fire   A firing using insufficient oxygen; carbon monoxide thus formed unites with oxygen from the body and glaze to form carbon dioxide, producing color changes in coloring oxides.

refractory   The quality of resisting the effects of high temperatures; also materials, high in alumina and silica, that are used for making kiln insulation, muffles, and kiln furniture.

rib   A tool of wood, bone, or metal, which is held in the hand while throwing to assist in shaping the pot or to compact the clay.

RO, R_2O_3, RO_2   The symbols or radicals for the three major groups of chemicals which make up a ceramic glaze. The RO radical refers to the base chemicals, such as the oxides of sodium, potassium, calcium, and lead which function in the glaze as fluxing agents. The R_2O_3 radical refers to the intermediate or amphoteric oxides, some of which may on occasion function either as bases or acids. The chief oxide of interest in this group is alumina (Al_2O_3) which always reacts as a refractory. The third radical RO_2 stands for the acid group which are the glass formers, such as silica (SiO_2).

rouge flambé   French, a type of Chinese copper-red reduction glaze (*sang de boeuf*) which is a mottled deep red with green and blue hues, also called a transmutation glaze.

rutile   An impure form of titanium dioxide (TiO_2) containing considerable iron. It will give a light yellow or tan color to the glaze with a streaked and runny effect. Used in large amounts it will raise the maturing temperature.

saggars   Round boxlike containers of fire clay used in kilns lacking muffles. The glazed ware is placed in saggars to protect the glaze from the combustion gases.

salt glaze   A glaze developed by throwing salt ($NaCl$) into a hot kiln. The salt vaporizes and combines with the silica in the body to form sodium silicate, a hard glassy glaze. A salt kiln is of a slightly different construction and is limited in use to the salt glaze.

sang de boeuf   French, meaning oxblood which describes the rich, deep-red hues produced by the Chinese in their copper-red reduction glazes.

sgraffito   Decoration achieved by scratching through a colored slip to show the contrasting body color beneath.

sherd   A broken fragment of pottery.

short   A body or clay lacking in plasticity.

shrinkage Contraction of the clay in either drying or firing. In the firing cycle the major body shrinkage for stoneware clays begins at approximately 900°C (1652°F). Earthenware clays will begin to fuse and shrink at slightly lower temperatures.

siccative Agent for drying the oils used in underglaze decoration.

silica Flint (SiO_2) produced in the United States by grinding almost pure flint sand.

silicate of soda A deflocculant. A standard solution of sodium silicate (commercial N brand) has the ratio of 1 soda to 3.3 silica. Specific gravity 1.395.

single fire A firing cycle in which the normal bisque and glaze firings are combined. The advantages are a great saving of fuel and labor, and development of a stronger bond between the body and glaze. These are partially offset by the need for greater care in handling the ware, and the danger of cracking, if in glazing the raw pieces absorb too much moisture. In a salt glaze, however, these disadvantages do not occur.

sintering A firing process in which ceramic compounds fuse sufficiently to form a solid mass upon cooling, but are not vitrified. An example is low-fired earthenware.

slip A clay in liquid suspension.

slip clay A clay such as Albany and Michigan clays containing sufficient fluxes to function as a glaze with little or no additions.

slip glazes A raw glaze largely composed of plastic clay.

spinel Chemically, magnesium aluminate ($MgAl_2O_3$), an extremely hard crystal arranged in an octa-hedron atomic structure. In ceramics, a spinel is a colored crystal used as a colorant in place of the metallic oxides because of its greater resistance to change by either the fluxing action of the glaze or the effects of high temperatures.

spray booth A boxlike booth equipped with a ventilating fan to remove spray dust which, whether toxic or not, is harmful.

spraying Applying glazes with a compressed-air-spray machine, the chief commercial method.

sprigging Applying clay in a plastic state to form a relief decoration.

stain Sometimes a single coloring oxide, but usually a combination of oxides, plus alumina, flint, and a fluxing compound. This mixture is calcined and then finely ground and washed. The purpose is to form a stable coloring agent not likely to be altered by the action of the glaze or heat. While stains are employed as glaze colorants, their chief use is as overglaze and underglaze decorations and body colorants.

stilt A ceramic tripod upon which glazed ware is placed in the kiln. Tripods with nickel-nichrome wire points are often used to minimize blemishes to the glaze. They are never used for high-fire porcelain which must be dry footed for greater support. Stilts may refer to the refractory posts used to support the kiln shelves.

stoneware A high-fired ware (above cone 8) with a slight or no absorbency. It is usually gray in color but may be tan or slightly reddish. Stoneware is similar in many respects to porcelain, the chief difference being the color which is the result of iron and other impurities in the clay.

stoneware clays Clays more plastic than a porcelain body, firing above cone 8 to a gray color.

talc $(3MgO \cdot 4SiO_2 \cdot H_2O)$ A compound used in most whiteware bodies in the low to moderate firing ranges as a source of silica and flux. It is slightly plastic and may be used to lower the firing range, if need be, of a stoneware or fireclay body.

terra cotta An earthenware body, generally red in color and containing grog. It is the common type body used for ceramic sculpture.

terra sigillata A sliplike glaze produced during the Etruscan and Greek periods. The finer slip particles were successively decanted off and collected. When applied, burnished, and fired, they gave a glaze-like surface. They were not completely waterproof.

throwing Forming pottery of plastic clay on a potter's wheel.

tin enamel A low-fire opaque glaze originally developed in Persia and carried to Spain by the Moorish conquests. The glaze is lead fluxed, occasionally combined with borax, with tin as an opacifier. The term tin enamel is given to a large body of ware produced in Spain from the eleventh to the fifteenth centuries, as well as the Italian Renaissance pottery, including the glazed terra cottas of della Robbia.

tin-vanadium stain A major yellow colorant produced by a calcined mixture of tin and vanadium oxides.

trailing A method of decorating, using a slip trailed out from a rubber syringe.

translucency The ability of a thin porcelain or whiteware body to transmit a diffused light.

turning Trimming the walls and foot of a pot on the wheel while the clay is in a leather-hard state.

underglaze Colored decoration applied on the bisque ware before the glaze is applied.

viscosity The nonrunning quality of a glaze, caused by glaze chemicals which resist the flowing action of the glaze flux.

vitreous Pertaining to the hard, glassy, and nonabsorbent quality of a body or glaze.

volatilization Action under influence of extreme heat of the kiln in which some glaze elements turn successively from a solid to a liquid, and finally into a gaseous, state.

ware In general, pottery or porcelain in either the raw, bisque, or glazed state.

warping Distortion of a pot in drying because of uneven wall thickness or a warm draft of air, or in firing when a kiln does not heat uniformly.

water glass Another term for a liquid solution of sodium silicate which is used as a deflocculant.

water smoking The initial phase of the firing cycle up to a dull red heat (1000° to 1100°F). Depending upon the thickness of the ware, this may take from 2 to 3 hours for thin pottery, to 12 hours for sculpture. The heat rise must be gradual to allow atmospheric and chemical water to escape. In some cases there will be organic impurities which will also burn out, releasing carbon monoxide.

wax resist A method of decorating pottery by brushing on a design with a warm wax solution or a wax emulsion. This will prevent an applied stain or glaze from adhering to the decorated portions. The wax may be applied to either the raw or bisque ware, over or between two layers of glaze.

weathering Generally the exposure of raw clay to the action of rain, sun, and freezing weather which breaks down the particle size and renders the clay more plastic.

wedging Kneading and cutting plastic clay, forcibly throwing down one piece upon the other in order to obtain a uniform texture free from air pockets.

white lead $[2PbCO_3 \cdot Pb(OH)_2]$ A major low-fire flux.

whiteware Pottery or chinaware with a white or light-cream colored body.

whiting Calcium carbonate ($CaCO_2$), similar chemically to limestone and marble; a major high-fire flux.

yellow base A glaze stain produced by a calcined mixture of red lead, antimony, and tin oxides.

zircopax A commercial frit used as an opacifier. It is composed of zirconium oxide, tin oxide, and silica. It gives less of a tint than tin oxide, but its price is considerably lower.

INDEX

INDEX

For ceramic terms, see Glossary, pp. 311-322. For ceramic chemicals, see pp. 202–218.

Numbers in italics refer to illustrations.

COLOR PLATES

Sung vase, *facing page 12*
Yung Chen vase, *facing page 13*
Iranian bowl, *facing page 44*
Peruvian bottle, *facing page 45*

Stoneware plate, *facing page 140*
Detail of mural, *facing page 141*
Raku bowl, *facing page 172*
Collection of bottles, *facing page 173*

artificial, 170, 239
procedure, 239
Reduction glazes, 170
Refractory compounds, 162, 242, 244
Refsgaard, Niels, *78*
Residual clays, 120
Rie, Lucie, *48*, 55
Robbia, Luca della, *30*
Rolf, Johnny, *61*, 62
Roman ceramics, 27
Rooden, Jan de, *61*, 62
Rörstrand Studios, 79, 87
Rosanjin, Kitaoji, *98*
Rothman, Jerry, *266*, *267*
RO, R_2O_3, RO_2 system, 196
Rutile, 215

S

Sakuma, Totaro, *101*
Salmenhaara, Kyllikki, 88
Salt glazes, 172
    contemporary, *173*
    firing techniques, 248
    historical, 44, 69
    kilns, 247
Scales, gram, 278
Scandinavia
    ceramics, 74–93
    design, 74, 80
    schools, 80, 90
Scheid, Karl, *69*, *72*
Scheid, Ursula, *73*
Schultze, Klaus, *71*, *72*
Sculpture (*see* Ceramic sculpture)
Sedimentary clays, 120
Seger cones, 290
Sgraffito, 29, 182
Shivering, 192
Shrinkage of clay, 125, 237
Silica (flint)
    function in glaze, 161
    sources of, 206
    types of, 126
Silicon carbide, 170, 215, 239, 243
Sillimanite, 215, 243
Silver compounds, 172, 215
Slab constructions, 145
Slip
    casting, 253
    clays, 122

decoration, 10, 43, 183
formulas, 255
glazes, 173
See also Engobe
Sluzarski, Peter A., *153*, *262–265*
Soda ash, 166, 216
Soda feldspar (*see* Feldspar)
Sodium compounds, 204, 216, 255
Soldner, Paul, *175*
Sperry, Robert, *185*
Spinel stains, 220
Spodumene, 126, 216, 286
Spray equipment, 278
Stains, 218, 220, 221, 297
Stålhane, Carl-Harry, *80*, *83*
Steatite, 216
Stoneware
    clays, 121, 286, 299
    glazes, 167, 294
    historical, 16, 18, 44
Storr-Britz, Hildegard, *73*
Studio equipment
    clay mixers, 276
    commercial sources, 302
    glaze equipment, 277
    kilns, 271
    wheels, 274
Sulphur gases, 166, 192
Supply dealers, ceramic
    in Canada, 306
    in England, 307
    in United States, 302
Suzuki, Osamu, *100*
Swedish ceramics, 79

T

Talc, 216
Taran, Irv, *154*
Tatsuzu, Skimaoka, *101*
Taub, Susanne, *58*
Tea ceremony, 96
Temmoku, 20
Temperature color scale, 288
Temperature equivalents (cones), 290
Terra sigllata, 10, 173
Throwing on the wheel
    problems in, 135
    techniques of, 130–143
Tin oxide, 206, 217